P9-AFO-986

Human Capital Over the Life Cycle

This book was prepared with financial support from the Accompanying Measures of the 5th Framework Programme of the European Commission and the SCHOLAR Institute at the University of Amsterdam, The Netherlands

Human Capital Over the Life Cycle

A European Perspective

Edited by

Catherine Sofer

TEAM, Université Paris I–Panthéon–Sorbonne, France

Edward Elgar
Cheltenham, UK • Northampton, MA, USA

Published by
Edward Elgar Publishing Limited
Glensanda House
Montpellier Parade
Cheltenham
Glos GL50 1UA
UK

Edward Elgar Publishing, Inc.
136 West Street
Suite 202
Northampton
Massachusetts 01060
USA

A catalogue record for this book
is available from the British Library

Library of Congress Cataloguing in Publication Data

Human capital over the life cycle: a European perspective / edited by Catherine
Sofer.
     p. cm.
   Includes bibliographical references.
    1. Human capital—Europe. 2. Human capital. 3. Labour demand—Europe. 4.
Occupational training—Europe. I. Sofer, Catherine.

HD4904.7.H85846 2004
331.12′5′094—dc21

                                           2003049262

ISBN 1 84376 067 3

Typeset by Cambrian Typesetters, Frimley, Surrey
Printed and bound in Great Britain by MPG Books Ltd, Bodmin, Cornwall

Contents

v

Figures

Tables

Contributors

Juan Cañada Vicinay, Laboratorio de Organización Industrial, University of Las Palmas de Gran Canaria.

Nathalie Damoiselet, Ministère de l'Education and University of Paris V–René Descartes.

Rhys Davies, Warwick Institute for Employment Research, University of Warwick.

Simone Dobbelsteen, Research Institute SCHOLAR Schooling, Labor Market and Economic Development, University of Amsterdam.

Peter Dolton, Institute of Education, Centre for Economic Performance, London School of Economics and University of Newcastle upon Tyne.

Peter Elias, Warwick Institute for Employment Research, University of Warwick.

Wim Groot, Research Institute SCHOLAR Schooling, Labor Market and Economic Development, University of Amsterdam.

Gérard Lassibille, Institut de Recherche sur l'Economie de l'Education (IREDU), University of Bourgogne and CNRS.

Ros Levacic, Institute of Education, Centre for Economic Performance, London School of Economics and University of Newcastle upon Tyne.

Louis Lévy-Garboua, TEAM, CNRS and University of Paris I–Panthéon–Sorbonne.

Henriëtte Maassen van den Brink, Research Institute SCHOLAR Schooling, Labor Market and Economic Development, University of Amsterdam.

David Margolis, TEAM, CNRS and University of Paris I–Panthéon–Sorbonne, INSEE-CREST and IZA.

Sylvie Mendès, LEO, University of Orleans.

Noortje van Mierlo, Research Institute SCHOLAR Schooling, Labor Market and Economic Development, University of Amsterdam.

Lucia Navarro-Gomez, University of Malaga, Spain.

Barbara Petrongolo, London School of Economics.

Erik Plug, Research Institute SCHOLAR Schooling, Labor Market and Economic Development, University of Amsterdam, Tinbergen Institute and IZA.

Kjell G. Salvanes, Department of Economics, Norwegian School of Economics and Business Administration, Statistics Norway and IZA.

María Jesús San Segundo, Universidad Carlos III de Madrid.

Véronique Simonnet, TEAM, CNRS and University of Paris I–Panthéon–Sorbonne.

Catherine Sofer, TEAM, CNRS and University of Paris I–Panthéon–Sorbonne

Michel Sollogoub, TEAM, CNRS and University of Paris I–Panthéon–Sorbonne.

Anna Vignoles, Centre for Economic Performance, London School of Economics.

Lars Vilhuber, US Bureau of the Census and York University.

Introduction

Catherine Sofer*

The objective of this book is to synthesize a wide range of research findings from a European research project 'Schooling, Training and Transitions (STT)',[1] organized and funded within the Targeted Socio-Economic Research Programme of the European Union.

At the Lisbon Summit in 2000, the European Council defined an ambitious ten-year strategy to make the European Union 'the most competitive and dynamic knowledge based economy in the world, capable of sustainable economic growth with more and better jobs and greater social cohesion'.[2] Subsequent monitoring has revealed only limited success in implementing certain key elements within this strategy, particularly in the sphere of lifelong learning. The process of equipping all of Europe's potential workforce with the skills, knowledge and expertise to enable them to contribute to economic growth and combat social exclusion represents a key area where substantial progress remains to be achieved.

A major reason for this disappointing progress lies in our limited knowledge of the nature and diversity of the education and training systems within the European Union and their interactions with the economies of the member states. To improve our understanding of the way these systems operate, a group of economists was constituted to conduct comparative research on the processes of human capital formation in the European education and training area and to study the interactions between these processes and the labour market. This group, of which I was the coordinator, worked together from 1997 to the end of 1999 to explore these issues. Adopting a lifecycle perspective, the group took advantage wherever possible of the range of research resources now available for analytical research on education, employment and training. Facilitated and funded by the European Commission under its programme of Targeted Socio-economic Research, the group prepared over 60 working papers.[3] These have been published in the STT project Working

* I wish to thank Andrew Clark for all the work he has done: critical comments on different chapters, rewriting in English, and coordinating the project of the book. I also wish to thank all the participants in the many workshops, which were organized within the STT project for the discussions that took place: this book would never have existed without them.

Paper Series. The main results have now been gathered together and are presented here in nine chapters.

'Transitions' serve as a useful unifying theme for this research project, as they link successive individual states over time: through school, from school to work, and between jobs. As the project gathered momentum, it became apparent that another common feature of the research is the links between the processes of human capital formation, obtained at any point in life, subsequent transitions and the present or future work career of individuals. We reflect this in the title of this book: *Human Capital Over the Life Cycle: A European Perspective*.

The objective of the project was to improve our knowledge about the factors underlying inequalities in education and the labour market. It seems to us that one of the most important challenges in Europe is to understand the link between education and training on the one hand and economic and social inequality on the other. The more we understand these links, the better placed we will be to tackle issues of inequality via the education and training system. We are aware that inequalities become apparent as individuals move through the schooling system, that they may develop further during an individual's career, and can take an extreme form with the phenomenon of poverty and exclusion in both childhood and adulthood. Three aspects deserve particular attention:

EDUCATIONAL INEQUALITY

Different individuals or different groups, within the same educational system, have varying chances of access to, or experience different outcomes from, the schooling system. Some of them experience various forms of 'wastage' in the education process, in that they choose to drop out or fail to engage with the process of education. Why do such outcomes arise? When does this situation begin? Are some characteristics of schooling systems more positive or some government incentives more effective in terms of reducing these inequalities or of limiting wastage?

DIFFERENCES IN ACCESS TO LABOUR MARKETS

The transition from school to work has increasingly become recognized as an important step in an individual's career development. Two reasons explain this widening interest. First, the transition process has become longer in many countries, which has implications for the inequalities in outcomes that become apparent around this time. While some young people find a job immediately after leaving school, others may experience a long and difficult transition before getting a steady job. The other reason is that this transition is suspected of having long-lasting effects upon the whole work career. Exploring the links between education and transition from school to work, which implies disentangling the effects of education from those other individual characteristics and experiences, is thus of substantial interest in its own right.

DIFFERENCES IN LIFELONG EARNINGS AND TRAINING

Finally, how can we understand differences in earnings over the life cycle? As there are an increasing number of panel data sets available in European countries, much can be said about the relationship between careers and earnings. Questions such as the links between initial education and training, the choice and characteristics of trainees, male/female differentials, or atypical employment and contracts can now be studied in a degree of detail and over time periods which permit us to probe these questions in depth.

We hope that this book will help to shed some light upon these issues. It may well be the case that we simply end up by posing more questions than we started with, but we hope that such questions will be based more firmly upon the up-to-date evidence provided in this publication. It is also worth stressing that, although the book appears to be an edited collection of readings, we have taken considerable care to integrate our work and to develop each chapter along common lines. In particular, we wanted the perspective to be systematically comparative. While our approach is essentially quantitative and theoretically rigorous, the value of good comparative research lies in the differences it reveals between countries. Through the variations that we observe, we gain a better understanding both of the limits of our theories and, more importantly, about the broader workings of the socio-economic system. However, big differences sometimes appear in the results for different countries, from similar models and using similar methods. These differences tell us many important things about the true scope of our theoretical models and, by deduction, about the influence of variations in the institutional context in our European countries. We inject a note of caution at times. Our work with data from different countries has taught us to question their comparability, and has given us strong incentives to increase pressure for the production of better quality data for European comparison purpose in the future. This being said, we did our best to provide systematically international comparisons in each chapter, with these comparisons being either the core of the chapter, or resulting from the confrontation of the results obtained from one or a few countries with those provided by an international review of existing papers on the same topics.

Another common link is the over-arching questions we have addressed.

Each chapter deals with optimal human capital investments and career choices at a specific point in the life cycle, from an individual or from a social point of view. Thus, we kept in mind the same general questions whatever the narrower issues considered in each chapter. What trends do we identify? How well do systems deliver? What are the labour market impacts of different choices in educational systems or among educational tracks? What do we learn from international comparisons? Are some results robust to the diversity of their institutional context? Where we find similarities or differences between countries, what do these imply in terms of policy implications and recommendations?

As economists, we focus particularly on optimal human capital investments and career choices. From a theoretical perspective, this means that we use as 'inputs' in our models variables like relative prices, costs and opportunities, and consider the relative efficiency of attaining a particular goal. This theoretical approach and the associated econometric 'tools' are useful when trying to derive broad comparative lines in the links between educational systems and the labour market. However, of course, they are much more limited if the objective was to explore in detail either the existing educational systems in the European countries, or the institutional aspects of their labour markets. This was not the case here. Similarly, social interactions in the shaping of 'preferences' for a particular educational track (for example in the choice of apprenticeship versus vocational school or gender differences in the choice of some particular jobs) are outwith our scope. From an empirical perspective, the different chapters in the book most often adopt a methodology that involves hypothesis formulation and testing. Individual level data (generally from large and rich data sets, facilitating the use of econometric methods) are used to test different theoretical hypotheses or questions raised in the particular phenomenon at stake: for example, several theoretical assumptions can be made about the relationship between the beginning of the work career and outcomes later in life. One can think of accumulation/disaccumulation of human capital, predictions based upon signalling theory and so on. Choosing between these different explanations, or refuting some of them, is a matter of empirical evidence. We follow this general approach throughout the book.

Finally, the book does not aim to cover all the aspects of the links between education and employment in every European country. This would have been ambitious in a book of 250 pages, and is certainly beyond the resources that were available to use as we undertook this task. The perspective adopted in the book is thus more limited. Though almost all the stages in the life cycle in relation to education are tackled, from early childhood to stages late in the work career, only some aspects are considered in detail here. These relate to three stages in the life cycle: first, the characteristics and effects of schooling systems, then transitions from school to work, and, finally, human capital and the work career.

SCHOOLING SYSTEMS

Differences in lifelong earnings may originate from an early point in an individual's life. The first chapter of this book deals with early childhood. Wim Groot, Henriëtte Maassen van den Brink, Simone Dobbelsteen and Noortje van Mierlo address the transfer of skills and competencies in the pre-school period. The authors suggest three reasons for an increased interest in early childhood education. The first reason is that nowadays in most European countries early childhood education services are widely accepted as an important stage in the education and social development of children. The second reason is the growing concern about the well-being and future of children from disadvantaged families. It is generally acknowledged that children from disadvantaged families face a restricted set of opportunities later in their lives. Thirdly, the increased interest in early childhood educational arrangements derives also from the increase in the labour force participation of women with young children, which in turn has led to a growing interest in the effects of women's employment in the pre-school years on outcomes for children. The aim of the chapter is to provide a survey of the research that has been carried out on the costs, benefits and returns of pre-school educational arrangements and to analyse their effectiveness. Two general conclusions emerge. The first is that one can find only few robust econometric results on the effects of early childhood education, although a fair amount of research has been done on this subject (both intervention programmes and childcare) on child development and on the effects of childcare on female labour supply. Moreover, little work has been done on the effects of childcare on firms and on the social costs and benefits of early childhood education. However, and this is the second general conclusion that they draw, the available research does seem to indicate that good quality care and good quality intervention programs can have substantial positive effects on the children who participate in these programmes.

Is expenditure on schooling causally and positively related to student educational and labour market outcomes? This is the question asked in Chapter 2 by Peter Dolton, Ros Levacic and Anna Vignoles. The research evidence for this is still under debate. For example, Hanushek et al. (1996)[4] find that in the US there is 'no strong or consistent relationship between school resources and student performance'. Others disagree, and find, also from the US, that school inputs[5] are positively related to outcomes, especially subsequent earnings (Card and Krueger, 1992).[6] A fair number of reasons might explain this mixed evidence on the effects of school quality. This chapter discusses these reasons from a methodological point of view and tackles the difficulties associated with the use of production function analysis. It then reviews and highlights the significant findings from the US and European literature on this issue. The authors also acknowledge the importance of school effectiveness. Mainly centred on class size, this body of research has largely neglected other school resources as explanatory factors for student attainment. Conversely, research using education production functions has systematically focused on the study of a causal relationship from school resources to student outcomes, but has paid little attention to the school process itself. The authors find that recent studies utilizing student level data, together with school and school district level resource input data, have found some school resource effects. Using a larger range of control variables, the authors are now also able to make progress in reducing omitted variables and endogeneity bias. These studies have produced some evidence that school quality variables exert a positive influence upon non-exam outcomes. However, a fair amount of work still needs to be done to improve the measures of school output. It also is necessary to overcome the problems of limited data on school resources, on the one hand, and to find reliable instruments to correct for endogeneity bias, on the other hand. Good quality studies that use individual level data tend to use panel data, and thus mostly relate to the performance of school systems that have now undergone significant changes. Therefore, their relevance for showing evidence of relationships between resources and pupils' examination attainment in the current system is questionable. There is no alternative to longitudinal data, though, if one wants to analyse the longer-term impact of the quality of schooling on earnings.

The aim of Chapter 3 is to provide a theory and description of schooling systems. Louis Lévy-Garboua, Nathalie Damoiselet, Gérard Lassibille and Lucia Navarro-Gomez provide a theory that distinguishes between education and training, in which these may be combined in varying proportions by schooling systems for the production of differentiated skills. The authors use data from 16 industrialized countries and the responses given by education experts to a questionnaire that they developed specifically for this study. They postulate a theoretical model in which a basic distinction is made between general education and vocational training. In this model they assume that education contributes to the production of the learning skill, which is considered a general investment for producing many other kinds of occupation-specific skills in combination with specific training. They propose a test for this model and then show that the diversity of marketable skills introduces a policy trade-off for schooling systems between education and non-learning skills. Students should be given a chance to receive further general education before they engage in vocational training. In the same way, they should be sorted in the different tracks according to some combination of their cognitive ability and occupation-specific talents. The authors conclude that early differentiation is good for education but not for the production of skills. They advocate a late horizontal differentiation of schooling systems, which, they argue, would induce a high demand for both education and training.

TRANSITIONS FROM SCHOOL TO WORK

In Chapter 4, María Jesús San Segundo and Barbara Petrongolo investigate the main determinants of the decision to stay on at school at age 16, relating this decision to local labour market conditions. It can be argued that high unemployment rates cause young people to postpone their labour market entrance, because of the resulting decrease in the expected gains from job search and, therefore, the opportunity cost of education. This results in a positive correlation between current youth unemployment and the probability of staying on at school. Conversely, higher youth unemployment, combined with higher adult unemployment, may imply tighter budget constraints for families, which could operate to discourage enrolment in secondary education. In their analysis, the authors identify these two contrasting effects of unemployment on the demand for post-compulsory education in Spain and the UK. Enrolment rates at age 16 are related to both the unemployment rate of youths who have not completed upper-secondary education and the general unemployment rate. They use two cross-sections of youths, interviewed in the Spanish Labour Force Survey (EPA) and the British Labour Force Survey, both in the second quarter of 1991. The use of both controls produces quite clear-cut results: staying-on rates are correlated positively with youth unemployment but negatively with adult unemployment for both males and females. However, the variable that plays the prominent role in the decision to stay on at school is the parents' level of education. These results argue in favour of policies aimed at improving the academic achievement of students from disadvantaged families, as developed in several European countries.

Chapter 5 relates early career experiences with later career success. David Margolis, Erik Plug, Véronique Simonnet and Lars Vilhuber provide an original comparative attempt to analyse the influence of early career experiences of young people in the labour market upon their labour market success or failure later in life. The subject of early-career experiences, in terms of access to a first job, or of the job mobility of young people, is already well developed in the literature. Very little attention, though, has been given to the effects of these experiences in the longer term (that is, more than five years after school leaving). This topic is approached from different perspectives. The authors undertake an econometric estimation using several measures of early career experiences with the aim of controlling for the omitted variable bias, and also considering a variety of different measures of later career success. They use long panel data sets from the United States, France, Germany and the Netherlands. As educational and labour market institutions vary widely from one country to another, they can test if workers with similar early career experiences experience similar career success in the different countries. They note that several different theories link early career variables to later career outcomes and show that there seem to be no 'general principles' that govern similarly the four labour markets considered. This implies that the role played by institutions and their inclusion in theoretical models should be an important topic for future research.

In Chapter 6, Sylvie Mendès and Catherine Sofer compare the access to the first job of apprentices and, more generally, the performances along the work career of ex-apprentices to those of workers who attended vocational school. Do firms value the skills resulting from in-firm training more than those acquired at school? The question then arises whether this specific type of learning facilitates transitions from school to work, as some of the German evidence, especially the low rate of youth unemployment, seems to indicate. However, other explanations are possible, such as demographic specificities, institutional arrangements that raise the returns to specific human capital for firms, or more generally the benefits from youth employment. From a theoretical point of view, the chapter first asks whether apprentices benefit mainly from firm-specific human capital or from positive selection mechanisms. The second question relates to a possible selection effect in the educational system: young people choosing apprenticeship over vocational school may well possess some characteristic that is correlated with the rate at which they obtain their first job. The authors find that apprenticeship seems to be an effective tool in the fight against youth unemployment. Correcting for the endogenous choice of education generally strengthens the results in favour of apprenticeship. Access to the first job appears to be easier for apprentices in every country analysed. In addition, and more generally, the quality of this first job is higher, where 'quality' is measured in terms of the permanence of the job. These are short-term findings, however. Over the longer run, the advantages of apprenticeship seem weaker, and are even found to disappear entirely in some of the research evidence considered in this chapter. One interpretation is that general human capital is of less value to firms at the beginning of the work career, but becomes more valuable over time as it facilitates adaptation to new types of work over the life cycle.

HUMAN CAPITAL AND THE WORK CAREER

In Chapter 7, Peter Elias and Rhys Davies provide an overview of the theoretical and empirical literature relating to employer-provided training and they consider the involvement of employers in skill formation across Europe. They stress that access to vocational training whilst in employment is regarded as a means of enhancing the flexibility of labour by increasing the productivity and employability of workers. This chapter considers the role of employers in the process of skill formation within the European Union. They use information from the Continuing Vocational Training Surveys, and show that there is considerable variation in the incidence of employer provided training within Europe. Especially, there is a significant divergence between the north and south of Europe. Differences in the industrial composition of employment between countries largely explain variations in training participation. However, the content of employer provided training is also shaped by the relationship between the structure of workforce skills delivered by national systems of initial vocational training and the associated production process used by employers. This implies that qualitative differences in employer provided training across countries must be studied alongside simple quantitative comparisons. The authors point towards the potential gains to be made from policy interventions, which would encourage the effective utilization of skills by employers and reduce their incentive to follow retrogressive forms of competition.

Chapter 8 moves on to labour contracts. Juan Cañada-Vicinay and Michel Sollogoub look at institutional regulation of the labour markets, and, more precisely, at the links between labour contracts and economic performance. They compare Spain and France, which both stand at the higher end of the labour standard index describing the strength of the legislation governing a number of aspects of the labour markets. At the same time, these two countries perform differently relative to the European average, with France having similar outcomes to the EU-15, while Spain is an extreme case of poor performance, especially regarding unemployment. The authors analyse how firms use two types of contracts, fixed-term and open-ended labour contracts, in the two countries. They pay special attention to the influence of education on the probability of obtaining permanent employment. They show from the Spanish example, where there was a change in the legislation in the 1990s, that the inflow into permanent contracts is driven more by the individual human capital endowment and business cycle variables than by legal changes. For France, on the one hand fixed-term contracts are found to facilitate integration into the labour market, and even sometimes provide a matching process leading to an open-ended contract but, on the other hand, they are found also to create inefficient working conditions in which employers and employees are insufficiently committed. These results raise the question of the effectiveness of government programmes aimed at integrating youths into the workforce (youth-employment contracts), which are generally based on fixed-term contracts. The limited duration of the contract may produce a risk of opportunistic behaviour by employers. The authors conclude that, to avoid this risk, government programmes should attempt to increase the employers' level of commitment to the employment relationship. Especially, their gain from a greater ease of firing might be compensated by an obligation to provide training, as in training-oriented contracts for example.

Finally, in Chapter 9, Kjell Salvanes looks at labour mobility. The author first presents the aggregate worker and job flows for Norway and compares the results with those from other European countries and the US. He then studies in detail the employment management policies for heterogeneous workers, using a panel data set for Norway for the 1986–94 period, matching workers and plants. The focus of the chapter is to analyse worker and job flows by education level. Two hypotheses can be made: high job creation/destruction rates and 'churning' rates may be due to job creation for highly educated workers and job destruction for low-educated workers and vice versa for replacements, or may result from high hiring separation rates for all skill levels. Distinguishing between education categories of workers allows the author to test these assumptions. He finds that re-employment separations are pro-cyclical, which suggests that this process consists mainly of quits, and that job destruction is counter-cyclical, which implies that it is mainly an employer-initiated phenomenon. Furthermore, these two processes also show different patterns with the educational level of workers. Re-employment separation rates do not vary monotonically with education level, while job destruction is declining in education level. The author also finds differences by education levels, cohorts and gender, in the level of job creation and job destruction rates, as well as in the level of re-employment rates. Another striking finding is that net job creation for highly-educated women is much higher than that for highly-educated men.

While the goals of the Lisbon Summit might appear now to be bold and ambitious, the very fact that we can undertake such productive and collaborative research to understand better the workings of our different educational systems and their longer-term impacts – making good use of data resources, many of which have been produced in a co-ordinated manner for the European Union – is testimony to the growing importance of our European identity. We hope that the results of the work presented here will be of interest to a fairly wide audience. While the general focus of our work lies within the disciplinary boundaries of comparative economic studies, we have written in a style that makes this work accessible to a wider audience, including policy makers, academics and others who have an interest in the ways in which the different educational systems across the European Union impart knowledge, foster citizenship and promote economic growth.

NOTES

1. The STT final report is available on the web site of the European Commission: http://improving-ser.sti.jrc.it/default/
2. Presidency Conclusions, Lisbon European Council, 23–24 March 2000.
3. Published in STT Working Papers Series, web site: *http://www.univ-orleans.fr/DEG/LEO/TSER*
4. Hanushek, E., S.G. Rivkin and L.L. Taylor (1996), 'Aggregation and the estimated effects of school success', *The Review of Economics and Statistics*, 78, 611–27.
5. School inputs include financial resources (such as expenditure per pupil) and real resources (such as pupil–teacher ratios or various measures of teacher education and experience).
6. Card, D. and A. Krueger (1992), 'Does school quality matter? Returns to education and the characteristics of public schools in the US', *Journal of Political Economy*, 100, 1–40.

PART I

Schooling systems

1. The economics of early childhood education: a survey[1]

Wim Groot, Henriëtte Maassen van den Brink, Simone Dobbelsteen and Noortje van Mierlo

1. INTRODUCTION

The development of skills and competences starts well before children reach the age of compulsory education. The transfer of skills and competences in the pre-school period is largely of an informal nature. At this age competences are mostly acquired in a (non-professional) educational situation, such as the family and neighbourhood in which the child grows up. However, there is a development in the direction of more formalized learning and nurturing situations for children in the pre-school age. The most prominent example of this is the increased use of formal childcare, as provided by day care centres, nursery schools and kindergartens. Broadly speaking the early childhood educational arrangements consist of childcare arrangements and social programmes aimed at the (pedagogical) development of children at an early age.

Three reasons can be given for this increased interest in early childhood education. These correspond with the two types of early childhood education just distinguished: general childcare arrangements and compensatory education programmes. The first reason is that nowadays in most European countries early childhood education services are widely accepted as suitable for the cognitive, socio-emotional and physical development of children. Spurred by new evidence from brain research that shows that stimulation and development of cognitive capabilities of infants and young children may have long-term consequences, there is a growing interest in formalized institutions and arrangements for child development at a very early age. The second reason is the growing concern about the well-being and future of children from (disadvantaged) families. It is widely acknowledged that children from disadvantaged families are faced with fewer opportunities in life than most other children. There is state dependency in unemployment, poverty, poor health and crime between generations of individuals from disadvantaged families. Early intervention programmes in education can interrupt this intergenerational transfer of poverty, unemployment and so on. Thirdly, the increased interest in early childhood educational arrangements is due to the increase in the labour force participation of women with young children. The increase in female labour force participation has to a large extent been made possible by the increased availability of childcare arrangements. Because of increasing labour force participation of women there is a growing interest in the effects of women's employment in the pre-school years on outcomes for children.

So on the one hand we have childcare arrangements, which are primarily aimed at the basic development of the child and at providing opportunities for women with young children to participate in the labour market. On the other hand, we distinguish affirmative action programmes that are aimed at increasing the chances in life of children from disadvantaged families, ethnic minority groups, low income households, single parent households and children with low educated parents.[2]

Pre-school arrangements are further to be distinguished from formal education. The essential difference between formal education and pre-school arrangements is that the former is compulsory and available at no or low cost for all eligible children, while the latter is not. As the age at which compulsory education starts varies (roughly somewhere between the age of three and seven), the ages at which children can participate in pre-school arrangements varies as well between OECD countries.

As pre-school arrangements can have different aims and results, we propose to distinguish between compensatory programmes with specific educational goals on the one hand and more general care arrangements on the other, whenever necessary. It should be noted that there is also a third group of pre-school provisions, that is sort of 'in-between' childcare and compensatory programmes: pre-school playgroups for children not specifically at risk. These are generally meant to stimulate the social and physical development of children by playing with peers, but they are not (or less) focused on compensation for disadvantages in early childhood experiences than early intervention programmes. They generally have fewer financial resources and lower-qualified personnel than compensatory programmes and do not enable the mother to work outside the home, as children usually spend only a few hours there. In some countries these pre-school playgroups form a part of the general childcare arrangements. In the presentation of the research on early childhood education we will specify the exact nature of the type of childcare under investigation that is, childcare (general, playgroups, kindergarten, nursery school) or intervention programmes.

Pre-school educational arrangements entail both costs and benefits. In line with the different aims of early childhood education distinguished above, we can make a distinction between the short term and long term benefits. The short term benefits include the contribution to the learning abilities of children and the increased opportunities for women to participate in the labour market.

In the long run there are (in)direct benefits for the child itself. If early childhood education improves the skills and abilities of children this will have a positive effect on the labour market position of the child at an adult age. Other positive effects in the long run include lower crime rates, less chance of being in poverty, better health status and so on. Children and parents may not be the only ones to benefit from early childhood education.

The aim of this chapter is to provide a survey of the research that has been done on the costs, benefits and returns of these arrangements and to analyse the (cost-) effectiveness of the pre-school educational arrangements. The results of this survey are used to analyse the policy issues related to early childhood education from an economic perspective.

2. RESEARCH ON EARLY CHILDHOOD EDUCATION AND CHILDCARE

Before discussing the main findings of research on this topic, we first want to discuss some methodological issues on investigating the effects of early childhood education and care. In order to assess the effect of specific pre-school programmes by comparing outcomes of participants with outcomes of non-participants, you have to make sure that you compare children and families that are similar with regard to all characteristics that may influence the outcomes (such as gender, age and family background). Only then you can be sure that any differences you find between the outcomes of participants and non-participants are caused by the programme. For instance, one should not compare school achievement of children from disadvantaged families that participated in a compensatory programme with school achievement of children from more advantaged families who therefore did not participate. Differences in social and economic characteristics between families of participants and non-participants can influence both the selection into participation and the outcome of the programme. If these differences are not controlled for in a proper way, the estimates of programme effectiveness will be biased.

The ideal case would be to first select a group of children and their families to be included in the research, and then randomly assign these individuals to an experimental group that will actually participate in the pre-school programme, and a control group that will not receive any treatment. If the assignment to treatment is really random, and both groups are similar with respect to other characteristics, any differences that you find in outcomes will be caused by participation in the programme. Unfortunately, only a few researchers have used random assignment of children and families into treatment to evaluate the effects of early childhood education and care (for example Berrueta-Clement et al., 1987; Barnett,1992; Campbell and Ramey, 1994).

If this type of experimental data is not available, it is difficult to assess whether any observed benefits of the treatment are due to the programme itself, or due to the selection of a specific group of participants. In this case, special statistical techniques should be used to control for both observed and unobserved characteristics of participants and non-participants. For instance, Reynolds and Temple (1995) use different (psychometric and econometric) techniques to estimate the effects of a pre-school programme (among others Heckman's inverse Mills ratio and Instrumental Variables). However, many studies in the literature that use non-experimental data have just ignored any possible selection bias. Other problems that often arise in evaluations of effects of pre-school arrangements are small numbers of observations, lack of data on longer-term outcomes, and survey attrition.

In this section the emphasis will be on empirical research on the returns of early childhood education and childcare for the child itself and its parents. The effects of early childhood education on firms and the social effects will be given less attention. The reason for this is a lack of empirical research in this area: we know fairly little about the social effects of early childhood education and childcare. The same holds for costs and benefits for firms.

In the following discussion of various studies on the effects of early childhood education and care, we will distinguish between three groups of outcomes: effects on the social and cognitive development of the child itself, on mother's (or other family members') labour force participation, and on other outcomes such as criminal behaviour, benefits for siblings and use of social security services. This survey on the effectiveness of pre-school arrangements is certainly not exhaustive, but attempts to provide an overview of recent good quality research into the subject. In addition, other reviews of studies concentrating on either childcare provision or compensatory pre-school programmes can be found in Clarke-Stewart (1991), Scarr and Eisenberg (1993), Farran (1990), Barnett (1992), Reynolds and Wolfe (1997) and Kimmel (1998).

2.1 Effects of Childcare on Child Development

In this section we will concentrate on the effects of childcare experiences on the cognitive and social-emotional development of the child. Various types of childcare are included: nurseries (subsidized and non-subsidized day and half-day nurseries) and childminding services (provided by childminders either at the home of the childminder or at the home of the child, who are supervised by professionals). They are typically paid for by parents themselves, but very often governments also finance part of the costs, for instance through subsidy programmes, or employers share the costs with their employees. Also included are pre-school playgroups that are offered as a general provision. So we ignore for the time being the specific arrangements offered to children at risk; these will be the focus of our discussion in the next section.

For several years, psychological research into the effects of childcare on the child's well-being and behaviour focused on possible negative effects of mother–child separation, as the repeated daily separations might harm psychosocial development. This was investigated by Strange Situation Tests: these claim to measure the quality of infant–parent attachment by observing the child's reaction to reunion with the parent following brief separation in an unfamiliar context (Ainsworth et al., 1978). Although some early studies reported disturbances in day care children's attachments, these results could not be replicated by other researchers. Moreover, 'attachment' studies generally suffered from non-random assignment of participants and from very small samples. A recent NICHD study (1997), using observations on more than 1100 infants, shows that childcare experiences only have negative effects in cases of poor quality, large amounts and in combination with poor maternal behaviour. This study also finds that Strange Situation Tests are equally valid to assess infant–mother attachments for children receiving different amounts of childcare, even though the more intensive childcare participants may be more used to separation from their mother.

In addition to studies investigating attachment to the mother using Strange Situation Tests, other studies have investigated different aspects of the emotional and social development of children, like peer relationships. Lamb and Sternberg (1990) present an overview of two decades of psychological research into the effects of childcare. They conclude that: 'If anything, children in nonparental care settings may be more sociable with peers and adults, presumably because they experience interactions with a greater variety of people.'

Several studies have also found effects of childcare on the cognitive development of children (for example O'Brien Caughy et al., 1994; Peisner-Feinberg and Burchinal, 1997). A review-study by Clarke-Stewart (1991) concludes that 'children in day care centres and pre-school programs tend to be more socially skilled and intellectually advanced than children at home with their parents, sitters, or in day care homes', where social and intellectual performance is measured by (among others) verbal ability, cognition, social competence, cooperation with adults and (unfamiliar) peers, or creativity with materials. Clarke-Stewart also discusses possible explanations for the positive effects of childcare experiences on child development. Research findings suggest that especially differences in the kind of attention and stimulation in centres and homes (the presence of peers, the training of care givers, and the use of specific programmes and curricula) influence the social and intellectual performance of children. Differences in the quality of attention and stimulation, and pre-existing differences between centre- and home-children and their families, also seem to contribute to some extent to the better performance of children in centre care.

Recent research finds some factors which could increase the risks concerning the developmental problems of children cared for in day care centres: the very young age of the child (Lamb, 1998; NICHD, 1998); the child's difficult disposition (for instance a choleric disposition) (Volling and Feagans, 1995); and a difficult home situation. The quality of the childcare arrangements compensates these risk factors and plays a crucial role on children's development (Hausfather et al., 1997). Research carried out by Andersson (1989, 1992) and Howes (1990) showed that the quality of the childcare has positive effects on the socio-emotional development and school performances of the child.

Most research on the effects of childcare experiences on child development that is presented in international journals is based on data from the United States. However, positive effects on children's intellectual development are also found for Sweden (Andersson, 1989 and 1992), Denmark (Teasdale and Berliner, 1991), Norway (Jungclaus et al., 1991), Germany (Tietze, 1987) and France (Jarousse and Mingat, 1992). Spence Boocock (1995) discusses evidence from 13 countries across the world on the impact of participation in childcare or pre-school educational programmes: from Australia, Canada, Colombia, France, Germany, India, Ireland, Japan, Singapore, South Korea, Sweden, Turkey and the United Kingdom. The findings for these countries also show that childcare is not harmful for child development, and may even have positive effects if the care provided is of good quality.

The comparison and generalization of the findings of various studies is hampered by the variability with respect to several factors. The effects of childcare are found to depend on the type of non-parental care considered (Osborn and Milbank, 1987), the quality of non-parental care (Zaslow, 1991; Peisner-Feinberg and Burchinal, 1997), the amount of non-parental care and the age at which a child first receives it (Andersson, 1989, 1992) and the socio-economic background of the child (O'Brien Caughy et al., 1994; Peisner-Feinberg and Burchinal, 1997). The effect of the latter may be indirect, via its influence on the quality of care that children receive (Phillips et al., 1994; Berger and Black, 1992).

Even more importantly, the ways in which outcomes are assessed, the composition and selection of comparison groups, and the statistical methods used to analyse the data, may also have large effects on the results found. For instance, none of the studies discussed has used samples of children that were randomly assigned into childcare or not. Nor has any of these studies investigated the possible influence of self-selection into childcare on their results, using specific statistical techniques. Therefore, it is possible that the positive effects of childcare that are found are due to (observable or unobservable) characteristics of the children or parents using childcare (see for instance Clarke-Stewart (1991), who concludes that pre-existing differences between centre- and home-children and their families seem to contribute to some extent to the better performance of children in centre care).

We therefore conclude that, on average, childcare (pre-school) children appear to do better than home-children on intellectual and social development. It remains unclear, however, to what extent these effects are due to the care provided or to pre-existing differences between both groups of children. Moreover, literature provides little guidance as to what is the optimal type, quality, amount, and timing of pre-school arrangements.

2.2 The Effects of Early Childhood Compensatory Programmes on Child Development

Early childhood compensatory programmes generally aim at improving the intellectual development of young children living in poverty by improving the educational and social environments of these children before they enter into formal (compulsory) education. Most research on early childhood intervention programmes is done in the United States. Since the early 1960s various experimental schemes for pre-school education have been initiated there. These programmes vary with respect to their target groups, the age of the children involved, their experimental design, scale, and so on. They are typically paid for by the government, with generally no or very low parental costs, as these programmes are especially meant for low-income families. Moreover, returns are expected not only to accrue to the participating families (for instance, improved school performance and higher earnings) but also to society as a whole (such as lower schooling costs later in life, higher tax-revenue through higher earnings, less welfare use and less criminal behaviour).

It is beyond the scope of this chapter to discuss all early childhood intervention programmes initiated since the 1960s. A nice historic overview of early childhood intervention (theoretical bases, different approaches, and discussion) can be found in Meisels and Shonkoff (1990). Moreover, not all programmes are equally appropriate to inform us on the success of early intervention programmes. Barnett (1992) points at serious design limitations and attrition problems of various studies evaluating compensatory pre-school education programmes in the US: small numbers of participants, severe attrition in the follow-up period, total absence of a formal evaluation of the programme, measurement of only specific and immediate outcomes, non-random assignment of participants to the control group, or no participants assigned to control groups at all. The last problem may arise if programme providers consider it 'unethical' to deny children in the control group access to services, or consider the testing of children in the control group as a loss of money: scientific considerations, like randomized assignment of participants, may conflict with service provision.

In addition to the numerous evaluations of specific intervention programmes (for example Berrueta-Clement et al., 1984, for the High/Scope Perry Preschool Project; Campbell and Ramey, 1994, for the Carolina Abecedarian Project; Currie and Thomas, 1995, for Head Start; Reynolds, 1997, for the Chicago Child–Parent Centers), several meta-analyses and review studies have summarized and discussed the returns of various early childhood interventions (see Royse et al., 1983; Casto and Mastropieri, 1986; Farran, 1990; Barnett, 1992; Karoly et al., 1998; see Reynolds and Wolfe 1997, for a 'review of reviews').

An early attempt to evaluate and compare longer term outcomes of compensatory programmes was done by the Consortium of Longitudinal Studies (1983). They re-analysed original data from 11 different intervention programmes, but also gathered follow-up data for these different programmes, as well as a meta-analysis of the raw data of 9 (of the 11) programmes by Royse et al. (1983), which show positive effects on (among others) school performance, self-esteem and occupational aspirations.

A more recent comparative study of the effects of various early intervention programmes is the one by Karoly et al. (1998). They investigate the costs and benefits of early childhood interventions by highlighting the findings from formal evaluations of ten of the most noteworthy early intervention programmes in the US. With their study they illustrate 'the range of interventions that have been studied, highlighting the types of effects that have been measured for these representative programs'. The ten programmes included in their study all satisfy criteria that are considered important for providing more-reliable estimates of both short-run and long-run programme effects: experimental design, preferably with random assignment to treatment and control groups, a sample size of 50 children or more in treatment plus control groups, a follow-up period, preferably past the period of programme intervention, and less than 50 per cent attrition at follow-up.

These ten programmes are: the Early Training Project, the High/Scope Perry Preschool Project, Project Head Start, the Chicago Child–Parent Center and Expansion Program, the Houston Parent–Child Development Center, the Syracuse Family Development Research Program, the Carolina Abecedarian Project, Project CARE (Carolina Approach to Responsive Education), the Infant Health and Development Project (IHDP), and the Elmira Prenatal/ Early Infancy Project (PEIP). Some programmes had less than 100 participants, only two programmes had more than 1500 participants (for example Head Start, since 1965 several projects, over 15 million children involved;

Chicago Child–Parent Center and Expansion Program, 1539 participants). Seven programmes used random assignment of participants, one used matched comparison groups, and another one used statistical controls for non-random participation. The programmes that started in the early 1970s tend to intervene at an earlier age in childhood than the older programmes, as the idea arose that intervention should take place as early in the childhood period as possible.

Karoly et al. conclude that every study produced at least one significant benefit for the child, and that most programmes produced benefits in even more than one domain. All studies that measured IQ found significant differences after treatment, although these differences disappeared within a few years. The (very-high-quality) Abecedarian program was the only one that showed lasting gains in IQ. Educational outcomes (such as academic achievement) showed longer-lasting benefits in all programmes, if measured, and the Chicago CPC and Abecedarian evaluations suggest that gains may be stronger the longer the duration of the intervention programme. Favourable results are also found for criminal activity, although this was only measured in four cases. Effects on employment, income, and welfare participation are only measured in the Perry Preschool programme, but they find promising results (also discussed in Berrueta-Clement, 1987, and Barnett, 1992).

We may conclude that the literature provides persuasive evidence that early intervention programmes, at least those of high quality, can produce significant and long-lasting benefits for children from disadvantaged families. However, Reynolds and Wolfe (1997) warn that the majority of empirical evidence in literature comes from high quality model programmes. The evaluations of these programmes may be limited in statistical power and generalizability, and need not be informative of the effectiveness of large-scale programmes.

The decision to spend public tax money on early intervention programmes will probably not just depend on any benefits produced, but much more on the returns of these programmes in relation to their costs. Only few studies have addressed the economic efficiency of various approaches to intervention, comparing costs with benefits. Barnett and Escobar (1987) review various studies on the cost-effectiveness of early intervention, and conclude that some studies provide credible evidence that early intervention is a good public investment. They also state that, unfortunately, the relative economic efficiency of alternative intervention programmes remains vague. Only two studies have explicitly investigated the effects of variations in characteristics of pre-school programmes, and found that group size, teacher preparation, and length of intervention appear to be important topics. Ruopp et al. (1979) found that teacher training was associated with better quality and higher gains in test scores, but had hardly any impact on cost. In contrast, teacher–child ratio was not related to quality or gains in test scores, but strongly determined costs.

Karoly et al. (1998) also present a cost–benefit analysis for two of the programmes discussed in their study: the Elmira Prenatal/Early Infancy Project and the Perry Preschool Project. Both programmes succeed in generating savings to government that exceed their costs. However, the net savings from the Elmira PEIP turned out to be substantial for higher-risk families, but negative for lower-risk families, which leads to the conclusion that targeting matters.

2.3   The Effects of Childcare Use on Mothers' Labour Force Participation

In economic models of household behaviour, household members can choose between working inside or outside the home, taking prices, productivity, wages and other income into account. Therefore, availability and costs of childcare will affect the labour force participation of the household members (see for example Gustafsson and Stafford, 1992). Empirical research concentrates on the influence of childcare costs on labour market activity of parents, especially mothers, and on the effect of prices, family income and earnings on the use of childcare. Both for Sweden (Gustafsson and Stafford, 1992) and the US (Blau and Robins, 1988; Ribar, 1992) evidence is found that lower costs of childcare lead to higher labour force participation of women and to a higher use of formal childcare. All three studies focused on the mother's decision to be employed; Gustafsson and Stafford also investigated the decision to work less or more than 30 hours. For Canada, Powell (1994) found no significant effect of childcare costs on labour force participation of married women, but a significant negative effect on the number of hours worked conditional on being employed. For a totally different sample of unmarried low-income women in the US, Berger and Black (1992) found no effect of childcare subsidies on the number of hours worked by these women. However, they did find that childcare subsidy programmes increased the probability that these women were employed, and also improved the quality of day care used by them.

Groot and Maassen van den Brink (1994), using Dutch data, find that the relationship between the use of childcare and labour force participation is mutual: the number of hours of childcare use significantly increases the number of hours the mother works, and the number of hours worked significantly increases the use of childcare (both paid and unpaid). However, the effect of the use of childcare on labour force participation is larger than vice versa.

Some studies in this literature have also investigated what factors influence the use of formal childcare. Groot et al. (1991) find a large negative effect of the price of childcare and a positive effect of household income on the probability that formal childcare is used. The choice between various types of childcare is influenced by the number of hours the mother works, household income, the number of children (both pre-school and school-age children), and the age difference between siblings (Lehrer, 1989; Groot et al., 1991). Most of these studies totally ignore possible effects of different childcare arrangements on the well-being of children, although quality of childcare is sometimes taken into account (Maassen van den Brink, 1994).

Earlier we made a distinction between childcare and compensatory programmes, and in the preceding pages we have only discussed effects on mothers' labour force participation of the former. However, some early intervention programmes take the form of full-day year-round educational day care and may therefore also effect the mother's labour supply. For instance, the Carolina Abecedarian and the IHDP intervention programmes both show higher employment of mothers during the pre-school period of their children (see Karoly et al., 1998).

We conclude that there appears to be strong evidence in various countries that childcare costs have an effect on both childcare use and on mothers' labour force activity, either by a higher probability of being employed or by an increase in the number of hours worked.

In some countries – such as the Netherlands – it is also common that employers supply childcare for their employees, or that they pay part of the costs. In this way, the employer may try to keep the employee in the firm, which prevents loss of investments in (firm-specific) human capital and costs of selection and training of new employees. It is also sometimes claimed that employer-sponsored childcare may increase the employee's job satisfaction and productivity, and may reduce employee absenteeism. However, in his evaluation of empirical studies on this subject, Miller (1984) concluded that such claims are not supported by credible research, and that more work has to be done. A more recent study by Kossek and Nichol (1992) investigated the effects of employer-provided on-site childcare on employee performance, absenteeism and attitudes. They found that childcare was more likely to significantly influence employee attitudes and membership behaviours (such as recruitment and retention), than employees' performance or absenteeism.

2.4 The Effects of Early Childhood Education and Care on Other Outcomes

The majority of studies on the effects of early childhood education and care have concentrated on (social and cognitive) development of the participating child itself, and on the labour force activity of the mother. Few studies, however, have addressed effects on other outcomes.

Seitz and Apfel (1994) claim that some early intervention programmes, namely the ones that focus on parents, may change the caregiving environment in a way that benefits all children. They found that siblings of intervention group children showed better school performance than siblings of control group children, although these siblings were all born after the programme's services had ended. These outcomes suggest the existence of selection effects.

The Perry Preschool Program is unique with respect to the number and variety of longer term outcomes that are measured. In addition to the effects on school success of participating children, as discussed earlier, the project also appeared to have significant effects on employment rates (at least at age 19), earnings and received public assistance, and criminal behaviour (Berrueta-Clement et al., 1984, and Barnett, 1992). Although the outcomes for criminal behaviour are questioned by Farran (1990), other pre-school programmes (that is, the Chicago Child-Parent Centers, the Syracuse Family Development Research Program, and the Elmira Prenatal/Early Infancy Project) also report significant differences in delinquency rates or number of arrests between participants and control groups (see Karoly et al., 1998). Not one of the pre-school programmes produced significant effects on teenage pregnancies.

Currie and Thomas (1995) investigated the health and nutritional status of Head Start participants in comparison with other children. They found no effects on child height-for-age, a long-run indicator of health and nutritional status, but did find higher immunization rates of participants, which they interpreted as evidence of greater access to preventive health services.

Until now we have only discussed studies evaluating pre-school programmes in developed countries. In contrast, pre-school programmes in developing countries generally put more emphasis on providing health and nutrition services to children in poverty, without or besides providing educational services. The World Bank increasingly directs funding to young children, by Early Child Development programmes, providing good health and nutrition and cognitive development services (see Young, 1996, and Human Development Network, 1998, for an overview). A study by van der Gaag and Tan (1997) showed that an Early Child Development programme (the PIDI-project in Bolivia) produced direct benefits such as lower mortality rates, progress in psychosocial development, and higher enrolment in primary school, which will lead to higher productivity of these children when they have grown up. Moreover, the project may lead to greater community participation and lower future fertility rates, but these benefits are much more difficult to quantify. Comparing quantifiable benefits of PIDI with its costs, benefit–cost ratios between 2.38 and 3.10 are obtained. They conclude that ECD programmes, if well targeted and successful in increasing school enrolment and achievement, are excellent economic investments.

3. EFFICIENCY AND EQUITY IN EARLY CHILDHOOD EDUCATION

There are two potential sources of impediments to equal access to early child-hood education: the price that parents have to pay for the arrangements and the availability of places at the facilities. These barriers to access are higher for some households than for others. The price may be a greater obstacle for low income families than for higher income households. Higher educated parents may also have more information and better contacts to arrange for a place at an institution for early childhood education. If early childhood education is organized by firms – as for example is to a large extent the case in the Netherlands – access to the arrangements may differ between employees and non-employees. It may also be more profitable for firms to arrange for child-care for workers in high skilled jobs than for workers in low skilled jobs. If so, this will create differences in access to childcare between workers.

Differences in family background lead to different starting positions for children once they enter education. Households offer a wide variety of learn-ing environments. In some households a lot of attention is paid to enhancing the cognitive skills of young children, while in others little or no attention is paid to child development. As a result some children are already at an disad-vantage the moment they enter the formal education system. The heterogene-ity in cognitive skills at the age at which children become eligible for compulsory education can have long lasting effects on their educational achievements and thereby on their future labour market and social position. This provides the rationale from an equity perspective to ensure that children enter the education system at roughly the same starting position in cognitive development. Early childhood education can contribute to these equal starting positions by compensating for the lack of attention paid by parents to the cognitive development of their children.

If access to early childhood education allows women to increase their labour supply, access to childcare will increase earnings differentials between women. Women who use childcare will increase their income relative to women who do not. This inequality will be even larger if higher educated women in high skilled and better paying jobs have more access to childcare than lower educated, low paid women in low skilled jobs.

The efficiency argument for subsidizing early childhood education is based on the notion than in the absence of subsidies the use of early childhood educa-tion is less than (socially) optimal. Government subsidies lower the price of early childhood education for the parents and increase the use of it. This may be especially relevant for parents who fail to see the importance of developing cognitive skills in their children.

From an efficiency point of view it is relevant to note that by investing in early childhood education social costs in the future might be avoided. If early childhood education leads to lower costs for unemployment benefits, health care or costs related to criminal activity, making costs for early childhood education avoids having to make these social costs in the future.

To determine the socially optimal use of early childhood education, we may also look at the goals of public policy. Two forms of public policy are of relevance here: educational policy and general socio-economic policy. The rationale for government intervention can be found in two important criteria for evaluation of (early) education systems: efficiency and equity.

From an efficiency point of view educational policy is concerned with the efficiency of the production of education. Two forms of efficiency in education can be distinguished: (1) learning efficiency and; (2) informational efficiency. Learning efficiency refers to the efficiency by which new skills are acquired. A more structured learning environment such as a school usually offers more opportunities for children to acquire cognitive skills. Early childhood intervention programmes are usually organized to provide a more structured learning environment to young children than is provided to them at home.

Informational efficiency refers to the efficiency by which information about the (cognitive) skills learned becomes known to others. A specific instrument for improving informational efficiency is certification. Certification means that particular skills are graded, or minimum skills are certified, so that other educational institutions or employers have more information about the expected achievements of prospective students and workers. A basic question is to what extent education systems are successful in realizing an efficient production of education for children.

Equity appeals to considerations of distributional justice. Opinions about what is equitable differ among individuals. It is therefore not possible to define a generally acceptable criterion of distributional justice. However, as was noted before, access to early childhood education is not equal for all. Furthermore, there is a wide variety in learning environments offered by households. This heterogeneity in learning environments by households leads to unequal starting positions for children at the age they enter formal education. Finally, the outcomes of the learning processes are not the same for everyone. As some children have more abilities, better access to education, and also are more efficient learners than others, educational outcomes differ. The differences between children and between educational institutions are a source of social inequality.

The equity argument calls for an education for everyone to match his or her abilities and interests in order to fully develop his or her potentials. At the very least, this calls for access to schooling irrespective of parental background, and hence elimination of informational, financial and motivational barriers. The argument may even be extended to call for compensating schooling efforts: more schooling resources devoted to those with the weakest potential future labour market position, and more support for low-ability children than for high-ability children. It would, for example, justify early childhood education for disadvantaged learners or more public subsidies to be given to these intervention programmes aimed at children from disadvantaged families.

There is a trade-off between equity and efficiency. For example, individuals with lower capabilities may be less efficient learners. While it may be efficient to invest more resources in able learners, equity considerations may lead one to prefer to spend resources on educating the most disadvantaged learners.

The efficiency argument calls for optimal development of individuals' abilities, and to some extent, generates similar conclusions as the equity argument. But from an efficiency point of view compensating schooling such as early childhood education must be justified by the individual and social returns of these investments in disadvantaged learners. Actually, the social returns may be high, if account is being taken of the effects on unemployment, health, crime and so on.

A caveat here must be made for the fact that parents of children who are eligible for compensating education programmes for young children are not always fully convinced of the benefits of these programmes. This may be an impediment to using early childhood education and thereby result in inefficient use of these arrangements. This might be avoided by bringing in elements of compulsion or by allocating subsidies in a way in which parents only benefit if their children participate in the early childhood education programmes.

4. CONCLUSION

From a historic perspective the aim of all forms of early childhood education – both intervention programmes and childcare – was to improve the cognitive skills of young children. With the increase in female labour participation a second aim has emerged: to enable women to combine children and paid work. It is also now widely recognized that children's experiences in their first years of life are highly formative for their future development.

As a result of the competing aims of early childhood education we have to distinguish between early childhood educational intervention programmes which are primarily aimed at the development and well-being of young children and childcare with an emphasis on allowing women to combine paid work and care for children. The competing goals of early childhood education are reflected in the different outcomes evaluated in this chapter.

A consequence of the competing objectives of early childhood education – child development and female labour supply – has been that different types of early childhood education are targeted towards different social groups. Early childhood education programmes are mostly – if not exclusively – intended for children from disadvantaged families (that is, low income households). The scope of childcare is wider and does not only include low income families. Rather the opposite, the use of childcare in many countries is higher among higher income households than among low income households. This is for a large part a result of the specific aim by which childcare is used: childcare is used to allow women with young children to be employed and earn an income. Investments in childcare appear to have large labour market impacts: a cross-country comparison shows that countries with generous childcare benefit systems are associated with high female labour force participation rates. Use of childcare therefore increases earnings differentials between households rather than reducing them, while early childhood educational intervention programmes are aimed at increasing opportunities for children from disadvantaged families and thereby reducing income inequality in the longer run.

In this chapter we have surveyed the literature on the economic effects of early childhood education. Critical questions in this respect include: how effective are different forms of early childhood education in preparing children for their future education and – eventually – for the labour market, what are the labour market impacts on early childhood education; and what trends can we identify in early childhood education?

Two general conclusions emerge from this survey. The first is that hard econometric evidence on the effects of early childhood education is scarce. This makes it difficult to draw any definite conclusions. If we look at the results of empirical research we further have to note that we have more knowledge on some of the aspects of early childhood education than on others. A fair amount of research has been done on the effects of early childhood education (both intervention programmes and childcare) on child development and on the effects of childcare on the female labour supply. Fairly little or no research has been done on the effects of childcare on firms and on the social costs and benefits of early childhood education. However – and that is the second general conclusion we draw – the available research does seem to indicate that good quality care and good quality intervention programmes can have substantially positive effects on the children who participate in these programmes.

This raises the issue whether the different types of early education should be integrated into one encompassing programme that combines the goal of fostering the cognitive development of children at an early age with the aim of allowing women with young children to participate in the labour market. Mothers of disadvantaged children may after all benefit even more from the opportunity to participate in the labour market, while parents who use child-care arrangements may very well be interested in pedagogical measures to develop the cognitive skills of their children. Strengthening the pedagogical objective of childcare may increase its attractiveness for young children and their parents.

The conclusion that early childhood education has positive effects on child development and female labour supply raises the question of whether governments should stimulate the use of early childhood education by subsidizing it? There are two aspects to this question: is there a motive for government intervention, and if there is, how should governments intervene?

Both from a perspective of educational policy and from the perspective of social policy there are efficiency and equity arguments for government intervention in early childhood education. The primary reason to provide educational intervention programmes to disadvantaged children is to improve their cognitive skills. These programmes are usually intended for children from families that neither have the means to pay for early childhood education themselves, nor a strong conviction that early childhood education is beneficial for their children. Combined with the positive effects of early childhood education on child development these provide strong arguments for governments to encourage and facilitate the use of early childhood education by children from disadvantaged families.

It is widely recognized that good quality childcare is a prerequisite to increase female labour supply. To increase the (female) labour force participation rate many countries have not only taken measures to improve childcare but have also provided for more generous entitlements for parental leave for parents. Both from a cost perspective and from the perspective of care arrangements, parental leave and childcare can be seen as substitutes. Care for young children can either be provided by parental leave for the parents themselves or by enabling parents to hire a place in a childcare institution. Both parental leave and childcare involve costs for parents, firms and/or the state. This raises the question of whether governments should focus on a further extension of parental leave measures or whether it is more efficient to aim at increasing childcare arrangements. The discussion in this chapter has shown that early childhood education probably has positive effects on the cognitive development of young children. Career interruptions from the labour market – for example through parental leave – have negative effects on future labour market chances and earnings capacity. Furthermore, parental leave is no substitute for early childhood education programmes aimed at the development of disadvantaged children. Also, there is substantial evidence to suggest that mother's educational qualifications – but not father's education – is positively related to children's educational attainment (see Haveman and Wolfe, 1995; Card, 1999 and Ermisch and Francesconi, 2001). One possible contributing factor is that higher educated mothers are more likely to participate in the labour market and to use childcare for their children. These arguments seem to suggest that a relative emphasis on childcare rather than on parental leave is to be preferred, especially if childcare has pedagogical objectives as well. As it is likely that in all European countries male and female labour force participation rates will gradually converge, the availability of childcare arrangements will continue to expand over the years to come. A second trend that can be foreseen is that early childhood intervention programmes will be integrated into childcare arrangements.

NOTES

1. We would like to thank Peter Dolton and the participants of the TSER/STT meeting on April 19 2002 in Warwick for their helpful comments on a previous version of this chapter. An extended version of this chapter – including detailed descriptions of the main findings of the studies herewith discussed – can be obtained from the authors on request.
2. This distinction between intervention programmes and general childcare arrangements does not fully describe all forms of early childhood education. It ignores forms of early childhood education such as music schools, sport schools, and ballet schools for young children. As the economic significance of these types of early childhood education have – to the best of our knowledge – never been studied, we will leave them out of our discussion.

REFERENCES

Ainsworth, M.D.S., M.S. Blehar, E. Walters and S. Wall (1978), *Patterns of Attachment: A Psychological Study of the Strange Situation*, Hillsdale, NJ: Lawrence Erlbaum.

Andersson, B.E. (1989), 'Effects of public day-care: a longitudinal study', *Child Development*, **60**, 857–66.

Andersson, B.E. (1992), 'Effects of day-care on cognitive and socioemotional competence of thirteen-year-old Swedish schoolchildren', *Child Development*, **63**, 20–36.

Barnett, W.S. (1992), 'Benefits of compensatory preschool education', *Journal of Human Resources*, **27** (2), 279–312.

Barnett, W.S. and C.M. Escobar (1987), 'The Economics of Early Educational Intervention: a review', *Review of Educational Research*, **57** (4), 387–414.

Berger, M.C. and D.A. Black (1992), 'Child care subsidies, quality of care, and the labor supply of low-income, single mothers', *The Review of Economics and Statistics,* **74** (4), 635–42.

Berrueta-Clement J.R., L.J. Schweinhart, W.S. Barnett, A.S. Epstein and D.P. Weikart (1984), 'Changed Lives: The Effects of the Perry Preschool Program on Youths Through Age 19', Ypsilant, MI: The High/Scope Press.

Berrueta-Clement, J.R., L.J. Schweinhart, W.S. Barnett and D.P. Weikart (1987), 'The effect of early educational intervention on crime and delinquency in adolescence and early adulthood', in J.D. Burchard and S.N. Burchard (eds), *Primary Prevention of Psycopathology, Volume 10, Prevention of Delinquent Behavior*, Newbury Park, CA: Sage Publications Inc., pp. 220–40.

Blau, D.M. and P.K. Robins (1988), 'Child-care costs and family labor supply', *The Review of Economics and Statistics*, **70** (3), 374–81.

Campbell, F.A. and C.T. Ramey (1994), 'Effects of early intervention on intellectual and academic achievement: a follow-up study of children from low-income families', *Child Development*, **65**, 684–98.

Card, D. (1999), 'The causal effect of education on earnings', in: O. Ashenfelter and D. Card (eds), *Handbook of Labor Economics*, Vol. 3, Amsterdam: Elsevier.

Casto, G. and M.A. Mastropieri (1986), 'The efficacy of early intervention programs: a meta-analysis', *Exceptional Children*, **52**, 417–24.

Clarke-Stewart (1991), 'A home is not a school: the effects of child care on children's development', *Journal of Social Issues*, **47** (2), 105–23.

Consortium for Longitudinal Studies (ed.) (1983), *As the Twig is Bent. Lasting effects of preschool programmes*, Hillsdale, NJ: L. Erlbaum Publisher.

Currie, J. and D. Thomas (1995), 'Does Head Start make a difference?', *American Economic Review*, **85** (3), 341–64.

Ermisch, J. and M. Francesconi (2001), 'Family matters: impacts of family background on educational attainments', *Economica*, **68**, 137–56.

Farran, D.C. (1990), 'Effects of intervention with disadvantaged and disabled children: A decade review', in S. Meisels and J. Shonkoff (eds), *Handbook of Early Childhood Interventions*, Cambridge, UK and New York: Cambridge University Press.

Groot, W. and H. Maassen van den Brink (1994), 'Kinderoprang verbetert inkomensparitie van vrouwen', *Economisch Statistische Berichten 4003*, 304–7.

Groot, W., H. Maassen van den Brink and H. Oosterbeek (1991), 'An empirical analysis of the determinants of child care arrangements in the Netherlands', Research Memorandum 9109, Center for Research in Public Economics, Leiden University.

Gustafsson, S. and F. Stafford (1992), 'Child care subsidies and labor supply in Sweden' *Journal of Human Resources*, **27** (1), 204–30.

Hausfather, A., A. Toharia, C. LaRoche and F. Engelsmann (1997), 'Effects of age of entry, day care quality and family characteristics on pre-school behavior', *Journal of Child Psychology and Psychiatry*, **38**, 441–8.

Haveman, R. and B. Wolfe (1995), 'The determinants of children's attainment: a review of methods and findings', *Journal of Economic Literature*, **33**, 1829–78.

Howes, C. (1990), 'Can the age of entry into child care and the quality of child care predict adjustment in kindergarten?', *Developmental Psychology*, **26**, 292–303.

Human Development Network (1998), OECD Development Center, http://www.oecd.org.dev.technics.

Jarousse, J.P. and A. Mingat (1992), 'La Formation du Capital Humain: Gestion par le Marche ou Gestion par L'Etat?', *Revue Economique*, **43** (4), 739–53.

Jarousse, J.P., C. Leroy-Audsouin and A. Mingat (1995), 'Les inspections de l'Education Nationale au niveau primaire: disparités, dotations, pratiques eteffets sur le fonctionnement des écoles et les acquis des élèves', *Revue Française de Pédagogie*, 1–34.

Jungclaus, R., T. Hartmann, G. Saake and C. Sernadas (1991), 'Introduction to TROLL – Textual Language for Object-oriented Specification', in G. Saake and A. Sernadas (eds), *Information Systems – Correctness and Reusability*, Technical Report 91–03, Technische Universitat Braunschweig, 97–128.

Kamerman, S.B. (1991), 'Child care policies and programs: an international overview', *Journal of Social Issues*, **47** (2), 179–96.

Karoly, L.A., P.W. Greenwood, S.S. Everingham, J. Houbé, M.R. Kilburn, C.P. Rydell,

M. Sanders and J. Chiesa (1998), 'Investing in our children: what we know and don't know about the costs and benefits of early childhood interventions', RAND Corperation, Santa Monica.

Kimmel J. (1998), 'Child care costs as a barrier to employment for single and married mothers', *Review of Economics and Statistics*, **10**, 287–99.

Kossek, E. and V. Nichol (1992), 'The effects of on-site child care on employee attitudes and performance', *Personnel Psychology*, **45**, 485–509.

Lamb, M.E. (1998), 'Non parental child care: context, quality, correlates and consequences', in W. Damon (series ed.) and E.E. Sigel and K.A. Renninger (vol. eds), *Handbook of Child Psychology*, vol. 4, *Child Psychology in Practice*, 77–133.

Lamb, M.E., and K.J. Sternberg (1990), 'Do we really know how day care affects children?' *Journal of Applied Developmental Psychology*, **11**, 351–79.

Lehrer, E. (1989), 'Preschoolers with Working Mothers: An Analysis of the Determinants of Child Care Arrangements', *Journal of Population Economics*, **2**, 251–68.

Maassen van den Brink, H. (1994), *Female Labor Supply, Child Care and Marital Conflict*, Amsterdam: Amsterdam University Press.

Meisels, S.J. and J.R. Shonkoff (1990), *Handbook of Early Childhood Interventions*, Cambridge, UK and New York: Cambridge University Press.

Miller, T.I. (1984), 'The effects of employer-sponsored child care on employee absenteeism, turnover, productivity, recruitment or job satisfaction: what is claimed and what is known', *Personnel Psychology*, **37** (2), 277–90.

NICHD Early Child Care Research Network (1997), 'The effects of infant child care on infant–mother attachment security: results of the NICHD Study of Early Child Care', *Child Development*, **68** (5), 860–79.

NICHD Early Child Care Research Network (1998), 'Early childcare and self-control, compliance and problem behavior at twenty-four and thirty-six months', *Child Development*, **69**, 1145–70.

O'Brien Caughy, M., J.A. DiPietro and D.M. Strobino (1994), 'Day-care participation as a protective factor in the cognitive development of low-income children', *Child Development*, **65**, 457–71.

Osborn, A.F. and J.E. Milbank (1987), *The effects of early education. A report from the Child Health and Education Study*, Oxford: Clarendon Press.

Peisner-Feinberg, E.S. and M.R. Burchinal (1997), 'Relations between preschool children's child-care experiences and concurrent development: the Cost, Quality and Outcomes Study', *Merrill-Palmer Quarterly*, **43** (3), 451–77.

Phillips, D.A., M. Voran, E. Kisker, C. Howes and M. Whitebook (1994), 'Child care for children in poverty: opportunity or inequity?', *Child Development*, **65**, 472–92.

Powell (1994), Queen's Institute for Economic Research Discussion, Paper 905.

Reynolds, A.J. (1997), *Success in Early Childhood Intervention*, Lincoln, NE: University of Nebraska.

Reynolds, A.J. and J.A. Temple (1995), 'Quasi-experimental estimates of the effects of a preschool intervention. Psychometric and econometric comparisons', *Evaluation Review*, **19** (4), 347–73.

Reynolds, A.J. and B. Wolfe (1997), 'Early intervention, school achievement and special education placement: findings from the Chicago Longitudinal Study', *Focus*, **19** (3), 25–8.

Ribar, D.C. (1992), 'Child care and the labor supply of married women. Reduced form evidence', *Journal of Human Resources*, **27** (1), 134–65.

Royse, D., B. Thyer, D. Padgett and T.K. Logan (1983), *Program Evaluation: An Introduction* (3rd edition), Belmont, CA: Brooks/Cole.

Ruopp, R., J. Travers, F. Glantz and C. Coelen (1979), *Children at the Center: Summary findings and their implications. Final report of the National Day Care Study*, Cambridge, MA: Abt. Associates.

Scarr and Eisenberg (1993), 'Child care research: issues, perspectives and results', *Annual Review of Psychology*, **44**, 613–44.

Seitz, V. and N.H. Apfel (1994), 'Parent-focused intervention: diffusion effects on siblings', *Child Development*, **65**, 677–83.

Spence Boocock, S. (1995), 'Early childhood programmes in other nations: Goals and outcomes', *The Future of Children*, **5** (3), 94–114.

Teasdale, T.W. and P. Berliner (1991), 'Experience of kindergartens in relation to educational level and cognitive abilities in adulthood: a geographical analysis', *Scandinavian Journal of Psychology*, **32**, 336–43.

Tietze, W. (1987), 'A structural model for the evaluation of preschool effects', *Early Childhood Research Quarterly*, **2**, 133–53.

Van der Gaag, J. and J.P. Tan (1997), *The Benefits of Early Child Development Programmes. An economic analysis*, Washington: The World Bank.

Young, M.E. (1996), 'Early Child Development: Investment in the Future', Report HDD, Washington, DC: Worldbank.

Zaslow, M.J. (1991), 'Variation in child care quality and its implications for children', *Journal of Social Issues*, **47** (2), 125–38.

2. The economic impact of schooling resources

Peter Dolton, Ros Levacic and Anna Vignoles

1. INTRODUCTION

Despite the strong belief amongst parents and educational professionals that expenditure on schooling is causally and positively related to student educational and labour market outcomes, the research evidence for this is equivocal (Burtless, 1996; Hanushek, 1986; Hanushek, 1997). For example, Hanushek et al. (1996) finds that in the US there is 'no strong or consistent relationship between school resources and student performance'. Others dispute such findings, criticising Hanushek's method of reviewing studies (Laine et al., 1996) and point to evidence, also from the US, that school inputs[1] are positively related to outcomes, in particular subsequent earnings (Card and Krueger, 1992).

There are a number of possible reasons for the mixed evidence on the effects of school quality, that is the impact of resourcing per pupil on outcomes. This chapter discusses the key methodological reasons for this mixed evidence and the difficulties associated with the use of production function analysis.[2] It then highlights the significant findings from the US and European literature on this issue. Although the focus of this chapter is production function analysis, we acknowledge the importance of a complementary field of research, on school effectiveness. School effectiveness research has been concerned with measuring differences in school effects on student attainment and searching for school process factors associated with differential effectiveness.[3] Apart from class size, this body of research has largely neglected school resources as explanatory factors for student attainment. In contrast, education production function research has largely focused on testing the hypothesis of a causal relationship from school resources to student outcomes. Apart from studies that include teacher quality variables, production function research has paid little attention to the school processes that intervene between inputs and outputs. Although we restrict our comments to education production function studies, we acknowledge that such studies should not exclude variables that school effectiveness research indicates are important, and thus the two research paradigms are not neatly separable.

2. METHODOLOGICAL ISSUES

This description is adapted from the work of Todd and Wolpin (2003). To fix ideas we consider that pupil attainment is determined by a production function relation, and we use the following notation.
Let :

A_{ijkt} – Pupil i attainment in class j, in school k at the end of time period t.[4]
X_i – Pupil i characteristics which may affect attainment.
S_{jkt} – Class j , school k resources at time t.
T_{ijt} – Teacher quality received by pupil i in class j at time t.
F_{it} – Family resources devoted to pupil i at time t.
μ_i – Individual i innate ability endowment.

Assuming educational attainment of the pupil to be a function of individual attributes and ability, school quality inputs, teacher quality inputs, as well as family inputs, then we may write the general production function type model of what determines pupil attainment as:

$$A_{ijkt} = g(T_{ijt}, X_i, S_{jkt}, \sum_t F_{it}, \mu_i) \tag{2.1}$$

Simplifying this production relation to consider the influence of initial attainment, prior to school, we suggest that

$$A_0 = g_0 (X, F_0, \mu) \tag{2.2}$$

where we drop the i subscript for the individual. The school feeds into the process both in terms of teaching quality T, and non-teaching resources, S, in the manner suggested by the production function. The schooling input decision for any pupil will be determined as a result of the pupil's ability and prior attainment, that is,

$$S_{jkt} = \varphi(A_{jkt-1}, \mu) \tag{2.3}$$

For notational convenience we will think of pupils' attainment being tested at the end of each school year t, so that A_t represents the attainment acquired in that year.
    There are a number of fundamental assumptions behind this model. Firstly, the school is assumed to know the form of the education production function and to maximize output, subject to its resource constraint. Secondly, all members of the school community, in particular the staff, subscribe to the school's utility function. Different utility functions, pursued by different

members of the school, can result in x-inefficiency from the consumer perspective (this may be the parent, student or government on behalf of society).

Lastly, the underlying school level utility function is an expression of a particular set of preferences with respect to which outputs are produced in the form of student attainment. For example, if a school wishes to maximize the sum of the progress of students in a measured cognitive outcome, then this might imply investing very little in students who are predicted to make slow progress. However, this type of utility function would conflict with one that values social equity and thus greater expenditure on pupils who have learning difficulties. Hence, internal resource allocation within a school reflects a set of preferences, which may be those of a single decision-maker or like-minded group, or which may emerge from overt and covert bargaining amongst decision-makers in the school community.

2.1   Specific Econometric Problems

2.1.1   Proxy variables
When precise measures of appropriate variables are not available it is possible to substitute one or more proxies for the missing variables. McCallum (1972) shows that when appropriate proxies are used this reduces omitted variable bias. However, often the proxy variables on offer may be very imperfect. Todd and Wolpin (2003) show that the inclusion of a 'crude proxy' that is related to included and omitted variables can confound the interpretation of observed inputs and can actually lead to more bias in model coefficients. The issue of proxy variables is very relevant to modelling the effect of school quality since representing the effect of unobservable school and parental decisions is particularly difficult. Information on whether the pupil receives free school meals or parental income may be taken as proxies for unobserved family decision variables. It is possible that if these proxy variables are too crude then this may actually induce bias into the estimation model.

2.1.2   Endogeneity
In non-experimental models, it is assumed, from the point of view of the pupil, that classroom and school resource allocations are randomly assigned. However it may well be that the unobservable effects which determine resource allocation may also be correlated with the unobserved variables which determine pupil attainment. In this sense the allocation of additional resources to any particular student, class or school may be endogenous. For example, schools with lower measured educational achievement may have systematically higher funding per pupil. Therefore, OLS regressions are likely to find a spurious negative correlation between outcomes and resources per pupil. An alternative endogenous relationship is that better-off parents select,

often by choice of residential area, better quality schools. An OLS regression may then attribute pupil cognitive achievement to higher resources when in fact part of this estimated effect is due to parental inputs not directly observed in the available data.

One recent example of the endogeneity problem is provided by Lazear (2001). He has suggested that one reason why the pupil–teacher ratio variable could have a counter intuitive sign in an educational production function relation is that smaller classes are usually allocated to the less able students. This factor could easily give rise to a spurious correlation between class size and educational attainment.

If school quality is endogenous then we have an additional important econometric modelling problem. Fortunately the different methods of attempting to tackle this modelling issue are directly analogous to those used in other areas of applied econometrics. There are three popular approaches to the problem of an endogenous treatment variable (Blundell, 2001). We confine our description of these approaches to how they would operate in our school quality case. The instrumental variables (IV) approach has been most widely used in this field of research.

Instrumental variables approach   This would consist of estimating an equation relating to school resources, which included explanatory variables that are excluded from the pupil attainment production function. Then the predicted value of the probability of receiving a given level of resources would be included in the pupil attainment equation instead of the actual resources received. This approach will give consistent parameter estimates of the parameters in the attainment equation, provided suitable IVs can be found. The difficulty of finding suitable IVs is well documented in other fields and the temptation of using too many weak instruments should be guarded against.[5]

In the absence of experimental data on this issue, the IV method provides perhaps the most fruitful prospect for good quality research. It is notable that a number of influential papers that have used IV have found positive effects from school inputs (Akerheim, 1995; Angrist and Lavy, 1999; Dewey et al., 2000; Figlio, 1997). A problem though with IV models is that they can only identify the effect of a change in school inputs for the particular sub-set of the pupil population that has experienced the variation in school inputs predicted by the instrument. An example comes from studies that have used rules about maximum class size as instruments. Such studies are actually measuring the effect of a random change in class sizes around the maximum possible class size (40 in the case of Angrist and Lavy, 1999). It is quite possible that changes in class size from 40 to 41 may have a significant effect, even if changes in class size from 30 to 31 (the range more relevant to the UK) do not. Furthermore, particular students may be clustered in the classes most affected by class size rules. If the characteristics of the target population (children in classes affected by class size rules at the margin) are not representative of the total population, results may be biased.

Control function   The control function approach is related to the IV approach. It involves again estimating a school resource equation as a first step and then including a selectivity correction term in the pupil attainment equation to provide consistent estimates of its parameters. The most common version of this approach is the Heckman Two-Step procedure.[6] This approach, in practice, also relies on having valid exclusion restrictions in the pupil attainment equation to ensure stable estimates of the pupil attainment equation.

Matching approach   This method would estimate an equation relating to whether a pupil received a particular educational treatment or resource, such as small class size. Computing predicted values of the whole sample on this variable allows us to match up, on this propensity score, for each treatment recipient. Provided the conditional independence assumption holds – that is, the outcomes, both hypothetical and real, for each person conditional on the exogenous regressors are independent of the treatment – then comparisons between those who receive the treatment and their matched counterparts are valid.[7] There are numerous different algorithms to do this matching but these details need not concern us here. The matching approach then computes a treatment effect, of the treatment on the treated, by a comparison of the pupil population who actually received small class sizes with the synthetic control population, who look like the treatment group but did not get small class sizes.

2.1.3   Unobserved heterogeneity, random effects and multilevel modelling

Another obvious area of methodological difficulty involves the treatment of unobserved heterogeneity. As specified in (1) this unobserved heterogeneity may be present at the level of the individual pupil i, the class j and the school k, and over time t, and at any combination of these levels in the data. The difficulty with this is how to estimate models in which these levels of unobserved heterogeneity may be explicitly recognized. The technique of multilevel modelling may be used to model the presence of any number of unobserved heterogeneity terms, provided the non-stochastic fixed effects assumption is made. This approach has been widely used in the school effectiveness literature.[8] Alternatively the random effects, stochastic error term at one level of the data may be handled by integrating out this unobserved heterogeneity. However, the analytical problems involved prevent this approach for more than one unobserved heterogeneity term. Hence, in practical terms, the estimation of equation (1) has distinct modelling limitations in terms of the scope for handling how the unobserved heterogeneity may be treated. In short, the estimated parameters must be partly a result of the modelling simplifications that have been assumed to facilitate estimation. This must be understood and appreciated in terms of appropriately qualified statements about the estimation results, which must always be stated as conditional on the validity of the modelling assumptions.

2.1.4   Functional form

Most regression models in the literature assume a linear (or log linear) functional form. This assumption implies that the effect of an additional unit of school inputs is the same both at very low and at very high initial levels of school inputs. Yet this linear functional form has been statistically rejected by the data in some instances (Figlio, 1999; Eide and Waehrer, 1998). It is difficult to determine whether functional form is a major issue, in terms of the wider empirical findings in the literature. However, high quality research in the future would clearly benefit from more rigorous statistical testing of the functional forms used. Another way of allowing for non-linearity is to test interactions between the independent variables (for example between home background and input per pupil). Studies that have examined the impact of school resources for students of differing levels of ability or of differing socio-economic background have often found some significant results (Dearden et al., 1997; Figlio, 1999; Wright et al., 1997). Further work needs to build on this approach to answer many more complex questions such as; do smaller class sizes benefit lower or higher ability children?

Having discussed the difficulties associated with modelling and estimating the impact of school quality on pupil outcomes, we now consider the empirical evidence on this issue.

3.   US EVIDENCE

In the US, economists have looked at the effect of resources on both educational and labour market outcomes (Card and Krueger, 1992; Hanushek et al., 1996; Burtless, 1996). Key papers in this literature suggest that certain school inputs do have a positive effect on pupils' earnings (Card and Krueger, 1992), although the evidence on the impact on earnings from smaller class sizes specifically is mixed. On the other hand, Hanushek (1986) and Hanushek et al. (1996) have claimed that school inputs do not have a positive effect on students' educational attainment. Yet a re-analysis by Laine et al. (1996) of these studies used by Hanushek, using different meta-analysis techniques, concluded that, despite data limitations, there is clear evidence of a positive relationship between school inputs and outcomes.

Of course from a policy perspective, it is crucial to know which particular resource measures may have a positive effect on pupil outcomes and hence class size is generally the variable of most interest to policy-makers. Only 15 per cent of the studies evaluated by Hanushek showed a positive significant link between smaller classes and educational attainment. However, Hanushek's assessment is somewhat undermined by the results from a unique random experiment, undertaken in Tennessee in 1986 (Finn and Achilles, 1990; Krueger, 1997; Krueger, 1999). In this experiment, children in kindergarten and grades 1 to 3 were randomly allocated to large (22–24 pupils) and small (14–16 pupils) classes. Teachers were also assigned randomly. Students' progress was assessed using a standardized test. After the first year, children in smaller classes did significantly better (by about 5–8 percentile points) (Krueger, 1997). The benefits were greater for minority and poor students. Subsequent tracking indicated that the achievement gains persisted through to the 7th grade. Krueger and Whitmore (1999) have found tentative evidence that the effect of smaller class sizes in this experiment was permanent, in that those who were in smaller classes were subsequently 20 per cent more likely to sit a college entrance examination. Hanushek (1997) however, has argued that the magnitudes of the effects found (and the cost of the class size reductions) do not justify wholesale reductions in class sizes across all grades or even across all primary school classes.[9] This view is confirmed in recent studies (Hoxby, 2000; Goldhaber et al., 1999), which have generally used sophisticated econometric techniques, and found a negative or insignificant relationship between class size and pupil outcomes.

Other input variables of great interest are overall expenditure, expenditure on teacher salaries and other teacher characteristics. Broadly the US evidence on the impact of expenditure per pupil is mixed. Marlow (2000) has come up with evidence of a possible explanation as to why additional expenditure may not have a direct positive effect on educational attainment. Marlow (2000) investigated the impact of competition and resources on school performance. Competition is measured by an index based on the number and concentration of different school districts within a particular US county. He found no statistically significant relationship between expenditure and outcomes but he did find that educational spending per capita was higher in counties with greater market power, that is, fewer competing school districts. This is consistent with the view that higher expenditure does not lead to better outcomes because expenditure tends to be allocated on the basis of reasons unrelated to performance.

However, the US evidence on teacher inputs is more positive. Hanushek et al. (1998) found a lower bound estimate that 7.5 per cent of the total variation in student performance is due to teacher effects. Yet identifying the specific teacher inputs that matter has been more problematic, raising serious issues for policy-makers about how to raise teacher quality. Whilst some studies (for example Dewey et al., 2000) found positive effects from greater expenditure on teacher salaries, the magnitudes were extremely small. Goldhaber et al. (1999) is perhaps the most useful study for policy-makers because it attempts to identify the effect of both observed and unobserved teacher and school characteristics on outcomes (10th grade mathematics scores). They found evidence that teacher behaviours/techniques were more important that resource inputs. For example, teachers who felt well prepared, who used oral questions frequently and who emphasized problem solving were more effective.

4. OTHER INTERNATIONAL EVIDENCE

Although the US literature is perhaps the most advanced in this field, there are some good quality European studies that attempt to evaluate the impact of school quality on outcomes. This chapter does not attempt a comprehensive review of all the international evidence, instead key messages are discussed.

4.1 Pupil and School Level Studies

The most recent and econometrically sophisticated studies from the UK are four papers utilising the National Child Development Study (NCDS) data (Dearden et al., 1997; Dolton and Vignoles, 1999; Dustmann et al., 1998; Feinstein and Symons, 1999). The NCDS provides panel data with individual level information on educational outcomes, prior attainment at 7 and 11, family background, and school quality; in particular type of school attended, its pupil–teacher ratio, and the child's class size at 16 for maths and English. All four studies use slightly different measures of attainment and outcomes.

The UK studies confirm the overwhelming importance of prior attainment/ability and family background variables in determining educational attainment. Three of the studies find some evidence of a positive effect from school resource variables on school attainment, and one of them of an effect on wages. For example, Dearden et al. found some school quality variables to be significant and correctly signed in wage equations. This finding came out of specifying interactions between the pupil–teacher ratio (PTR) and school type, and PTR and ability. The PTR did have significant and negative effects for men who attended certain types of school (secondary modern schools)[10] and lower ability women, illustrating the basic point that resources may be differentially effective for different types of student. Dustmann et al. found that a lower PTR increases the probability of a student staying on at school after 16. We conclude that some positive effects from school quality variables on educational outcomes have been found using UK data, although there is little evidence of strong resource effects.

Little evidence exists in the UK that relates pupil labour market performance with the level of educational resources devoted to their education in financial terms, partly due to the lack of appropriate data. One exception is the study on school-to-work transitions conducted by Dolton et al. (1999) using the Youth Cohort Surveys (YCS). The authors find that where Local Education Authority expenditure per pupil was higher the individuals were less likely to be unemployed on leaving school. Further work by Dolton et al. (2002) has suggested that school resources have stronger effects on school outcomes than labour market outcomes but that the latter are still evident.

Even more recent work by Gibbons and Machin (2001) has found that pupils located in schools in higher income areas did significantly better than pupils in schools in less well off areas. However, he argues that there is no causality here since, once the specific characteristics of the area are taken into account (especially neighbourhood composition and residential selection on prior school performance), there is no longer a relationship between average incomes and school performance. In other words, it is the characteristics of the people living in a particular area, not the incomes they earn, that determine school performance. This study is informative because it links teacher resources to outcomes. They find a wrongly signed negative relationship between number of teachers per pupil in schools and pupil attainments, even allowing for prior attainment, local area characteristics and other factors. However, once they allow for lagged school performance, they find weak significant positive effects from teacher inputs, and indeed from higher educational expenditure. They note that these resource variables are not nearly as important as other variables, including location variables. The latter explain around five times as much of the variance in primary school performance as do the resource variables. They also note the small magnitude of the resource effects. A one standard deviation increase in the number of qualified teachers per 100 pupils (0.486 in 98/99) would increase average school performance by just around 1.3 percentage points. They calculate this cost to be around £360 million. An additional expenditure of 10 per cent per pupil would cost around £684 million, and generate an increase in average school performance of just 0.4 percentage points.

4.2   Recent Class Size Studies

Two recent class size studies have found this variable to be negatively and significantly related to pupil attainment in primary schools. Goldstein and Blatchford, using longitudinal data, studied over 9000 children in the first three years of school (ages 4 to 7) in 368 classes in 220 schools in England (Blatchford et al., 2002). Two measures of output are used: a Literacy Baseline test and a specially developed test of numeracy (maths). Control variables are the prior attainment (baseline) tests in literacy and maths, child's term of entry to school, age, gender and eligibility for free school meals (an indicator of family poverty). Class size was recorded in each term and the average class size over the school year used as the appropriate measure. The methodology is notable for using multilevel modelling and for non-linear modelling of class size. In both literacy and maths there was a larger effect of smaller classes on low achievers, whose achievement declined with class sizes up to 30. For high and middle attainers, there was little further negative impact of larger classes above 22.[11] The authors report that a decrease in class size of 10, at sizes below 25, was associated with a gain of about 1 year in the achievement of low attainers and of 5 months for other pupils. Preliminary analysis indicated that an increased number of adults in the class (for example teaching assistants) had no effect on attainment.

A recent paper by Dolton (2002) is the first to attempt to isolate the disruptive element associated with the peer group effects of streamed classes by ability. By use of class list data he computes a proxy index variable for disruption for the class that each pupil is in using the number of pupils in that class with special educational needs. His results provide limited evidence from one school in which, for English, pupils are not streamed but for maths they are. He finds that without the disruptive index a pupil attainment equation has a counterintuitive sign on class size. However if the disruption index is added to the same equation then smaller classes produce better pupil attainment (having conditioned for attendance, family background and other factors). This chapter provides first limited evidence of the Lazear (2001) conjecture on the importance of peer group effects for educational production function mis-specification.

4.3 Instrumental Variable Studies

Angrist and Lavy (1999) examine the impact of class size reductions in Israel in the early 1990s. Their instrument relies on the so-called Maimonides' rule, which states that class sizes in Israel cannot exceed 40. This random discontinuity in class size makes a satisfactory instrument, although of course it generally only measures the local area treatment effect, namely the impact of marginal class size changes either side of 40. The authors find that a 1 per cent decrease in class size generates a 1.7–3.6 per cent gain in test scores. Of course Israeli class sizes are, on average, larger than most OECD countries so extrapolation of these results is problematic.

5.   CROSS-COUNTRY EVIDENCE

5.1   Education Production Function Studies

A small group of studies estimates education production functions for data on
outputs, resources and other variables for a cross-section of countries. As
Woessmann (2001) argues, the endogeneity problem is less likely to occur
with cross-country data as resources to do not move across national borders in
large amounts in response to differences in achievement, nor do parents, in the
main, exercise cross-border school choices. The output measures are taken
from international studies of comparative educational performance of pupils at
the same age and grade level conducted by the International Association for
the Evaluation of Educational Attainment (IEA).

Gundlach et al.'s (2001) study does not estimate an education production
function but instead calculates a set of indices of school sector output and real
inputs for 11 OECD countries from 1970 to 1994. These countries participated
in both the 1970 and 1994 international studies of student attainment. The
increase in real education spending 1970–94 in the 11 countries varied from
6.8 per cent in the Netherlands to 17.2 per cent in Italy. In most countries the
index for output (benchmarked scores on the IEA tests) declined slightly. It
rose only in Italy, Sweden and the Netherlands, by at most 5 per cent
(Sweden). Overall there was a negative rank correlation of –0.47 between
changes in schooling output and changes in the relative price of schooling.

Lassibille and Navarro-Gomez (2001) fit an education production function
for 14 countries. Output is measured by the average scores in maths for pupils
in grades 7 and 8 (used as separate dependent variables) in the Third
International Mathematics and Science Study (TIMSS). The independent variables are the pupil–teacher ratio, instructional time, size of the private sector,
degree of decentralization (as measured from schools' responses to a TIMSS
questionnaire) and the degree of integration (measured by the proportion of
the years of compulsory education spent in non-differentiated schools). They
find that differentiated national educational systems had a positive effect on
maths attainment. However, the pupil–teacher ratio had a relatively small but
negative and significant effect on maths scores. Instructional time and the
degree of decentralization were insignificant, while a larger private sector had
a positive and significant effect.

Woessmann's (2001) study is more sophisticated as it uses pupil level data
from TIMSS on 260 000 students from 39 countries. Resource variables
include expenditure per student, class size, pupil–teacher ratio, headteachers'
reporting of adequacy of materials, instruction time and teachers' age, gender,
experience and years of education. Since resource allocation within countries
is subject to endogeneity, class size is instrumented on the average grade level

class size of the school, but there is no attempt to correct for selection of school by parents. The major finding of the study is that institutional variables matter more for pupil attainment than resourcing variables. Of the institutional variables, centralized examinations, curriculum and textbooks had a positive significant effect on attainment, as did the decentralization of decision making on purchasing supplies and hiring teachers. However, greater educational expenditure at country level and smaller class size at school level were associated with lower maths and science scores. The pupil–teacher ratio was insignificant. Instruction time had a small positive and significant effect. Headteachers' rating of resource adequacy was significant and 'correctly' signed. Women teachers and teacher experience and level of education all had a significant positive effect, while the teacher's age had a negative impact.[12]

5.2 Macro-level Studies of Education Resources and Economic Growth

At the macro level there has certainly been a large amount of research into the relationship between the stock of human capital (within a country) and economic growth. Early literature in this field used quite crude measures of the stock of human capital, such as primary or secondary school enrolment rates (Romer, 1990; Barro, 1991; Mankiw et al., 1992). However, enrolment rates or average years of schooling are not good proxies for the stock of human capital, since the quality and educational value of a year of education will vary between countries. Hence researchers have also attempted to evaluate the impact of the quality of schooling on economic growth, normally including resource measures of school quality (such as the pupil–teacher ratio) in economic growth models. Some results suggest that at the primary school level, smaller pupil–teacher ratios may lead to better quality education and hence more rapid economic growth but that secondary school inputs are unimportant (Barro, 1991).

Hanushek and Kim (2000) have explored this issue further. They looked at the relationship between economic growth and the academic achievement or cognitive skills of a nation's population, as measured by standardized test scores. Using data from the International Association for the Evaluation of Educational Achievement (IEA), and the International Assessment of Educational Progress (IAEP) on 39 countries, Hanushek and Kim (2000) estimated the effect of cognitive skills in mathematics and science on the growth in average real per capita GDP between 1960 and 1988. They, like Bishop (1989), concluded that cognitive skills are an important determinant of labour productivity: a one standard deviation increase in test scores resulted in a one percentage point increase in average annual real growth. However, when they then related the differences in cognitive skills between countries to specific measures of school resources (pupil–teacher ratio, recurrent educational

expenditure and total educational expenditure) they found that these variables
were not important determinants of science and mathematics skills.[13] Thus the
limited international evidence seems to support the view that better resourcing
does not necessarily result in better academic or labour market outcomes.

On the other hand, Gupta et al. (2002) also used cross-country comparisons to
examine the determinants of enrolment rates, using an IV approach. They found
that countries that invest a greater proportion of income in education do have
higher enrolment rates. It is unclear if these results apply to an OECD country
context, since they come from a mixed sample of OECD and non-OECD countries. However, they found that a 1 per cent increase in educational expenditure
had a 0.2 per cent increase in enrolment rates.

6. CONCLUSION

Education production function research in Europe has been hampered by the
lack of good quality data. More recent studies utilizing student level data,
together with school and school district level resource input data, have
detected some school resource effects. The larger range of control variables
has also enabled these studies to make progress in reducing omitted variables
and endogeneity bias, and they have used more sophisticated and varied model
specifications. These studies have produced some evidence of school quality
variables impacting positively on non-exam outcomes. However, many of the
measures of school output used in these studies lack high construct validity
and they have not been able to overcome the twin problems of limited resource
data and the lack of obvious instruments to overcome endogeneity bias. Such
studies do suggest that interaction effects are of potential importance in detect-
ing differential resource effects for students according to gender and ability.
Studies that utilize school level data would obviously miss such effects. One
problem is that good quality studies that use individual level data tend to be
longitudinal in nature and relate to school systems some time in the past. Their
relevance for relationships between resources and pupils' examination attainment in the current system is questionable. However, if one is interested in the
longer-term impact of the quality of schooling on earnings there is no alternative to longitudinal data.

NOTES

1.   School inputs include financial resources (such as expenditure per pupil) and real resources
     (such as pupil–teacher ratios or various measures of teacher education and experience).
2.   In this chapter we will ignore the wider benefits of learning outcomes on health etc.

3. See Ridder and Brown (1991) and Sammons et al. (1995) for a survey.
4. For notational convenience we will think of pupils' attainment being tested at the end of each school year t, so that A_t represents the attainment acquired in that year.
5. See Bound et al. (1995).
6. See Heckman (1979).
7. See Rosenbaum and Rubin (1983) for a proof of this result.
8. See Goldstein (1995).
9. Hanushek et al. (1998) also conduct their own analysis, using data from the Harvard/ UTD Texas Schools Project, to analyse the impact of class size. They find significant class size effects for 4th and 5th graders only. The magnitudes of such effects are so small they account for less than 0.1 per cent of the total variation in student achievement.
10. These schools catered for the bottom 80 per cent of the ability/socio-economic distribution
11. Class sizes above 35 were not included in the study.
12. Missing variables were imputed so long as students had at least 25 variables with non-missing values. Dropping observations with imputed data individually for each imputed variable and re-estimating did not change the results in any significant way.
13. Hanushek and Kimko (2000) also find that variations in school resources do not have strong effects on test performance.

REFERENCES AND FURTHER READING

Akerheim, K. (1995), 'Does class size matter?', *Economics of Education Review*, **14** (1), 229–41.

Angrist, J. and V. Lavy (1999), 'Using Maimondes' rule to estimate the effects of class size on scholastic achievement', *Quarterly Journal of Economics*, **114** (2), 533–75.

Barro, R.J. (1991), 'Economic growth in a cross section of countries', *Quarterly Journal of Economics*, **CVI** (2), 407–44.

Bishop, J.H. (1989), 'Is the test score decline responsible for the productivity growth decline?', *American Economic Review*, **79** (1), 178–97.

Blatchford, P., H. Goldstein, C. Martin and W. Browne (2002), 'A study of class size effects in English school reception year classes', *British Educational Research Journal*, **28** (2), 171–87.

Blundell, R. (2001), 'Estimating the returns to education: models, methods and results', Mimeo: Royal Statistical Society.

Bonesronning, H. (1994), 'Efficiency variation among Norwegian high schools: consequences of equalization policy', *Economics of Education Review*, **13** (4), 289–304.

Bound, J., D.A. Jaeger, and R.M. Baker (1995), 'Problems with instrumental variables estimation when the correlation between the instruments and the endogenous explanatory variable is weak', *Journal of the American Statistical Association*, **90** (430), 443–50.

Burtless, G. (ed.) (1996), *Does Money Matter? The effect of school resources on student achievement and adult success*, Washington DC: The Brookings Institution.

Card, D. and A. Krueger (1992), 'Does school quality matter? Returns to education and the characteristics of public schools in the US', *Journal of Political Economy*, **100**, 1–40.

Coleman, J.S., E.Q. Campbell, C.J. Hobson, J. McPartland, A.M. Mood, F.D. Weinfeld and R.L. York (1966), *Equality of Educational Opportunity*, Washington, DC: Government Printing Office.

Dearden, L., J. Ferri and C. Meghir (1997), 'The effects of school quality on educational attainment and wages', *Institute for Fiscal Studies Working Paper*, W98/3.

Dewey, J., T.A. Husted and L.W. Kenny (2000), 'The ineffectiveness of school inputs: a product of misspecification', *Economics of Education Review*, **19** (1), 27–45.

Dolton, P. (2002), 'Evaluating Educational Inclusion', University of Newcastle, mimeo.

Dolton, P. and A. Vignoles (1999), 'The impact of school quality on labour market success in the UK', *University of Newcastle Discussion Paper*, 98–03.

Dolton, P. and A. Vignoles (2000), 'The effects of school quality on pupil outcomes: An overview' in H. Heijke and J. Muyksen (eds), *Education, Training and Employment in the Knowledge Based Economy*, AEA Macmillan.

Dolton, P., A. Chevalier and S. McIntosh (2002), 'The Effect of School Resources on School and Early Labour Market Outcomes', Institute of Education, mimeo.

Dolton, P., G. Makepeace, S. Hutton and R. Audas (1999), *Making the Grade: Education, the labour market and young people*, York: Joseph Rowntree Foundation.

Dustmann, C., N. Rajah and A. van Soest (1998), 'School quality, exam performance and career choice', *Tilburg Centre for Economic Research Discussion Paper*, 98/6.

Eide, E. and G. Waehrer (1998), 'The role of option value of college attendance in college major choice', *Economics of Education Review*, **17** (1), 73–82.

Feinstein, L. and J. Symons (1999), 'Attainment in secondary school', *Oxford Economic Papers*, **51**, 300–321.

Figlio, D.N. (1997), 'Did the "tax revolt" reduce school performance?', *Journal of Public Economics*, **65** (3), 245–69.

Figlio, D.N. (1999) 'Functional form and the estimated effects of school resources', *Economics of Education Review*, **18**, 241–52.

Finn, J.D. and C.M. Achilles (1990), 'Answers and questions about class size: a statewide experiment', *American Educational Research Journal*, **27**, 557–77.

Gibbons, S. and S. Machin (2001), 'Valuing Primary Schools', Centre for the Economics of Education Discussion Paper No. 15, London School of Economics.

Goldhaber, D.J., D.J. Brewer and D.J. Anderson (1999), 'A three way error components analysis of education productivity', *Education Economics*, **7** (3).

Goldstein, H. (1995), *Multilevel Statistical Models*, London: Arnold.

Goldstein, H. (1997), 'Methods in school effectiveness research', *School Effectiveness and School Improvement*, **8**, 369–95.

Gundlach, E., L. Woessmann and J. Gemlin (2001), 'The decline of schooling productivity in OECD countries', *Economic Journal*, **111**, 135–47.

Gupta, S., M. Verhoeven and E.R. Tiongson (2002), 'The effectiveness of government spending on education and health care in developing and transition economies', *European Journal of Political Economy*, **18** (4), 717–37.

Hanushek, E. (1986), 'The economics of schooling: production and efficiency in public schools', *Journal of Economic Literature*, **24** (3), 1141–77.

Hanushek, E. (1994), *Making Schools Work: Improving Performance and Controlling Costs*, Washington: Brooking Institute.

Hanushek, E. (1997), 'Assessing the effects of school resources on student performance: an update', *Education Evaluation and Policy Analysis*, **19** (2), 141–64.

Hanushek, E. and D. Kim (2000), 'Schooling, labor-force quality, and the growth of nations', *American Economic Review*, **90** (5), 1184–208.

Hanushek, E., J.F. Kain and S.G. Rivkin (1998), 'Teachers, schools and academic achievement', *NBER Working Paper*, **10**.

Hanushek, E., S.G. Rivkin and L.L. Taylor (1996), 'Aggregation and the estimated effects of school success', *The Review of Economics and Statistics*, **78**, 611–27.

Heckman, J. (1979), 'Sample selection bias as a specification error', *Econometrica*, **47**, 153–61.

Heckman, J., A. Layne-Farrar and P. Todd (1996), 'Does measured school quality really matter? An examination of the earnings–quality relationship', in G. Butless (ed.), *Does Money Matter? The Effect of School Resources on Student Achievement and Adult Success*, Washington, DC: The Brookings Institute.

Hoxby, C.M. (2000), 'The effects of class size on student achievement: new evidence from population variation', *The Quarterly Journal of Economics*, November, 1239–85.

Jesson, D., D. Mayston and P. Smith (1987), 'Performance assessment in the education sector: educational and economic perspectives', *Oxford Review of Education*, **13** (3), 249–66.

Krueger, A. (1997), 'Experimental estimates of education production functions', *NBER working paper*, 6051.

Krueger, A. (1999), 'Experimental estimates of education production functions', *Quarterly Journal of Economics*, **CXIV**, 497–532.

Krueger, A.B. and D.M. Whitmore (1999), 'The effects of attending a small class in the early grades on college-test taking and middle school test results: evidence from Project STAR', *Economic Journal*, **111** (468), 1–28.

Laine, R.D., R. Greenwald and L.V. Hedges (1996), 'Money does matter: a research synthesis of a new universe of education production function studies', in L.O. Picus and J.L. Wattenbarger (eds), *Where Does the Money Go? Resource allocation in elementary and secondary schools*, Thousand Oaks, CA: Corwin Press, 44–70.

Lassibille, G. and M.L. Navarro-Gomez (2001), 'Organization and efficiency of education systems: some empirical findings', *TSER Programme on Schooling, Training and Transition*.

Lazear, E. (2001), 'Educational Production', *Quarterly Journal of Economics*, **CXVI** (3), 777–803.

Lord, R. (1984), *Value for Money in Education*, London: Public Money.

McCallum, B. (1972), 'Relative asymptotic bias from errors of omission and measurement', *Econometrica*, **40** (4).

Mankiw, N.G., D. Romer and D.N. Weil (1992), 'A contribution to the empirics of economic growth', *Quarterly Journal of Economics*, 407–37.

Marlow, M.L. (2000), 'Spending, school structure and public education quality. Evidence from California', *Economics of Education Review*, **19**, 89–106.

Mayston, D.J. (1996), 'Educational attainment and resource use: mystery or econometric misspecification?', *Education Economics*, **4** (2), 127–42.

Ridder, S. and S. Brown (1991), *School Effectiveness Research*, The Scottish Office, HMSO.

Romer, P. (1990), 'Endogenous technological change', *Journal of Political Economy*, **99** (5), S71–S102.

Rosenbaum, P. and D. Rubin (1983), 'The central role of the propensity score in observational studies for casual effects', *Biometrika*, **70** (1), 41–55.

Sammons, P., J. Hillman and P. Mortimore (1995) 'Key characteristics of effective schools: A review of school effectiveness research', *Institute of Education*, OFSTED.

Todd, P. and K. Wolpin, (2003), 'On the specification and estimation of the production function for cognitive achievement', *The Economic Journal*, **113** (485), 3–33.

Vignoles, A., R. Levacic, J. Walker, S. Machin and D. Reynolds (2000), *The Relationship Between Resource Allocation and Pupil Attainment: a review*, London: DFEE.

Woessmann, L. (2001), 'Schooling resources, educational institutions and student performance: the international evidence', *Education Next*, Summer, Keil Institute of World Economics Working paper, 1–29 plus tables.

Wright, S.P., S.P. Horn and W.L. Sanders (1997), 'Teacher and classroom context effects on student achievement: implications for teacher evaluation', *Journal of Personal Evaluation in Education*, **11**, 57–67.

3. An economist's view of schooling systems*

Louis Lévy-Garboua, Nathalie Damoiselet, Gérard Lassibille and Lucia Navarro-Gomez

1. INTRODUCTION

The aim of the present chapter is to provide a simple theory and description of schooling systems from an economic perspective. The theory distinguishes between education and training, which may be combined in various proportions by schooling systems for the production of differentiated skills. The description is based on a core sample of 16 industrialized countries which was determined by the availability of comparable data from various sources and the answers given by education experts to a questionnaire tailored to our needs.[1] The 16 countries forming our sample are Austria, Canada, France, Germany, Greece, Hungary, Italy, Japan, the Netherlands, Norway, Portugal, the Russian Federation, Spain, Sweden, the UK and the USA.

The considerable differentiation typically observed in schooling systems is inconsistent with the assumption of homogeneous human capital made in much of economic literature. Thus Section 2 presents a simple economic theory of schooling systems relaxing this assumption and making an important distinction between the provision of general education and vocational training. In Section 3, we show a variety of indexes of average education, skill (human capital at market value), and types of differentiation and screening for our main sample of 16 countries. Then Section 4 relates productive efficiency at country level with the differentiation of schooling systems. Our main conclusions are summarized in Section 5.

2. A SIMPLE THEORY OF SCHOOLING SYSTEMS

A schooling system is the institution which allocates social knowledge primarily to young individuals. Drawing on Becker's (1964) seminal distinction between general and specific human capital, we may say that schooling provides both general knowledge and occupation-specific knowledge. General knowledge can be used in all firms and all occupations, while occupation-specific knowledge can be used in all firms but only in specific occupations (note that firm-specific knowledge cannot be provided by the schooling system). We focus our attention here on the dual provision of general and occupation-specific, that is vocational, knowledge by schooling systems above the common-core syllabus.

The standard assumption of homogeneous human capital and capacities tends to understate the extent of optimal differentiation of schooling systems.[2] Under this standard assumption, a differentiated schooling system would be described as a common-core syllabus followed by a variety of vocational curricula of optional length. But this is not a good description of what schooling systems actually offer. What is being observed is that students may decide to receive further general education before they engage in vocational training. Further education is seen as a general but optional prerequisite for enhancing the acquisition of skills by vocational training.

2.1   The Basic Model

It will be assumed that the schooling system provides, above the common-core education, both further general eduction E and a variety of skill-specific training T_i, $i = (1,....,s)$ at unit price. Each pupil combines school inputs with his own capacities to embody one of the s differentiated skills S_i. We write the skill i's individual production function as

$$S_i(E,T_i) = t_i A(E) T_i^{\beta}, \tag{3.1}$$

where t_i (>0) is a given i-specific capacity, called 'talent', $A(E)$ designates the individual's general ability, and $0 < \beta < 1$. The crucial assumption we make is that the general ability is not entirely given by birth and cultural transmission, but also captures the learning skill acquired through 'education'

$$A(E) \equiv S_0(E) \tag{3.2}$$

with $S_0'(E) \geq 0$, and $S_0(0) = 1$.

The general learning skill uniformly raises the marginal productivity of training in the acquisition of all non-learning skills. It is assumed to be a non-decreasing concave function of the amount of further education, for instance

$$S_0(E) = 1 + aE^{\alpha}, \tag{3.3}$$

with $a > 0$, $0 \leq \alpha < 1$.

The parameter a describes the student's cognitive ability by the end of the common-core education.

We shall further assume that there is a small number of paths leading to the production of any skill due to large set-up costs in the production of education. For instance, E might only take two values, 0 or 1, if students are given a choice among pure training and one period of general education followed by training. We do not make the same assumption for training because training is partly supplied by firms as a joint product of their activity. Thus, the amount of training is chosen optimally by each individual. Finally, we assume decreasing marginal returns on both education and training, and the Inada condition $S_i'(E,0) = +\infty$. The rational behaviour of a student is described by the choice of skill type i and school inputs E and T_i which maximize the net returns from his general education and vocational training on the discrete set of educational options $E = (0,1,...,n)$

$$\max_{i,E,T_i} \quad p_i S_i(E,T_i) - E - T_i \tag{3.4}$$

subject to (3.1), (3.2), (3.3), and non-negativity constraints on the amount of training $T_i \geq 0$. The Inada condition ensures that some training will always be provided $T_i > 0$. It should be noted that the i-specific talent t_i and the price of skill (that is, specific human capital) i, p_i, cannot be independently identified.[3] Henceforth, in the following paragraphs, we drop the latter variable and adopt a nominal definition of specific talents (that is, $p_i t_i$). Thus a 1 per cent increase of the rate of return to skill i results in an equal rise of i-specific talent for all students, and a 1 per cent increase in the borrowing rate of a student, reflecting the latter's diminishing opportunities, entails a 1 per cent decline of all his nominal talents. Although the present analysis emphasizes variations of specific talents among students, we should not forget that variations of the rates of return on skills and of the average borrowing rate may also have large aggregate effects on the outputs of schooling systems in a cross-country comparison. The conclusions that would be drawn from the model by omitting price effects would only hold for countries of similar income level per capita insofar that the distribution of opportunities may then be assumed to vary little between these countries.

For space limitations, all proofs are omitted here but are available on request. The solution of programme (3.4) has intuitive appeal. Students' rational behaviour may be described as if they first chose the specific occupation for which they have more (nominal) talent. Then, they choose the optimal mix of education and training conditional on this choice of occupation. The main proposition follows:

PROPOSITION 1
If cognitive abilities and skill-specific talents differ among students but are

perfectly known both by themselves and by schools, it is not optimal to sort students into the more general and the vocational path on the basis of their cognitive ability alone. The optimal sorting rule is described by the following condition, which combines information on cognitive ability and skill-specific talents:

$$\left(\beta^{\frac{\beta}{1-\beta}} - \beta^{\frac{1}{1-\beta}} \right) t_i^{\frac{1}{1-\beta}} \left[(1 + a)^{\frac{1}{1-\beta}} - 1 \right] > 1.$$

Moreover, students who prefer the education-cum-training path always engage in longer specific training and, a fortiori, in longer studies than those engaged in pure training. The latter prediction is in line with countless observations of complementarity between education and training. Besides, since the more talent a student has for a skill, the more he will be inclined to opt for education (proposition1), this has an important corollary:

COROLLARY
The differentiation of vocational studies increases the demand for general education (and longer studies), for given distributions of cognitive abilities and skill-specific talents.

We believe that this corollary provides a strong and, to some extent, new rationale for the vocationalization and lengthening of studies, as well as the 'massification' of further general education that took place in industrialized countries.

2.2 Screening

In actual practice, schools and universities screen students who are not perfectly aware of their cognitive ability and skill-specific talents. Because the general ability applies to a great many tasks, it will often be detected early in the course of common-core (that is, primary and lower secondary) education. On the other hand, the assessment of an individual's return-maximizing skill-specific talent must often await the later differentiation of curricula since each talent can only be detected on a single set of tasks. The present discussion is summarized by the following assumption:

ASSUMPTION
Students' return-maximizing skill-specific talents cannot be detected as early as their cognitive ability.

The presence of a lag between the times when general ability and talents can be detected precisely generates a trade-off between the first-best choices of education and skill.

PROPOSITION 2
As far as education *is concerned, early screening by general ability is optimal as soon as this can be detected. However, such early screening is inefficient as far as the production of* skills *is concerned, for which screening should occur later on.*

The postponement of screening until the upper secondary level, where talents can be assessed with some precision, has often been advocated as a means of reducing inequality. However it may also be justified for efficiency reasons if abilities and talents are not strongly correlated. Its adoption by market economies entails a vocationalization of schools at the relative expense of general education. Thus our theory relates the potential decline of educational standards to the postponement of differentiation by ability until occupation-specific talents can be assessed.

3. AN ECONOMIC DESCRIPTION OF SCHOOLING SYSTEMS

In order to show the relevance of our theoretical distinction between education and training for understanding the productive efficiency of schooling systems, we must measure these two outputs of schooling systems and how the latter differentiate in matching heterogeneous capacities and skills. The appropriate indicators have been derived from available statistics and the answers of selected education experts to a questionnaire. Twenty-three experts[4] from 16 OECD countries completed this questionnaire in 1997. These 16 countries form the main sample that will be used below for statistical analysis.

3.1 The Production of Education and Skills

Average scores obtained in standardized tests are commonly taken to be good indicators of school performance, assuming that the distribution of abilities between pupils is the same in all countries. However, the theoretical discussion of Section 2 makes it clear that they are not concerned with vocational training and essentially describe the average level of the general ability produced by general education. A better indicator of market skills, or total human capital per pupil, should reflect the market value of school outputs.

Various measures of the production and distribution of human capital
(education-cum-training) and its education component appear in Table 3.1 for
our sample of 16 industrialized countries. The most comprehensive index of
total human capital per pupil at 1994 market value[5] (HTOT) is shown in
column 1. It was derived from OECD's statistics (OECD 1996: tables R11.1,
R12.1) on the distribution of graduate output between four highest completed
levels of education (lower secondary, upper secondary, non-university and
university sector). Each level was imputed a market value index through the
mean earnings of employed male graduates of 25 to 64 years of age at this
level relative to the mean earnings at upper secondary level (OECD 1996:
table R22.1). A proxy for the same total human capital index one generation
back (HTOT0) was obtained by weighting the same value indexes with the
distribution of the population 25 to 64 years of age between the four levels of
graduation (OECD: table C1.1). The derived estimate of the rate of human
capital growth per pupil in a generation (that is, IH = (HTOT −
HTOT0)/HTOT0) is given in column 2. Inequality of the distribution of
human capital is summarized in column 3 by the variance of the 1994 value
indexes between the four levels of graduation (INEQ). The objective growth
of human capital is paralleled in column 4 with a subjective indicator for the
decline of educational standards, derived from the informed opinion of the
selected experts. While all of the sampled countries have undergone positive,
and often substantial, growth in one generation, education experts frequently
expressed the opinion that educational standards had declined. An interpretation of the latter's perception will be given in Section 4. Finally, this description of the output of schooling systems is completed in column 5 by the scores
obtained in standardized mathematics and science tests by pupils at grade
seven (SCORE), who are theoretically 13 years old. These results were gathered in 1994–95 for a sample of 24 countries by the International Association
for the Evaluation of Educational Achievement in its third international study
on mathematics and science. These countries include our own sample of 16
countries, with the exception of Italy. We consider this last variable to be a
good aggregate index of the general ability produced by education.

Clearly, HTOT and SCORE do not describe the same schooling output. The
rank correlation (Spearman's rho) between these two variables is only 0.134
(n = 14) and the assumption that they are stochastically independent cannot be
rejected. By plotting these two variables along two axes, Figure 3.1 shows that
a parabolic relation would fit the data better than a straight line.[6] Greece,
Portugal and Spain, which are the least developed countries of the sample,
rank low along the two dimensions, Japan is clearly the highest performer in
the production of education and Norway has the lead in the production of
skills. If the three low-performers were left out of the diagram, the slope would
even become slightly negative. Whereas differences in opportunities generate

Table 3.1 *The production and distribution of education and skills in 16 schooling systems*

Country	Total human capital per pupil at 1994 market value (upper secondary = 100) HTOT	Rate of growth of human capital in a generation (%) IH	Inequality INEQ	Opinion on the decline of educational standards DECLINE	Score in math. and science tests in grade seven SCORE
Austria	102.4	4.1	0.152	1	509
Canada	112.0	5.1	0.252	1.5	494
France	117.7	11.6	0.277	0	492
Germany	109.8	0.3	0.203	0.5	484
Greece	102.8	5.8	0.221	2	440
Hungary	105.8	n.a.	0.234	2	502
Italy	100.6	15.6	0.188	2	–
Japan	117.3	n.a.	0.215	1	571
Netherlands	104.7	3.8	0.192	0	516
Norway	127.4	16.8	0.165	1.5	461
Portugal	96.7	24.8	0.392	1	423
Russian Fed.	116.3	n.a.	0.219	1	501
Spain	102.8	16.0	0.248	1	448
Sweden	107.8	1.2	0.223	1	478
UK	117.9	13.4	0.263	1	463
USA	115.6	3.3	0.349	2	476

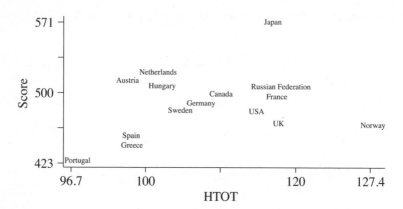

Figure 3.1   *Comparing the performance of schooling systems along two dimensions: education and skills*

a positive correlation of education and skills, a negative correlation between education and skills emerges from distinctive patterns of differentiation across countries.

3.2   Differentiation and Screening

If we use our theoretical distinction between one single general ability and many kinds of occupation-specific talents, we see that the sorting of students, whether it is by ability or by talent, must produce sharply different social outcomes. Since general ability as opposed to occupation-specific talents possessed by an individual determines the extent of students' market opportunities, only the differentiation by ability unambiguously produces a ranking of students. We may speak of vertical differentiation on one hand, and horizontal differentiation on the other. In our questionnaire, the amount of vertical differentiation is attested by the use of three potential means of sorting students by their general ability: a standardized test, grades and the reference of the school. The amount of horizontal differentiation can be traced by the use of two common means of assessing occupation-specific talents: preferences of the family or the student, and choice of optional courses. These five criteria of differentiation were listed separately by experts for lower secondary and upper secondary levels. This information is summarized below by Table 3.2, which indicates the frequency of use of each of these means of differentiation in our sample of 16 countries.[7]

The first three columns indicate that the vertical differentiation of students is equally present in the lower and the upper levels of secondary schooling and the last two indicate that horizontal differentiation prevails at the upper level.

*Table 3.2   The frequency of use of various means of differentiation in lower
secondary and upper secondary levels*

Means level	By standardized test	By grades	By reference of the school	By preference of family or student	By optional courses
Lower secondary	1*	7	5.5	4.5	1.5
Upper secondary	0.5	6	5.5	12.5	9.5

Note: * The range of variation of all the indicators is 0–16.

This shows that education takes place at both levels and training eventually starts at the upper level. Moreover, the figures demonstrate that sorting by ability dominates sorting by talent in the lower level, while the reverse is true in the upper level. This is consistent with our assumption that the general ability can be detected rather early but the occupation-specific talents can hardly be known before the specific training has taken place.

Another proof of the last assertion can be found in the increased severity of screening between the lower and upper levels of secondary education. Screening scores have been derived from our survey among education experts by adding up three indicators of downstreaming, class repeating and drop-out,[8] each measured on an ordinal 0–4 scale (detailed figures can be found in Damoiselet and Lévy-Garboua 2000, 2001).[9] The resulting index measures the amount of screening taking place at each level of education on a 0–12 scale in a way which allows comparison between levels. Screening increases from a score of 3.2 in the lower level to 4.7 in the upper level of secondary education and this difference is significant at the 1 per cent confidence level ($t = 2.82$, d.f. 28).

The addition of frequencies of use for all five means of differentiation yields country scores of total differentiation at the two levels of secondary education (DIFLOW, DIFUP). Total differentiation increases with level without exception. This picture is confirmed by a t-test of difference between the means of the lower and the upper levels. The mean scores of total differentiation are 1.2 for the lower level and 2.2 for the upper level, and they are unequal at the 5 per cent confidence level ($t = 2.168$, d.f. 30).[10] This result is consistent with the theoretical prediction that students should be sorted by a combination of ability and talents, which optimally requires postponement of differentiation until talents can be assessed with sufficient precision. Figure 3.2 plots the total differentiation scores at the two levels of secondary education. It separates two groups of countries without ambiguity. Canada, Greece, Italy, Japan, Norway, Portugal and Spain have no differentiation of any kind at the lower secondary level (DIFLOW = 0). These countries have in common that all pupils must follow a common-core syllabus from the time of entry into primary education to the end of compulsory education (Lassibille and Navarro-Gomez, 2000). At the other end of the spectrum, France, Germany, the Netherlands and the USA are strongly differentiated at both levels of secondary education. In between lie countries with intermediate levels of total differentiation. On the basis of their patterns of horizontal and vertical differentiation (detailed figures are shown in Damoiselet and Lévy-Garboua 2000, 2001) these countries may be further classified in two groups by closer inspection. Hungary and Sweden offer no kind of horizontal differentiation. Austria, Russia and the UK form a residual group of average differentiation whether we take the distribution of total differentiation between levels or between vertical and horizontal means.

4. THE PRODUCTIVE EFFICIENCY OF SCHOOLING SYSTEMS

In this section we test two implications of our theory of schooling systems, namely proposition 2 and the corollary of proposition 1:

a) Since ability can be detected earlier than talents, it is not optimal to make an intensive use of differentiation too early, say at the lower secondary level, for producing skills. However, it will be optimal to do so for producing education;

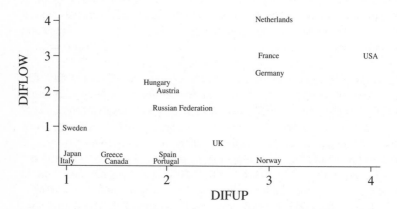

Figure 3.2   Comparing total differentiation of schooling systems in the lower secondary and upper secondary levels

b) Horizontal differentiation enhances the aggregate demand for general education and training.

4.1 A First Set of Results

Table 3.3 presents the results of regressions for the output measures that appeared in Table 3.1. The explained variables in Table 3.3 are HTOT (column 1), SCORE (column 2), INEQ (column 3) and DECLINE (columns 4–5). These are all explained essentially by two supply variables, the amount of differentiation at the lower secondary and upper secondary levels (DIFLOW, DIFUP), and by one demand variable, the average level of human capital one generation back (HTOT0).

The first set of implications amounts to the prediction of a negative effect of DIFLOW on HTOT (acting as a proxy for average skills) and a positive effect on SCORE (acting as a proxy for average education). The second implication is a positive effect of DIFUP (acting as a proxy for horizontal differentiation) on HTOT (acting as a proxy for aggregate education-cum-training). Both sets of implications are confirmed in columns 1 and 2 of Table 3.3. The three coefficients describing these effects are significant at the 5 per cent level with the predicted sign. The trade-off between education and skills is strikingly illustrated by the offsetting effects of lower-level differentiation and upper-level differentiation on these two outputs. Lower-level differentiation is good for the production of general education (SCORE) and bad for the

Table 3.3 Regression analysis of schooling outputs

	HTOT	SCORE	INEQ	DECLINE	DECLINE
HTOT0	0.648	1.191	–0.003	0.013	–
	(4.72)**	(2.11)	(1.34)	(0.66)	–
DIFLOW	–3.494	15.870	–0.010	–0.348	–0.243
	(3.15)*	(3.58)**	(0.57)	(2.14)	(2.63)
DIFUP	5.428	–15.170	0.046	0.077	–
	(2.95)*	(1.98)	(1.52)	(0.29)	–
STTPRIM	–	–	–	–	–0.079
	–	–	–	–	(2.68)
Constant	36.162	367.939	0.453	0.044	2.641
	(2.83)*	(6.75)**	(2.15)	(0.02)	(5.59)
Observations	13	12	13	13	13
R-squared	0.83	0.74	0.26	0.40	0.61

Notes:
Absolute value of t-statistics in parentheses
* significant at 5% level; ** significant at 1% level

production of occupation-specific skills (HTOT). Late differentiation is good for the production of skills. Looking back at Figure 3.1 and Table 3.1, Norway turns out to be the best performer because it has managed to suppress school-leavers at lower secondary level and has developed a large vocational non-university sector. These results are obtained on a small sample and must be treated with caution. However, the qualitative conclusions were replicated with similar but different variables and samples. An instance of this is given by the comparison of column 5 with column 4 in Table 3.3.

Comparison of columns 4 and 2 shows that the perception of declining standards (see, on the same topic, Baudelot and Establet, 1989) addresses the relative decline of education in the total output of schooling systems. This interpretation is confirmed by the regression of column 5. The STTPRIM designates the ratio of students to teaching staff in primary education for 1994, as given by OECD (1996: table P32 (public and private)). This is positively related to early differentiation if education expenditures are constrained. For a given budget, larger class size is the price for having more differentiation that obviously uses more teachers.[11] Therefore, DIFLOW and STTPRIM both capture aspects of early differentiation and have a negative effect (significant at the 5 per cent level) on DECLINE. Indeed, the selected experts did not stress the decline of educational standards in France, Germany and the Netherlands which have strongly early-differentiated schooling systems on both accounts. The converse is true for Italy.

By introducing the level of human capital one generation back in the regressions, the dynamics of education and human capital can be analysed. The coefficient of this variable is positive and smaller than one in column 1 of Table 3.3, but close to one in column 2. These results suggest the convergence of the human capital or skill output of schooling systems but the lack of convergence of the education output., For instance, Table 3.1 shows that Canada, Germany, the Netherlands, Sweden and the USA have been expanding slowly in comparison with developing countries like Italy, Portugal, and Spain. Finally, the results of column 4 in Table 3.3 suggest that the dispersion of human capital within countries (INEQ) is not increased by early differentiation.

4.2   A Second Set of Results

Our first results may be open to criticism in that they are based on a small sample of countries and on qualitative or even subjective explanatory variables. Fortunately, we were able to replicate, on a larger sample and with more and well-accepted indicators, the regression analysis concerning the scores obtained in standardized mathematics and science tests (SCORE) by pupils in grade seven and grade eight. Twenty-four countries are included in this analysis, encompassing the 16 countries of our main sample. In the 12 non-differenti-ated systems,[12] all the pupils had normally completed the same curriculum when they took the tests; while the pupils in the 12 differentiated systems[13] had been sorted into several streams after completing the common-core syllabus (see Lassibille and Navarro-Gomez (2000) for a full description of the differentiation and other variables). On average, pupils in differentiated systems perform better than pupils in non-differentiated systems. For example, at grade seven, pupils in the first systems achieved a score of 502, while the second achieved only 477.

In order to show the extent to which the characteristics of the two systems affect pupils' achievement, in Table 3.4 we regress the mathematics test scores in grades seven and eight on the following 'objective' variables: the ratio of the length of common-core syllabus to the length of compulsory education (an index of non-differentiation of systems which takes value 1 for non-differen-tiated systems and values smaller than one for differentiated systems), the pupil/teacher ratio, the instructional time from the first year of primary educa-tion up to the age when pupils took the tests, the percentage of pupils enrolled in the private sector, and the degree of decentralization of systems, estimated on the basis of the share of central government funding. The test scores in the seventh and eighth grades are adjusted within the framework of a fixed-effect model. To take into account the correlation between the results obtained in each grade, the variance–covariance matrix is corrected for heteroscedasticity by clustering observations by country (see, for example, Greene, 1997). Given the availability of data, the estimation covers 14 countries, yielding 28 obser-vations. Among these, seven countries have differentiated and seven have non-differentiated education systems.

Differentiated systems obtain better results than non-differentiated systems, all things being equal. The effect of the structure of the system is far from negligible, as the timing of differentiation of pupils into streams explains about 15 per cent of the difference in scores between pupils. Since the differ-entiation index retained here is mainly concerned with early (vertical) differ-entiation, this finding confirms the results obtained in Table 3.3 (column 2), namely that early differentiation is good for education. The generally accepted idea among educators that non-differentiated systems are the best way to maximise the production of education is probably wrong. Even the superiority of these systems for reducing social inequalities at an early age seemed ques-tionable in Table 3.3.

The results in Table 3.4 also show that the pupil/teacher ratio has a negative impact on pupils' scores after allowing for differentiation. This result is similar to those obtained by other studies (see, for example, Hanushek, 1986). The total number of school hours, which differs widely across countries, has no signifi-cant effect on achievement in mathematics. However, the instructional time in

Table 3.4 Adjustment of mathematics test scores in grades 7 and 8

	Coefficient	t-stat.	Coefficient	t-stat.
Constant	569.315	9.11	620.496	14.81
I_1	−83.024	2.66	−187.817	2.17
Pupil/teacher ratio	−5.438	2.05	−5.633	3.08
Instructional time (up to 13 or 14 years of age)	0.009	0.73	n.a.	n.a.
Instructional time in primary level	–	–	0.012	1.52
Instructional time in secondary level (up to 13 or 14 years of age)	–	–	0.004	0.91
Size of private sector	0.609	2.06	0.796	3.68
Degree of centralization	−0.057	0.27	0.118	0.37
Adjusted R^2	0.392	–	0.452	–
F	10.82	–	18.76	–
Number of observations	28	–	28	–

Note: Fixed-effect model corrected for heteroscedasticity by clustering observations by country.

Sources: International Bureau of Education (1997), OECD (1996) and UNESCO (1996) for instructional time; UNESCO (1996) for the size of private sector; OECD (1996) for the degree of centralization.

primary education explains the good performance of certain countries better than the instructional time in secondary education. These results confirm that marginal returns are decreasing in the acquisition of learning skills. Furthermore, the regression results indicate that countries where private education is more widespread perform significantly better than countries where it is more limited. Once again, private education widens the choice set of families and children and thus operates like another kind of differentiation by choice (this point is developed in Damoiselet and Lévy-Garboua, 2000, 2001). Finally, centrally managed education systems perform as well as decentralized ones, after controlling for differentiation.

5. CONCLUSION

This chapter has made a basic distinction between general education and vocational training. Education contributes to the production of the learning skill, which is a general investment for producing many other sorts of occupation-specific skills in combination with specific training. The diversity of marketable skills introduces a policy trade-off for schooling systems between education and non-learning skills. If the objective was to maximize the net returns to education alone, students should be sorted by their cognitive ability alone. But if the objective is to maximize the net returns to both education and many kinds of specific training, then students should be given an option to receive further general education before they engage in vocational training and be sorted between these alternative paths according to some combination of their cognitive ability and occupation-specific talents. Early differentiation is good for education but is bad for the production of skills. Furthermore, the horizontal differentiation of schooling systems at a later stage induces a rising demand for both education and training.

NOTES

*   We thank Mariá-Jesus San Segundo for her helpful comments.
1.   We are grateful to Wim Groot and Jean-Jacques Paul for helping us in the preparation of the questionnaire and the selection of experts. Many thanks to the 23 education experts who gave generously of their time and effort to answer our questionnaire.
2.   Some amount of differentiation is optimal, even if human capital and capacities are assumed homogeneous, when students differ in capacities (see Damoiselet, 1998).
3.   If human capital yielded a constant rental price w_i over an infinite duration of life and if r was the constant individual's borrowing rate, the price of skill i for an individual of unit i-specific talent would be: $p_i = w_i/r$.
4.   Since the list of topics reflected the economic issues raised by schooling systems, due weight was given to their economics background in the selection of experts.
5.   See Damoiselet and Lévy-Garboua (2000, 2001) for a detailed description of this indicator.

6. This statement is unambiguously supported by the data. We regressed SCORE on a quadratic function of HTOT and found strong non-linearity.
7. Frequencies may vary by steps of 0.5 because, in some countries, two experts responded to the questionnaire independently and disagreed in their answers.
8. 'Down-streaming' means that a student may switch from a higher education level to a lower education level. 'Class repeating' means that a student will not be given access to the next level if he or she does not meet the academic requirements. Lastly, 'drop-out' describes a student leaving an institution of education without a diploma or certificate.
9. 0 – never, 1 – not very often; 2 – sometimes; 3 – frequent; 4 – very frequent.
10. This index of total differentiation gives more weight to ability than talent since the questionnaire mentions three criteria of vertical differentiation and only two criteria of horizontal differentiation. An equal weighting of the two kinds of differentiation would still reinforce our conclusion.
11. The substitution between differentiation and the reduction of class size is further attested by the absence of correlation between the expenditure per student and the ratio of students to teaching staff at the secondary level.
12. Australia, Canada, Denmark, Greece, Iceland, Japan, Norway, Portugal, the Russian Federation, Scotland, Spain, Switzerland.
13. Austria, the Czech Republic, France, Germany, Hungary, Ireland, Korea, the Netherlands, New Zealand, Sweden, the United Kingdom and the United States.

REFERENCES

Baudelot, C. and R. Establet (1989), *Le Niveau Monte,* Paris: Seuil.
Becker, G.S. (1964), *Human Capital*, 1st edition, New York: Columbia University Press for the NBER.
Damoiselet, N. (1998), 'Effets des systèmes scolaires sur le comportement éducatif individuel', *L'Actualité Economique*, (**74**), 29–61.
Damoiselet, N. and L. Lévy-Garboua (2000), 'L'efficacité de la différenciation et de la sélection scolaire: une comparaison économique des systèmes éducatifs', *Economie Publique*, (**6**), 17–39.
Damoiselet, N. and L. Lévy-Garboua (2001) 'Comparaison des systèmes éducatifs: une approche économique', in Raymond Boudon, Nathalie Bulle and Mohamed Cherkaoui (eds), *Ecole et Société: les paradoxes de la démocratie*, Paris: PUF, pp. 241–68.
Greene, W. (1997), *Econometric Analysis*, 3rd edition, London: Prentice-Hall International, Inc.
Hanushek, E.A. (1986), 'The Economics of Schooling: Production and Efficiency in Public Schools', *Journal of Economic Literature*, (**24**), 1141–77.
International Bureau of Education (1997), *World Data on Education: 1993–1994*, Geneva: International Bureau of Education.
Lassibille, G. and L. Navarro Gómez (2000), 'Organization and Efficiency of Education Systems: some empirical findings', *Comparative Education*, (**36**), 7–19.
OECD (1996), *Education at a Glance*, Paris: OECD.
UNESCO (1996), *Statistical Yearbook*, Paris: UNESCO.

PART II

Transitions from school to work

4. School-leaving and unemployment: evidence from Spain and the UK

María Jesús San Segundo and Barbara Petrongolo[1]

1. INTRODUCTION

In the second half of the twentieth century, primary and secondary education became practically universal in most developed countries. OECD research (1998, 2001) has recently concluded that there is a clear tendency towards convergence in human capital stocks, at least for some basic indicators such as the percentage of the population completing secondary education.

European countries have mostly followed this general tendency. The COM (1993) Report (White Paper) established ambitious goals for EU countries to reach human capital levels similar to those of their main economic competitors. Recent summits have reinforced the objective of raising Europe's competitive position in the knowledge society. However, available data shows that several European countries still face significant challenges. Of special relevance here are the ongoing deficits in upper-secondary completion rates for young generations. The Annual Employment Reports show that progress is uneven among member countries, with regard to the objectives of promoting lifelong learning and reducing early school-leaving (COM, 2000).

In this chapter we investigate the main determinants of the decision to stay on at school at age 16, with special emphasis on the role played by local labour market conditions. On the one hand, it can be argued that high unemployment rates drive young people to postpone their labour market entrance, by reducing the expected gains from job search and therefore the opportunity cost of their educational investment. This produces a positive effect of current youth unemployment on the probability of staying on at school.

On the other hand, higher prime-age unemployment may imply tighter budget constraints for families with teenage children, therefore discouraging enrolment in secondary education. Furthermore, an increase in adult unemployment may increase the probability of expected future unemployment, which arguably reduces the returns to education, and hence the demand for schooling. The combination of these two factors implies a negative correlation between unemployment and enrolment rates (see Micklewright, Pearson and Smith, 1990).

Previous work on the demand for education at different levels has already studied the relationship between enrolment rates and economic conditions, providing somewhat mixed evidence. It may be argued that this results from the lack of adequate unemployment controls (in some cases), as well as the level of aggregation used to characterize local labour markets.

In our analysis, we identify the two contrasting effects of unemployment on the demand for post-compulsory education in Spain and the UK. Enrolment rates at age 16 are related to both the unemployment rate of youths who have not completed upper-secondary education (as a proxy for the opportunity cost of remaining in the schooling system) and the general unemployment rate (as an indicator of budgetary restrictions and/or signal of poor employment prospects in the future). The use of both controls produces quite clear-cut results: staying-on rates are correlated positively with youth unemployment but negatively with adult unemployment for both males and females.

We use two cross-sections of youths, interviewed in the Spanish Labour Force Survey (EPA) and the British Labour Force Survey, both in the second quarter of 1991. In both cases, census data allows us to match individual record files with very detailed information on unemployment rates by sex, age and educational qualification at the provincial level (Spain) or the regional level (UK). The local (provincial or regional) labour market is the most apt alternative to schooling for 16-year-olds, most of whom live with their parents.

The chapter is organized as follows. Section 2 presents a brief overview of enrolment rates at the secondary level in the OECD. Section 3 analyses the main empirical implications of human capital models and provides a survey of previous results. Section 4 presents the estimates of probability models for the education of youngsters in Spain and the UK. The last section concludes and summarizes the main findings.

2. SECONDARY EDUCATION AND UNEMPLOYMENT IN THE OECD

A country's stock of human capital is hard to measure precisely. Over the last few decades the most commonly used proxy for human capital has been the educational attainment of the population. This is measured as the highest completed level of education amongst adults of working age.

The situation of developed countries can then be compared in terms of how many people have completed upper secondary education (or higher education). At the end of the 20th century, OECD countries still differed widely in terms of average educational attainment. Over 60 per cent of the population has completed at least upper secondary education in the majority of countries; in other countries, such as Italy, Spain, Portugal, Mexico and Turkey, more than half of the adult population has not reached that level. These human capital indicators are positively correlated with GDP per head, as shown by Figure 4.1.

Recent research (OECD, 1998) has warned of the difficulties that adults who have not completed upper secondary education face. They are more likely to be unemployed and to have unstable and badly-paid jobs (Katz and Murphy, 1992), and experience serious difficulties in developing new skills. From the point of view of economic policy, we should therefore be concerned about youngsters who leave secondary education as soon as legally possible, typically around age 16.

In Figures 4.2 and 4.3 we compare enrolment rates at ages 16 and 17 in most OECD countries for 1999. At least 20 countries had enrolment rates of 90 per cent or higher for 16-year-olds. Spain and the UK are below the OECD average (89 per cent) and the EU average (91 per cent), with rates of 84 per cent. For 17-year-olds, 9 countries reach rates of 90 per cent or more, while the Spanish figure is 79 per cent and the UK only reaches 73 per cent. In general, Mediterranean countries, together with the United Kingdom, have significantly lower enrolment rates at all ages than do their main economic competitors.

These graphs also depict youth unemployment rates, which exhibit a slight negative correlation with enrolment rates. In the following sections we

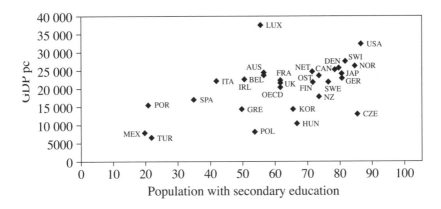

Source: OECD (2001).

Figure 4.1   GDP per capita and human capital stock in 1999

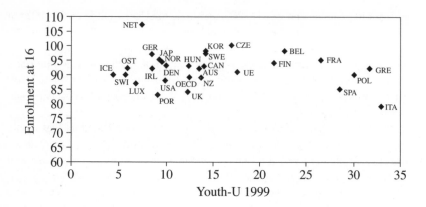

Source: OECD (2001).

Figure 4.2   Secondary schooling and unemployment in the OECD (1)

explore the effects of unemployment on education demand in more detail for both Spain and the UK. It is possible that the unfavourable situation faced by youngsters in the labour market has reduced the gap between enrolment rates in Spain and other OECD countries. However, British and Spanish participation rates in upper-secondary education remain low, assuming that both countries aim to converge to the EU average level of human capital over the next few years.

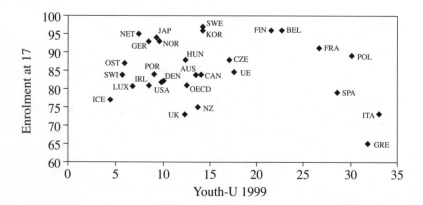

Source: OECD (2001).

Figure 4.3   Secondary schooling and unemployment in the OECD (2)

3. HUMAN CAPITAL THEORY: MODELS AND EMPIRICAL ESTIMATES

3.1 Empirical Implications of Human Capital Models

To explain the individual demand for education, traditional consumption models (in which the quantity demanded depends on the prices of education and other goods, and on the income and preferences of the consumer) compete with investment models, among which human capital models stand out. The latter theory is based on the assumption that individuals choose their optimal number of periods of schooling by comparing the present value of the costs of this educational investment with the present value of the future benefits which it generates.

Human capital models generate certain important predictions with respect to education demand. In particular, reductions in costs, or increases in benefits, will induce an increase in educational investment. It is often considered that the high unemployment rates in certain European countries (especially in Spain), caused by recent economic crises, have been responsible for the growth in post-compulsory education. However, human capital theory does not necessarily yield a positive relationship between unemployment and investment in education.

From a theoretical point of view, there are a number of possible effects of unemployment on schooling. On the one hand, it is often assumed that high rates of youth unemployment provide an incentive for students to remain in education, in that the opportunity cost of study is reduced. An alternative argument is that the increase in current observed unemployment may raise expectations of future unemployment, thereby causing a reduction in the expected earnings of investment in education. This latter provides a disincentive to staying on at school (Micklewright et al., 1990). Likewise, an increase in unemployment will lead to family budget constraints potentially reducing investments in human capital, especially if the unemployment is mainly long term (as has been the case in Spain in recent years).

In this study we investigate the determinants of the decisions taken by young people at the end of the compulsory schooling period. We wish to test the relative weight of family socio-economic factors, as well as labour market variables, on these decisions.

The estimation of the effects of unemployment on schooling in the abundant empirical literature depends on the identification of the relevant local labour market. For example, the only realistic alternative to education for 16- or 17-year-olds is the labour market closest to the family home. In the Spanish case, this may be identified as the province of residence rather than the region, as the latter covers too broad a geographical area, given that young people are little inclined to leave the family home. However, this is not true for individuals who are somewhat older. For university students the national market may be more relevant than provincial or regional labour markets. It is not surprising therefore that analyses of university demand find few significant relationships between regional unemployment and schooling.

It is also worth noting that many studies lack precise indicators of the unemployment rates which are most relevant for young people's decisions. In many cases only the overall rate of unemployment is included in the analysis; it is difficult to say whether this adequately reflects the opportunity cost of studying for the individuals in question. In the analysis below, we attempt to identify accurately different unemployment indicators affecting young people's investment in human capital. First, different rates will be used for men and women where possible, as their labour market situations have differed markedly over recent years. Second, various indicators of unemployment will be used to try to identify the diverse effects that unemployment has on education demand. Youth unemployment rates will be used for individuals who have not completed secondary education, as these rates constitute the best measure of the opportunity cost of continuing to study after completing compulsory education. Finally, the models also incorporate overall unemployment, by gender, as an indicator of current unemployment expectations and of possible budget restrictions which families may face as a result of unemployment.

3.2 Review of the Empirical Literature

There has been an abundance of empirical literature on the acquisition of human capital and how it is related to the labour market. Here we concentrate on certain studies which have analysed the first decisions regarding investment in post-compulsory education: in European countries these decisions are sometimes taken at the end of compulsory secondary education, while in the US the relevant stage is the step up to higher education. In other instances, the first decision refers to the choice of a track or a programme within secondary education. It should be borne in mind that this choice may take place relatively early (at age 12 or 14) in the Netherlands, Belgium, Germany, France and Italy.

3.2.1 United States
The US literature is abundant, although the results with respect to two key decisions are quite varied: that of leaving school by certain young people under the age of 18, and that of the transition from secondary education (compulsory) to higher education (post-compulsory). Analyses using time series data began with Duncan (1965). Studying cohorts of young people

aged 16–17 after the Second World War, the author found that school-leaving rose when unemployment decreased, and fell when there were fewer opportunities in the labour market. Later, Mattila (1982) also found a positive effect of unemployment (for males aged 25–34) on the enrolment of males aged 16–19. However, studies which use data across the 50 states produce quite varied results. Whereas Corman and Davidson (1984) find a positive effect of regional (global) unemployment on enrolment, Grubb (1988) finds that the demand for higher education is not very sensitive to variations in the labour market.

More recently there has been a proliferation of analyses of education demand using individual data. Hill (1979) finds that the probability of leaving secondary education depends significantly on mother's education and on the individual's ability (measured via tests). The improvement in local labour markets at the end of the 1960s significantly reduced school-leaving for young Whites. Rumberger (1983) found a positive relationship between unemployment and the probability of young Blacks and Hispanics staying on in the education system. Rees and Mocan (1997) incorporate a number of characteristics of the residential zone and students' schools into their analysis. Larger class sizes appear to be associated with higher exit rates from secondary education. Growth in unemployment reduces school-leaving, especially among young Hispanics in New York.

It is worth highlighting the work of Betts and McFarland (1995), using data from 818 Community Colleges over a 20-year period. They identify a positive relationship between unemployment and enrolment in short-term higher education. The rate of unemployment used (that of young people with secondary education certificates) can be interpreted as an indicator of the opportunity cost of continuing to study. However, in another recent study based on individual data, Kane (1994) does not find any significant relationship between local unemployment and the enrolment decisions of young Whites and Blacks.[2] Corman (1983) only finds significant negative effects in the case of university graduate unemployment (the expectations effect) on university enrolment by females aged 18–22.

A special mention should be given to the work of Willis and Rosen (1979), who estimate the structural version of the human capital model. They find evidence of behaviour on the part of individuals consistent with the maximization of the present value of future income when it comes to making the decision of whether or not to invest in higher education (after having completed secondary education). Their results confirm that the usual estimations of earnings equations may suffer from self-selection biases. Their model, however, does not incorporate individuals' unemployment expectations.

3.2.2 United Kingdom

In the case of the UK, education is only compulsory up to age 16, as in Spain, and empirical studies have concentrated on the decisions of young people at that age to continue education. The first study we highlight is that of Pissarides (1981), who, using time series data, finds a positive effect of overall unemployment, not youth unemployment, on male enrolment. Similar results are found in Rice (1987), Bennett et al. (1992), and Micklewright et al. (1990) (although insignificant) in analyses of individual data for 16- and 17-year-olds. It seems, in these cases, that the principal effect of unemployment is to reduce the opportunity cost of studying, which in turn provides incentives for schooling.

With regard to the effects of the family's socio-economic level on education demand, it should be pointed out that the human capital of the parents always plays an important role, whereas family income is significant in the models of Micklewright et al. (1990), but not in those of Rice (1987), Micklewright (1989) or Bennett et al. (1992).

3.2.3 Spain

In the Spanish case, Mora (1989) finds a positive relationship between aggregate unemployment and first-year university schooling in a time series analysis of the period 1962–83. Studies using individual data are very scarce and have concentrated on higher education. No important effects of unemployment on university enrolment have been found. Neither González and Dávila (1998), using data from the 1991 Family Budget Survey (EPF), nor Albert (2000), using various years of the Labour Force Survey (EPA) find significant effects of regional unemployment on the behaviour of university students. Modrego (1987) is the only study to find a negative impact of graduate unemployment on university enrolment of longer duration (that is, degree courses as opposed to diplomas, which are shorter), using 1991 Census data for the province of Vizcaya. The latter result seems to reveal a relationship between the decision to continue with higher education and the local perception of the likely labour market returns to these studies.

Work on secondary schooling is even scarcer. Petrongolo and San Segundo (1999) find a positive effect of youth unemployment (at the provincial level) on young people's staying on decisions at the ages of 16 and 17. These results are found for both 1981 and 1991, using individual data from the Family Budget Surveys (EPFs) combined with labour force data from the Censuses. As in other studies, overall unemployment (provincial) is negatively correlated with education demand. The results are thus consistent with the human capital model: see also Petrongolo and San Segundo (2002), where multinomial logit models are estimated using data from the 1991 Labour Force Survey (EPA).

3.2.4 Other European countries

Oosterbeek (1990) applies the Willis and Rosen model to the Netherlands and finds that the family's socio-economic origin does not affect the demand for higher education, whereas ability and the economic earnings from the investment are important. However, parents' education and social background play an important role in decisions prior to higher education.

In a recent study, McIntosh (2001) uses time-series data to analyse the demand for upper-secondary education in four European countries: England, Germany, the Netherlands and Sweden. The two key findings are the importance of prior academic performance, and the small positive effect of youth unemployment on education participation rates.

4.   THE DETERMINANTS OF THE PROBABILITY OF STAYING ON AT SCHOOL IN SPAIN AND IN THE UK

We are now in a position to assess the effect of family characteristics and local labour market conditions on the demand for post-compulsory education in Spain and the UK. Our data sets combine individual data (from the Labour Force Surveys) with regional or provincial unemployment data taken from the census.

The first two columns of Tables 4.1 and 4.2 present the parameter estimates from logit regressions of the probability of staying on at school at age 16 or 17 in Spain. The right-hand side of these tables show analogous results for the UK. Preliminary analyses suggested that the effects of most family controls were similar for males and females; we therefore present results from pooled data, although we retain interactions between both measures of unemployment and gender dummies.

In both countries it can be shown that females have a higher probability of remaining in the schooling system, and that both the occupational and educational level of the household head appear as strong determinants of enrolment in secondary education.[3] This finding is consistent with the results obtained by Micklewright (1989) for the UK, Heckman and Hotz (1986) for Panama, Kodde and Ritzen (1988) for the Netherlands, Kane (1994) for the US, and González and Dávila (1998) for Spain (Higher Education). All of our estimates indicate that father's, and especially mother's, education exercises a powerful influence on teenagers' educational demand. The effect of father's education seems to diminish somewhat above the secondary education level in Spain. Interestingly, Alba and San Segundo (1995) and San Segundo (1997) both show that increases in human capital beyond the secondary schooling level do have a positive effect on parents' income, but they do not seem to affect the educational demand of children. This result suggests that parents' low education (below secondary

Table 4.1   Staying on at school: effects of parents' education

| | SPAIN | | UK | | |
	(1)	(1 F)	(1)	(1 F)	
Mother primary	0.6431	0.6391	–	–	–
	(7.6)	(7.4)			
Mother lower	1.0780	1.1053	0.6729	0.6315	Mother
secondary	(7.4)	(7.4)	(7.5)	(7.0)	O-level
Mother upper	1.8091	1.7540	1.0409	1.0968	Mother
secondary	(7.1)	(6.8)	(5.9)	(6.2)	A-level
Mother	2.0157	2.0090	1.2835	1.2578	Mother
university	(6.3)	(6.2)	(8.8)	(8.5)	degree
Father primary	0.4927	0.4764	–	–	–
	(5.4)	(5.2)			
Father lower	0.8652	0.8844	0.4015	0.4207	Father
secondary	(5.7)	(5.7)	(3.9)	(4.0)	O-level
Father upper	1.4026	1.3694	0.3225	0.3903	Father
secondary	(7.4)	(7.2)	(2.8)	(3.4)	A-level
Father university	1.2253	1.1531	0.8890	0.9117	Father
	(4.8)	(4.5)	(6.3)	(6.4)	degree
Fixed effects	NO	YES	NO	YES	
Pseudo R^2	0.145	0.155	0.146	0.161	
N° of Obs.	6860	6860	4137	4137	

Notes:
Estimated models include sex and age dummies, parents' employment status, number of family
members 16 and older, number of younger siblings, and the regional/provincial variables included
in Table 4.2.
Dependent variable = 1 if the youngster stays on at school.

education) acts as a cultural rather than an economic barrier in determining
children's education.

In addition, we can interpret these results in light of the significant differences in returns to education between social groups. In the Spanish case, San
Segundo and Valiente (2003) find that the return to upper secondary schooling
varies from 46 per cent for workers whose father has a higher education degree
to 15 per cent for those whose father had not completed primary education.

Other results, which are not explicitly presented in Table 4.1, reveal that
in Spain, father's unemployment has a significant negative effect on the probability of staying on at school, whereas mother's unemployment attracts an
insignificant coefficient. For the UK, however, parents' worklessness does
not reduce the demand for schooling. Also, as expected, family size exerts a

Table 4.2 Unemployment effects

	SPAIN				UK			
	(1)	(2)	(3)	(4)	(1)	(2)	(3)	(4)
Male x male general unemployment rate	-4.2786	1.9154		-3.1539	-3.0472	0.9992		-2.9511
	(2.9)	(2.9)		(4.8)	(1.6)	(0.7)		(1.5)
Female x female general unemployment rate	-3.2689	-1.4239		-3.0044	-15.3256	7.6750		-15.3083
	(3.3)	(2.5)		(3.0)	(2.0)	(2.4)		(2.0)
Male x male youth unemployment rate	4.2737		1.9694	3.7070	5.6940		4.0206	5.6573
	(4.7)		(4.8)	(4.0)	(3.5)		(3.2)	(3.4)
Female x female youth unemployment rate	1.6993		-0.3215	1.5248	11.9723		5.4527	12.0183
	(2.2)		(0.7)	(2.0)	(3.3)		(3.6)	(3.3)
Stock of university graduates				6.0547				0.3247
				(3.0)				(0.1)
Pseudo-R^2	0.145	0.141	0.142	0.146	0.146	0.142	0.145	0.146
N° of Obs.	6860	6860	6860	6860	4137	4137	4137	4137

Note: Regressions include all of the individual and family characteristics described in Table 4.1.

negative influence on the probability of staying on at school. This negative effect is especially associated with the presence of younger siblings in Spain. It appears that the number of family members younger than 16, and therefore unable to work, reflects household budget constraints. In the UK, however, budget restrictions seem to be picked up by the number of adults.

The last set of variables to be introduced relate to the characteristics of the province of residence. For 1991, the availability of data from the census of population allowed us to match individual files with more detailed information on unemployment rates by province (or region in the UK), sex, age and educational qualification, and a number of other local indicators. We therefore include in our probability models both the adult unemployment rate (by province and gender), and the unemployment rate of youngsters who have only completed lower secondary education (the compulsory stage). This latter should proxy the opportunity cost of schooling for those entering post-compulsory education.

It can be argued that the labour market situation in the province of residence plays an important role in the decision of staying on at school. First, entering the local market would seem to be the relevant alternative to school for 16-year-olds, who rarely live away from their parents. Secondly, provinces can be considered as self-contained labour markets where young workers live and may look for a job. The search channels mostly used by youngsters, such as local newspaper and public unemployment offices, do in fact operate at a provincial level.

There is considerable variation in unemployment across Spanish provinces, ranging from 4 per cent to 31 per cent for males and from 9 per cent to 47 per cent for females in 1991. The 1991 census provides detailed information about unemployment rates for youngsters who enter the labour market with different qualification levels. The significance of these rates in explaining the decision to leave education will be explored below.

Before explicitly analysing the impact of regional variables in the model, column 1F of Table 4.1 adds province- or region-level fixed effects. Given that the specification in which local labour market variables are included may produce an overestimate of the level of significance of the parameters of interest (see Moulton, 1986), we replace such variables in regression (1F) with province–region dummies. These regional effects on enrolment are jointly significant.

Regressions 1–3 in Table 4.2 then introduce explicit regional characteristics that may explain the significance of the fixed effects in Table 4.1. It is worth noting that the estimated coefficients for the variables that measure individual and family characteristics, as well as their significance levels, remain practically unchanged. The results with respect to the relationship between local unemployment and the demand for education are fairly unambiguous. Youth unemployment has a positive impact on the staying-on decision, while the overall unemployment rate has a negative impact for both males and females. Therefore, we conclude that youth unemployment rates adequately measure the opportunity costs of studying versus working, by reducing the returns to job search in local labour markets, while adult rates proxy unemployment. According to human capital theory, a decline in opportunity costs should increase education demand, while an increase in the expected unemployment rate should reduce it. While both of these effects have a larger quantitative impact on enrolment rates in the UK than in Spain, it is worth noticing that the family controls are more important in Spain than in the UK.

If we only use one unemployment measure in our models, the results are mixed: see regressions (2) and (3). In Spain, for males, local unemployment appears to have a positive significant impact on the probability of undertaking post-compulsory education, both for the overall unemployment rate (in regression 2) and for youth unemployment (regression 3). For females, the estimated unemployment coefficients are all negative, although only that corresponding to the general unemployment rate (regression 2) is statistically significant. The fact that labour market conditions have a limited impact on women's decisions to quit the educational system can be at least partly explained by their low rates of labour market participation. OECD (1993) reports that in 1991 young women (aged 25–34) who had not yet completed secondary education had very low participation rates in both Spain (43 per cent) and the rest of Europe (47 per cent).

For the UK, only female adult unemployment rates have a positive effect on the staying-on probability in regression (2). Youth unemployment (in regression 3) has a clearer effect: both males and females are significantly more likely to remain in the schooling system when the local labour market is slack. The effect of youth unemployment on enrolment seems stronger in the UK than in Spain.

Finally, we note in regression 4 that our basic unemployment effects remain practically unchanged when a measure of the human capital stock of the provinces/regions is introduced. The percentage of adults with a university degree has a significant positive effect on the probability of staying on at school in Spain, but not in the UK. This variable can proxy cultural and socio-economic determinants of the demand for education, but it can also be interpreted as a measure of supply restrictions. The number of places available in secondary education in each province (and its geographic distribution) is very likely to be determined by the number of teachers, and therefore the intensity of educational demand in the past. There is therefore a high degree of inertia in educational inequalities between provinces. Other province indicators such as the pupil/teacher ratio, average income or population density were also included in the regressions, but they did not attract significant coefficients.

Table 4.3   Predicted probabilities of staying on at school in Spain and the UK

	Spain	UK
Reference individual*	53%	58%
Female	62%	65%
Parents with secondary education	88%	79%
Parent with degree	96%	88%
High unemployment area	60%	69%
High human capital area	59%	58%

Note:
* Young male aged 16, whose parents have no qualifications, the mother being out of work and the father being a private sector employee, and whose household includes one individual under 16 and four individuals ages 16 or more. We also impose that the province of residence has average levels of unemployment (15.5% for adults and 31% for youngsters), and low levels of human capital (4% of the population have a university degree).

5.   CONCLUDING REMARKS AND POLICY COMMENTS

This chapter has analysed the impact of family characteristics and labour market conditions on the demand for secondary education after the age of 16. The decision to undertake post-compulsory education has been shown to depend critically on the cultural and social background of the household. Table 4.3 shows the predicted probabilities of staying on at school, which vary markedly with parents' education, especially in Spain. For the reference individuals (whose parents have the lowest qualifications) the probabilities are only 53 per cent (Spain) and 58 per cent (UK). If both parents have completed secondary education, the probabilities rise to 88 per cent and 79 per cent, respectively. With higher education degrees they rise further to 96 per cent (Spain) and 88 per cent (UK).

It is also likely that secondary school students partially base their decisions regarding additional education on unemployment rates. The direction of these effects confirms our prior beliefs: the impact of local labour markets on enrolment rates mostly works through the opportunity cost effect of staying in the schooling system. Once both youth and adult unemployment rates are introduced, the two counteracting effects of unemployment on the demand for education can be better assessed. Table 4.3 shows that labour market conditions have a larger effect on UK than on Spanish enrolment rates, and that family controls have a greater impact in Spain than in the UK. However, in both countries the effects of unemployment on educational demand are of smaller magnitude than those from family human capital variables.

In general, we can conclude that high youth unemployment rates may explain some of the rise in enrolment, and at the same time the improvement of grant policies has probably eased the budgetary constraints faced by students coming from lower socio-economic backgrounds. However, the main determinant of the decision to stay on at school beyond the age of 16 seems to be parents' education.[4]

Recently, several European countries have followed financing policies aimed at improving the academic achievement of pupils from disadvantaged family backgrounds. In Belgium, additional funding is awarded for schools with at least 10 per cent of students with social or cultural problems. Target groups are formed by immigrant pupils as well as those whose mothers did not continue their education beyond the age of 18 (EC, 2000). In France, financing models award additional staff for *zones d'education prioritares* which are established taking into account not only unemployment rates but also the proportion of families in which neither parent has secondary education. In the United Kingdom, the Excellence Challenge policy aims to help young people (aged 13–19) at risk of under-achieving to enter post-16 education and higher education and to successfully complete the courses they take. Opportunity grants are given to pupils, depending on family income and parents' education. Priority is given to those with little or no history of family participation in higher education.

It is still probably too early to know if these policies have been successful, but, following on from our results, we expect them to produce a reduction in the educational inequalities that currently hold in European countries.

APPENDIX

The Data Sets

The Spanish data used in this chapter is drawn from the Spanish Labour Force Survey (Encuesta de Población Activa), carried out every quarter on a sample of some 60,000 households. It is designed to be representative of the total Spanish population, and contains very detailed individual information about labour force and schooling status of people aged 16 and over. In particular, the EPA provides abundant information on family characteristics of youngsters.

The sample used in this chapter refers to 16- and 17-year-olds surveyed in the second quarter of 1991. Focusing only on youngsters who were 16 at the end (in the spring) of an academic year could create problems for our analysis. A large part of the sample would be made up of people who were 15 at the beginning of the school year, hence they could not enter the labour market, and would be likely to stay at school until the end of the year. Therefore, we decide to include both 16- and 17-year-olds in our analysis. It can be calculated that 36.3 per cent of those aged 16 or 17 left school in 1987, while less than ten years later only 18.2 per cent of the sample left the educational system.

Table 4A.1 reports some descriptive statistics of the sample used. Enrolment rates are computed including all those who declared that they were receiving some education during the previous four weeks, either within the general or the vocational system.

The probability models estimated include, first of all, a group of dummy variables that reflect father's and mother's educational levels. The next set of variables summarizes the socio-economic status of the father (employer, professional, civil servant or wage earner in the private sector). Two dummies indicate whether either parent is out of work at the time of the survey. Two more variables control for those cases in which the youngster's father or mother are not present in the household. Finally, the size of the household is introduced through two variables which measure the number of family members who are 16 and older, and those who are younger and therefore cannot work; this last group can proxy budget constraints faced by large families.

The right-hand sides of Tables 4.1 and 4.2 report results for the UK. The regression specification adopted is as similar as possible to that estimated for Spain, with the only significant difference being a coarser classification of local labour markets, based on 19 regions. This choice was mainly due to the fact that the UK Labour Force Survey does not allow – for confidentiality reasons – the local district of residence to be disseminated. But given the smaller size of the territory, and the presumably higher mobility of UK youths, we believe this broader disaggregation of labour markets can still adequately represent the local job-finding opportunities of school leavers.

Table 4A.1   Descriptive statistics

	Spain 1991	UK 1991
Staying-on rate	0.723	0.620
Females	0.498	0.473
Seventeen years	0.505	0.499
Ed. Mother primary	0.563	–
Secondary – 1st stage	0.098	0.272
Secondary – 2nd stage	0.042	0.058
University ed. Mother	0.047	0.114
Ed. Father primary	0.500	–
Secondary – 1st stage	0.080	0.188
Secondary – 2nd stage	0.073	0.144
University ed. Father	0.078	0.149
Father – employer	0.056	0.054
Father – professional	0.073	0.072
Father – civil servant	0.130	0.030
Father – pr. wage earner	0.393	0.409
Father – out of work	0.247	0.191
Mother – out of work	0.728	0.351
Family members >16 yrs	4.133	3.346
Family members <16 yrs	0.976	0.850
Father – not present	0.083	0.164
Mother – not present	0.018	0.068
Number of observations	6860	4137

Sources: Labour Force Surveys (2nd quarter, 1991). Samples of 16- and 17-year-olds

Furthermore, unemployment indicators similar to those used in the Spanish case (the general and the 16–24 unemployment rates) pose serious problems of correlation in the UK. As a consequence, we measure youth unemployment by the unemployment rate of teenagers aged 16 and 17. This reduces the degree of correlation and solves the collinearity problems found before.

NOTES

1. We wish to thank Alberto Vaquero for help with the data. This research is part of a EU-TSER project on *Schooling, Training and Transitions – An Economic Perspective*. Address for correspondence: M.J. San Segundo (mjsan@eco.uc3m.es), Dept. of Economics, Universidad Carlos III, c/ Madrid 126, 28903 Getafe (Madrid), Spain.
2. Although unemployment always attracts a positive coefficient in the ten models estimated, and for Whites it is significant in two of these.
4. Tables 4.1 and 4.2 do not present all of the parameters estimated, due to space constraints.
5. Family income is found to be insignificant in most studies of the UK, and in the analysis of the Spanish Family Budget Survey for 1991 (Petrongolo and San Segundo, 2000).

REFERENCES

Alba, A. and M.J. San Segundo, (1995), 'The returns to education in Spain', *Economics of Education Review*, **14** (2), 155–66.

Albert, C. (2000), 'Higher education demand in Spain. The influence of labour market signals and family background', *Higher Education*, **40** (2), 147–62.

Bennett, R., H. Glennester and D. Nevison (1992), 'Investing in skill: to stay on or not to stay on?', *Oxford Review of Economic Policy*, **8** (2), 130–45.

Betts, J. and L. McFarland (1995), 'Safe port in a storm. The impact of labor market conditions on community college enrollments', *The Journal of Human Resources*, **30** (4), 741–65.

Bowles, S. and V. Nelson (1974), 'The inheritance of IQ and the intergenerational reproduction of economic inequality', *Review of Economics and Statistics*, **56** (1), 39–51.

COM (1993), *Growth, Competitiveness and Employment*, Brussels.

COM (2000), *Joint Employment Report 2000*, Brussels.

Corman, H. (1983), 'Postsecondary education enrollment responses by recent high school graduates and other adults', *Journal of Human Resources*, **18** (2), 247–67.

Corman, H. and P. Davidson (1984), 'Economic aspects of post-secondary schooling decisions', *Economics of Education Review*, **3**, 131–9.

Duncan, B. (1965), 'Dropouts and the unemployed', *Journal of Political Economy*, **73**, 121–34.

European Commission (2000), *Financing and Management of Resources in Compulsory Education*, European Commission, Luxembourg.

González, B. and D. Dávila (1998), 'Economic and cultural impediments to university education in Spain', *Economics of Education Review*, **17** (1), 93–103.

Grubb, W.N. (1988), 'The decline of community college transfer rates', *Journal of Higher Education*, **62** (2), 194–222.

Heckman, J. and V. Hotz (1986), 'An investigation of the labor market earnings of Panamanian males', *Journal of Human Resources*, **21** (4), 507–42.

Hill, C.R. (1979), 'Capacities, opportunities and educational investments: the case of the high school dropout', *Review of Economics and Statistics*, 9–20.

Kane, T.J. (1994), 'College entry by Blacks since 1970', *The Journal of Political Economy*, **102** (5), 878–911.

Katz, L. and K. Murphy (1992), 'Changes in relative wages, 1963–1987', *Quarterly Journal of Economics*, **107** (1), 35–78.

Kodde, D. and J. Ritzen (1984), 'Integrating consumption and investment motives in a neoclassical model of demand for education', *Kyklos*, **37** (4), 598–606.

Kodde, D. and J. Ritzen (1988), 'Direct and indirect effects of parental education on the demand for higher education', *The Journal of Human Resources*, **23** (3), 356–71.

Mare, R.D. (1980), 'Social background and school continuation decisions', *Journal of the American Statistical Association*, **75** (370), 295–305.

Mattila, J.P. (1982), 'Determinants of male school enrolments: a time-series analysis', *Review of Economics and Statistics*, **6**, 242–51.

McIntosh, S. (2001), 'The demand for post-compulsory education in four European countries', *Education Economics*, **9** (1), 69–90.

Micklewright, J. (1989), 'Choice at sixteen', *Economica*, **56**, 25–39.

Micklewright, J., M. Pearson and S. Smith (1990), 'Unemployment and early school leaving', *The Economic Journal*, **100**, 163–9.

Modrego, A. (1987), 'Demanda de Educación. Resultados de la estimación de un modelo para la provincia de Vizcaya', *Ekonomiaz*, **19**, 87–96.

Mora, J. (1989), *La demanda de Educación Superior*, Consejo de Universidades, Madrid.

Moulton, R. (1986), 'Random effects and the precision of regression estimates', *Journal of Econometrics*, **32** (3), 385–97.

OECD (1993), *Education at a Glance*, OECD, Paris.

OECD (1998), *Human Capital Investment. An International Comparison*, OECD, Paris.

OECD (2001), *Education at a Glance*, OECD, Paris.

Oosterbeek, H. (1990), 'Education and earnings in the Netherlands: an empirical analysis', *European Economic Review*, **34**, 1353–75.

Petrongolo, B. and M. San Segundo (1999), '¿Incentiva el paro juvenil la escolarización secundaria?', *Ekonomiaz*, **43**, 10–37.

Petrongolo, B. and M. San Segundo, (2002), 'Staying-on at school at sixteen. The impact of labor market conditions in Spain', *Economics of Education Review*, **21**, 353–65.

Pissarides, C.A. (1981), 'Staying-on at School in England and Wales', *Economica*, **48**, 345–63.

Rees, D. and N. Mocan (1997), 'Labor market conditions and the high school dropout rate: Evidence from New York State', *Economics of Education Review*, **16** (2), 103–9.

Rice, P. (1987), 'The demand for post-compulsory education in the UK and the effects of educational maintenance allowances', *Economica*, **54**, 465–75.

Rumberger, R. (1983), 'Dropping out of high school: the influence of race, sex, and family background', *American Educational Research Journal*, **20**, 199–220.

San Segundo, M.J. (1997), 'Decentralisation and Diversification in Spain', *Higher Education Management*, **9** (3), 89–100.

San Segundo, M.J. and A. Valiente (2003), 'Returns to Schooling and the Socioeconomic Background of the Family in Spain', *Education Economics*, **11** (1), 39–52.

Willis, R. and S. Rosen (1979), 'Education and Self-Selection', *Journal of Political Economy*, **87** (5), S7–S36.

5. Early career experiences and later career success: an international comparison

David Margolis, Erik Plug, Véronique Simonnet and Lars Vilhuber

1. INTRODUCTION

This chapter represents an attempt to untangle the links between the early career experiences of young people in the labour market and their labour market success or failure later in life. Although the subject of early-career experiences, such as 'excessive' job mobility or taking a long time to find a first job, has already been treated in the literature,[1] very little attention has been given to the effects at a much longer term (that is, at least five years after school leaving) of these experiences. Most of these studies focus on a single measure of early career experiences and consider the effects from a short-term perspective. Furthermore, these studies tend to consider only one output measure, typically log hourly wages.

We approach this topic from two different perspectives. First, we use a large set of measures of early career experiences in an attempt to control for the omitted variable bias that has made interpretation of many previous results risky and we consider a variety of different measures of later career success. Second, we use long (at least 10-year) panel data sets available in the United States, France, Germany and the Netherlands. As the countries have vastly differing institutions, we can see if workers in different labour markets are treated in the same manner when they have similar early career experiences.

This chapter is organized as follows. Section 2 provides some very brief theoretical foundations for the analyses undertaken here and situates the chapter relative to the work of Gardecki and Newmark (1998). Section 3 describes the different data sets that are exploited in the econometrics, and Section 4 discusses the descriptive statistics from the different countries to provide a basis for interpreting the results. Section 5 presents the results from the various estimations. Section 6 concludes.

2. LITERATURE AND THEORY

The theoretical literature in labour economics has much to say about why early career experiences should be observable as affecting later career success. This section very briefly divides the literature into four main strands: information-based learning models, sorting models, human capital models and contracting models. An additional class of models based on job search theory has no *ex-ante* implications for the early–late career link[2], although we will refer to this framework below in our interpretation. Finally, unobserved individual heterogeneity can also be considered a class of models, although it is treated here as a catch-all category for all other (non-specified) theories. We end the section with a comparison of our chapter to that of Gardecki and Newmark (1998), the closest paper in the literature to our approach.

2.1 Information-based Learning Models

The information-based learning models[3] maintain that, since information is not symmetric and complete in the labour market, agents will learn about unknown characteristics over time. Since the fastest updating of beliefs about characteristics occurs with the earliest observations, early career experiences could play an important role in determining later posterior distributions of beliefs over unknown characteristics, which should be correlated with observable output measures. One implication is that, as time goes by, the early-career experiences play a less and less important role in the determination of the posterior distribution of beliefs.[4]

2.2 Sorting Models

Sorting models (Roy, 1951; Spence, 1973), like learning models, assume that initially information is not symmetric and complete. However, sorting models differ in that, as information is revealed about the worker, the market assigns him or her to the appropriate job. Econometrically, these models imply that the early career experiences will have an impact on the type of job the person has in the future, and that the importance of these initial experiences in determining later career outcomes does not diminish over time.[5]

2.3 Human Capital Models

These models, originating with Becker (1993), suggest that worker characteristics change over time as they learn new things or as their old knowledge becomes outdated. The Ben-Porath (1967) life-cycle version implies that the greatest investments in learning will be made at the beginning of the career, where their returns can be reaped over a longer time in the future. Other refinements of these models have typically been based on decomposing human capital into different types.[6] The empirical implications of this type of model depend on the variant retained. In the sector-specific approach, fewer different sectors for a given number of days worked implies the accumulation of more human capital, and an equivalent reasoning holds for occupational capital models. In models where the human capital does not depreciate over time, the significance of these effects should remain constant, as the skills learned early in the career can still be used later. In models where human capital depreciates, the capital garnered at the beginning of a career becomes less and less relevant over time, and thus measures of it should become less and less significant.

2.4   Contracting Models

Contracting models are based on the idea that, at the start of an employment relation, firms and workers come to an agreement on the conditions and requirements of the job, and the associated remuneration. There is an enormous literature surrounding these models, and the implications for the relation between observable early career events and later career outcomes depend entirely on the question being specifically addressed. For example, in the bonding model of Lazear (1979), the tournament model of Lazear and Rosen (1981) and the internal labour markets models,[7] one expects to see faster early-career earnings growth associated with higher later-career earnings. On the other hand, contract renegotiation models[8] have empirical implications for the link between early career variables and later career outcomes that are identical to learning-based models.[9]

2.5   Gardecki and Newmark (1998)

Gardecki and Neumark (1998) represent a (rare) recent example of a paper that considers the link between early career experiences and later career outcomes for the United States and that uses the same data as us. There are a number of important differences between their approach and ours. First, whereas we use information on all jobs to construct our measures of labour market insertion, they restrict their attention (in their main analysis) to the most recent job at interview time. Second, whereas Gardecki and Neumark concentrate on a fixed calendar date (1990–92), we have fixed the time since labour market entry to five years and more, each year generating a new observation on each individual. Third, Gardecki and Neumark consider the transition to occur at the latest when individuals leave two-year colleges, considering any education occurring after this transition to be training, while we focus less on the specific (high-)school-to-work transition and more on the actual entry into the labour market, irrespective of the educational attainment at the time of that insertion. Finally, Gardecki and Neumark consider 'churning' measures over the five years following the exit from school, whereas we consider only a two-year period.

3. DATA

In this section, we discuss briefly the data upon which our estimations are performed.

3.1 The United States

The data used here were extracted from the 1979–93 National Longitudinal Survey of Youth[10] (NLSY) data files. We exclude all oversamples, as well as the military subsample. To be included in the regressions, an individual needs to have been in school at the time of the 1979 interview; this allows us to observe the transition into the labour force. The individual's permanent exit from school is computed by requiring an exit from school to be followed immediately by at least two full years during which the individual never returned to school.[11]

In order to gather sufficient post-schooling data, we require the exit from school to occur before 1987, which leaves a minimum of six post-schooling years from which to compute outcome measures. The date of school exit is then taken to be the first interview for which these conditions are met.[12] This criterion is satisfied by 78.28 per cent of the 4043 available persons. A number of individuals have missing data, leaving us with a maximal sample size (depending on the regression specification) of 2974 individuals.

3.2 France

The French data are drawn from the Déclarations Annuelles des Données Sociales[13] (DADS), or Annual Social Data Reports, from 1976 through 1996. These data are a 1/25th random sample of the French population, selected by the individual's birth date. It should be noted that data from 1981, 1983 and 1990 were not made available to us, and as such we restrict our attention to school leaving cohorts 1976–78, 1984–87 and 1991. For one-tenth of the DADS data, we observe the level of education (in eight degree categories, including 'no known educational certification') and the age at school leaving with a supplementary data set to the DADS called the Echantillon Démographique Permanent (EDP), or Permanent Demographic Sample. We restricted our attention to this subset of the DADS.[14]

3.3 Germany

In Germany, we use the German Socio-Economic Panel[15] (GSOEP, 1984–96),
a 13-year household panel survey, restraining our attention to 16- to 45-year-
old German nationals or foreigners residing in western Germany. For reasons
of attrition, only 6300 individuals (approximately) are present in any given
year out of 11 081 potentially eligible individuals.[16]

We kept only those people who left school between 1984 and 1991, which
left us with 2551 individuals, of which 1396 were men. As the year and the
month of school leaving were not directly available as survey variables, we
used the survey's monthly activity calendar and the same school ending definition as in the United States.

Our analysis sample represents a relatively small subsample of the initially
available data. Of the 1396 men in our sample, only 624 were present four
years after the end of schooling and provided information regarding their early
career events, while 356 were present eight years after. These numbers are
reduced to 474 and 240, respectively, when we consider only people who are
working at the time of the interview four to eight years after the end of
school.[17] For the women (1155 in the sample), 487 were present four years
after the end of school and provided information on their early career experiences and 265 of them were present eight years after school leaving, but only
355 and 147, respectively, were employed at the interview date.

3.4 The Netherlands

For the Netherlands, we use the OSA Labour Supply Panel Survey[18]. These
data include information on individual schooling duration, labour market
status and earnings for the following years: 1985, 1986, 1988, 1990, 1992,
1994 and 1996. Each wave contains about 4500 observations and is intended
to be representative for the Dutch labour force.

We construct our insertion variables based on information from the 1985,
1986, 1988 and 1990 waves; from these waves we are able to identify 199,
523, 70 and 90 school leavers, respectively, whom we follow for at least two
years.[19] We construct the variables that refer to the later career outcomes from
all seven waves of the OSA data. Linking the 884 school leavers to their later
working career, we are left with 662 observations, of which 318 are female.

4.   DESCRIPTIVE STATISTICS CONCERNING EARLY
       CAREER VARIABLES

In this section, we characterize the early career experiences in our four countries and describe the samples on which we estimate our models.[20]

4.1 Job Search Variables

We calculate two measures of job search experiences: time to first job and time to first job of at least six months.[21] There are several definitional differences across the countries. In the United States, France and Germany, we exclude workers who do not find their first job of at least six months within five years of leaving school from the analyses.[22] In the Netherlands, the job search variables are top-coded at five years, with a correction for military service.[23]

Overall, the United States clearly has the shortest observed time to first job, at 0.304 years (around 16 weeks) on average for men and 0.362 (around 19 weeks) for women. This is consistent with the differing labour market institutions, since school leavers are ineligible for most sorts of government transfers in the United States.[24] The Netherlands is close behind, with an average time to first job of 0.671 years (35 weeks) for men and 0.514 years (27 weeks) for women, while in France and Germany it takes, on average, over a year to find the first job.

Much of the difference between the European and US data can be attributed to the treatment of mandatory military service.[25] Taking these differences into account, men typically seem to find their first jobs faster than women, and the time to first job (net of the expected time spent in the military) varies for men from 0.30 in the US to 0.36 in France[26] to 0.44 in Germany to 0.67 in the Netherlands.[27]

Differences across countries for women, on the other hand, should not be directly affected by military service. Women in the United States and the Netherlands clearly find their first jobs faster than in France or Germany.[28] Some of this effect, notably the differences between the United States and Germany, may be due to differences in female labour force participation rates.

There is also very little variability in the time to first job in the United States relative to the European countries, and in particular relative to France and Germany. As with the means, part of this difference in variability may be due to the treatment of military service. Still, the differences persist for the women, and there is little difference within France and Germany across sexes in the variance of time to first job. The sum of this evidence implies substantially less variability in the United States in underlying reservation wages or offer arrival rates.

In considering the time to the first job of at least six months, the United States again stands out; men only take an additional 8.4 weeks (on average) and women an additional 7.6 weeks to find a stable job, while the figures for France (23.2 and 23.5 extra weeks) and Dutch men (25.6 extra weeks) suggest that the earliest jobs are less stable in these countries. Given our earlier results, this is likely due to a higher exogenous separation in France and faster early career job-to-job mobility for Dutch men.[29]

4.2 Earnings Growth

In all of our countries, we calculated earnings growth as

$$\text{earnings growth} = \frac{(w_{t+1} - w_t)}{w_{t+1}},$$

where w_t refers to the relevant earnings measure in period t.[30] Overall, we find that the fastest earnings growth occurred in the Netherlands, where first year earnings were on average 27 per cent lower than second year earnings for men, and 12 per cent lower for women. Average earnings growth was lower for men in Germany with respect to the Netherlands (14 per cent), but marginally higher for women (also 14 per cent). Our earnings growth measures for the United States suggest slower average earnings growth than in Germany and the Netherlands, with women having earnings that are sufficiently decreasing over time so as to induce, on average across individuals, a decline in our measure of earnings growth. At the other end of the spectrum, our measure of earnings growth for France is largely negative on average for both men and women, but this is clearly driven by a few outliers.[31]

4.3 Employment Variables

We constructed several measures of early career employment, each measured over six month periods beginning at the time of school leaving. These variables were the number of different employers, the time spent in employment and the average job duration (measured as the share of time employed divided by the number of employers times the length of the interval).

For all of the countries in our sample and for both sexes (with the exception of Dutch women and, to a much lesser extent, Dutch men), young people spent more and more time in employment as time elapsed following the end of schooling. Part of this effect is mechanically related to the time to first long job measures, since by construction the six months following the first long job will have 100 per cent employment. Nevertheless, this measure suggests that unemployment is not evenly distributed throughout the insertion period, and that either workers tend to spend less and less time unemployed, or that fewer and fewer workers spend any time unemployed, as the labour market insertion progresses.

There does not appear to be any common pattern across countries in terms of the number of different employers visited during the first two years of one's career. In the United States, the trend is essentially decreasing, which suggests that jobs are becoming more and more stable over time (as would be implied by standard job search theory). On the other hand, the number of different employers is monotonically increasing on average in France, while in the Netherlands there is no clear pattern.[32] These differences suggest that care should be taken when trying to transpose results, such as those found in Gardecki and Neumark (1998), from American data based studies to the European context, as the base descriptive statistics are not even comparable.

4.4 Occupational and Industry Mobility Variables

Certain recent modifications of human capital theory suggest that, for a given number of employers, those individuals who change occupation or industry more often will acquire less human capital in any given industry that may be of use later in life. In addition, Neal's (1999) analysis of the complexity of early career mobility suggests that workers who often switch occupation or sector are having problems finding an adequate match, which delays the start of their real careers. With these theories in mind, we constructed measures of the number of different occupations and industries experienced during the first two years after the end of schooling, measured in six month intervals.[33]

The patterns in the means of the data do not suggest that workers settle in to an industry or occupation within their first two years on the labour market. Only in the case of American women is there a trend in industry mobility that looks somewhat monotonically declining. For French men and women, the tendency is toward an increase in the number of different occupations and industries experienced.

5. RESULTS

In this section, we present the results of estimating models of the effects of early career experiences on later career outcomes. For each country, we estimate linear models of the form $y_{it} = x_i\beta_1 + z_{it}\beta_2 + \varepsilon_{it}$, where y_{it} is the later-career earnings outcome of interest (log hourly wages, log monthly earnings or log full year equivalent (FYE) earnings), x_i is a vector of measures of early-career experiences, and z_{it} is a vector of other covariates measured at the same date as the dependent variable y_{it} that control for other characteristics such as age, seniority, education, region, industry and occupation. For the percentage of time spent in employment, we use a standard Tobit specification based on the latent model specified above, bounded above by 1 and below by 0, with the same control variables.

Below we present results for our early career variables in three sections: time to first job and earnings growth variables; number of employers, share of time employed and average duration variables; and number of occupations and number of industries variables.[34] Although we attempt to interpret each set of coefficients in turn, the general implication of our results is clear: there is significant variation in the relations between early career variables and later career outcomes, even when considering the same right- and left-hand side variables, when looking across countries and across sexes. Put simply, institutions (broadly defined) matter.

5.1   Time to First Job and Earnings Growth Measures

Table 5.1 shows our results for the variables time to first job, time to first job of at least six months and earnings growth between first and second post-exit years. For the United States, we use instead three semester-on-semester earnings growth measures.

The first thing to note is the lack of significance of the time to first job for the determination of the hourly wage in the United States, Germany and the Netherlands. However, this variable becomes larger, significant and of essentially a constant value (for men) for Germany in the log monthly income and log FYE earnings measures. This suggests that, in Germany at least, those who took longer to find their first job tend to work more hours, and thus have higher monthly and annual earnings. The positive coefficients on monthly earnings for men and women in Germany, however, are not found in the Netherlands for women, nor are they found in France for either men or women. The French results imply that men and women who find their first jobs faster in France tend to earn more later in their careers.

The fact that the effect of time to first job on women's earnings becomes more positive both in France and in Germany when going from monthly to FYE earnings is reasonable in light of the results on employment probabilities. Long times to first jobs in Germany are associated with higher subsequent employment probabilities (as they are for American women), and since time to first job is positively associated with monthly earnings, the relation is strengthened through the covariance of days worked with time to first job. In France, the opposite relation between time to first job and percentage of time employed holds (as in the Netherlands and for American men), namely that those who take longer to find a first job are less likely to be employed later in their careers.

The French (and Dutch women's) results are consistent with a search theoretic model. A person with a higher discount rate will have a lower reservation wage. This leads to faster job finding at the beginning of the career and quicker job acceptances later in the career as well, and thus a negative correlation in France between time to first job and employment probability. However, since the reservation wage is lower, earnings for high discount rate people should be lower, and Table 5.1 suggests that they are.

Table 5.1   Time to first job and early-career earnings growth measures

Dependent variable[1]	Early-career variable	United States[2]		France[3]		Germany[4]		Netherlands[5]	
		Men	Women	Men	Women	Men	Women	Men	Women
Log hourly wage	Time to first job	0.1012	0.0920			0.0117	0.0131	0.0230	0.0162
		(0.1800)	(0.2138)			(0.0157)	(0.0140)	(0.0441)	(0.1648)
	Time to first job of at least 6 months	-0.0599	-0.0271			-0.0313*	-0.0047	-0.0191	-0.0070
		(0.0711)	(0.0697)			(0.0125)	(0.0139)	(0.0304)	(0.1029)
	Earnings growth between first and second post-exit years					0.0035	-0.0492*	0.0873	0.0303
						(0.0118)	(0.0220)	(0.0746)	(0.3233)
	Wage growth between first and second post-exit semesters	0.1135*	0.0502						
		(0.0495)	(0.0444)						
	Wage growth between second and third post-exit semesters	0.0893*	0.0191						
		(0.0309)	(0.0124)						
	Wage growth between third and fourth post-exit semesters	0.0119	0.0435						
		(0.0181)	(0.0326)						
Log monthly income	Time to first job			-0.0101*	-0.0647*	0.0343*	0.0057	0.0129	-0.0276
				(0.0046)	(0.0085)	(0.0131)	(0.0143)	(0.0515)	(0.2047)
	Time to first job of at least 6 months			0.0072*	0.0445*	-0.0320*	0.0133	-0.0292	-0.0492
				(0.0016)	(0.0032)	(0.0105)	(0.0133)	(0.0355)	(0.1279)
	Earnings growth between first and second post-exit years			0.0007*	-0.0001	0.0035	0.0534*	0.0066	0.4854
				(0.0001)	(0.0002)	(0.0105)	(0.0210)	(0.0870)	(0.4017)
	Wage growth between first and second post-exit semesters								

Table 5.1 continued

Dependent variable[1]	Early-career variable	United States[2]		France[3]		Germany[4]		Netherlands[5]	
		Men	Women	Men	Women	Men	Women	Men	Women
	Wage growth between second and third post-exit semesters								
	Wage growth between third and fourth post-exit semesters								
Log full-year equivalent earnings	Time to first job			-0.0219* (0.0026)	-0.0485* (0.0054)	0.0345* (0.0170)	0.0108 (0.0180)		
	Time to first job of at least 6 months			0.0050* (0.0010)	0.0289* (0.0021)	-0.0350* (0.0135)	0.0128 (0.0179)		
	Earnings growth between first and second post-exit years			0.0006* (0.0001)	-0.0009* (0.0001)	0.0025 (0.0130)	0.0311 (0.0240)		
	Wage growth between first and second post-exit semesters								
	Wage growth between second and third post-exit semesters								
	Wage growth between third and fourth post-exit semesters								
Employment probability[6]	Time to first job	-0.0180 (0.0304)	0.0518 (0.0659)	-0.0048 (0.0600)	-0.1369 (0.0774)	0.1462 (0.0877)	0.4816* (0.1086)	-0.0030 (0.0358)	-0.2222* (0.0920)
	Time to first job of at least 6 months	-0.0320* (0.0093)	-0.0097 (0.0194)	0.2007* (0.0214)	0.2525* (0.0283)	-0.4554* (0.0632)	-0.3194* (0.0870)	-0.0168 (0.0236)	0.1252 (0.0477)
	Earnings growth between first and second post-exit years			0.0029* (0.0009)	0.0014 (0.0013)	-0.0210 (0.1081)	-0.1282 (0.1588)	-0.0342 (0.0632)	-0.2761* (0.1166)

Wage growth between first and second post-exit semesters	-0.0093 (0.0086)	-0.0010 (0.0110)
Wage growth between second and third post-exit semesters	0.0046 (0.0051)	0.0052 (0.0027)
Wage growth between third and fourth post-exit semesters	0.0000 (0.0031)	0.0055 (0.0088)

Notes:

1. Least squares standard errors in all regressions are corrected for arbitrary heteroskedasticity.
2. Regressions control for log hours, years of education, age, age^2, seniority, seniority^2, rural residency, nonwhite, married, 6 entry cohorts, 9 years, 4 regions, 8 sectors and 6 occupations.
3. Regressions control for 8 educational categories, age, age^2, age^3, age^4, seniority, seniority^2, Paris region, 8 entry cohorts, 13 years, 8 sectors and 6 occupations.
4. Regressions control for 9 educational categories plus years of education, age, age^2, age^3, age^4, seniority, seniority^2, 8 entry cohorts, 9 years, marital status, 4 firm sizes and 3 occupations.
5. Regressions control for years of education, age, age^2, age^3, age^4, seniority, seniority^2, firm size, firm size^2, 10 entry cohorts, 7 years, cohabitation, 6 sectors and 6 occupations. Hourly wages and monthly income measured in levels, not logs.
6. US: Linear probability model of percentage of time employed with heteroskedacity–consistent standard errors. Regression controls as note 2. France, Germany and Netherlands: Tobit of percentage of time employed bounded above by 1 and below by 0. France: Regressions control for 8 educational categories, age, age^2, age^3, age^4, 8 entry cohorts and 13 years. Germany: Regressions control for 9 educational categories, plus years of education, age, age^2, age^3, age^4, 8 entry cohorts, 9 years and marital status.

Sources:
United States:	NLSY and authors' calculations.
France:	DADS and authors' calculations.
Germany:	GSOEP and authors' calculations.
Netherlands:	OSA and authors' calculations.

The German results are consistent with a sorting model with heterogeneous workers and heterogeneous jobs.[35] Here, the jobs that pay higher initial wages offer flatter seniority profiles, and these jobs are relatively abundant and attract less stable workers.[36] Unstable workers will take jobs quicker but be less likely to be employed at any given time. Those who took longer to find their jobs will be, on average, more stable and have more seniority than those who found jobs faster. Which group has the highest expected wages at any point is a function of the model parameters, but since we are observing our individuals 5–20 years after they started looking for jobs, it is probable that seniority returns dominate, thus giving the observed positive sign on wages in Germany and for American women.[37]

The results concerning the first stable job tend to go in the opposite direction to those concerning the first job.[38] In the United States, Germany and the Netherlands, taking a long time to find one's first job of at least six months is associated with lower wages and (generally) lower values of the other earnings measures. This suggests that low reservation wages are driving these results. That said, the negative coefficients on employment probabilities suggest that long periods between the first job and the first job of at least six months may also be due to heterogeneity in worker stability. The French results, unlike the other three countries, suggest a positive link between a time to first job of at least six months and later earnings. There exist several models that could explain such a result.[39]

Finally, the early career earnings growth results suggest, in the vast majority of cases, that workers who managed faster earnings growth at the beginning of their careers tend to earn more later in their working lives. This could indicate efficient on-the-job search, heterogeneous career ladders, good quality matches or a simple autocorrelation in the earnings series,[40] but not all of these explanations have straightforward implications for the link between early career earnings growth and later career employment rates. The French and American results can be interpreted as being generally consistent with a Jovanovic (1979) matching model.[41] The German and Dutch results, on the other hand, might be considered consistent with a model of internal labour markets (tournaments), where there is stiffer competition higher up the hierarchy, and an up-or-out promotion rule.[42]

5.2 Number of Employers, Share of Time Employed and Average Duration Measures

Table 5.2 presents the coefficients on the number of employers, share of time employed and average job duration measures from our various models. Each of our measures is broken into six-month intervals, which allows us to see whether it is the earliest experiences alone that count, or whether the entire

Table 5.2 Number of employers, share of time employed and average duration measures*

Dependent variable[1]	Early-career variable	United States[2] Men	United States[2] Women	France[3] Men	France[3] Women	Germany[4] Men	Germany[4] Women	Netherlands[5] Men	Netherlands[5] Women
Log hourly wage	Number of employers in first 6 months	0.0581 (0.0304)	-0.0741* (0.0341)					0.0670 (0.1196)	-0.3398 (0.2657)
	Number of employers in months 6–12	-0.0005 (0.0356)	-0.0072 (0.0362)					0.4167* (0.1267)	-0.1626 (0.3000)
	Number of employers in months 12–18	0.0259 (0.0361)	-0.0168 (0.0413)					0.4050* (0.1210)	0.5023 (0.2614)
	Number of employers in months 18–24	0.0001 (0.0353)	-0.0085 (0.0361)					0.0400 (0.0695)	0.0238 (0.2673)
	Share of time spent in employment in first 6 months	-0.5020* (0.2345)	0.7944* (0.2686)			-0.0024 (0.0059)	0.0070 (0.0056)	0.1136 (0.2925)	-0.3970 (0.8334)
	Share of time spent in employment in months 6–12	0.0173 (0.2482)	0.0477 (0.2648)			-0.0072 (0.0072)	0.0006 (0.0067)	-0.4509 (0.3305)	0.6710 (0.6892)
	Share of time spent in employment in months 12–18	0.0338 (0.2667)	0.5292 (0.3071)			0.0099 (0.0068)	-0.0082 (0.0062)	-1.1211* (0.2171)	-0.6052 (0.6288)
	Share of time spent in employment in months 18–24	0.5279 (0.2738)	-0.1026 (0.2790)			-0.0032 (0.0061)	0.0153* (0.0050)	-0.2754 (0.2463)	0.9631 (0.8278)
	Average job duration during first 6 months	0.5911* (0.2228)	-0.4973* (0.2420)					0.1919 (0.4849)	0.0060 (1.3200)
	Average job duration during months 6–12	-0.0477 (0.2211)	0.1637 (0.2367)					0.4901 (0.5657)	-0.8035 (1.1789)
	Average job duration during months 12–18	0.2118 (0.2292)	-0.3166 (0.2746)					1.8210* (0.4378)	0.8643 (1.3400)
	Average job duration during months 18–24	-0.1131 (0.2292)	-0.0192 (0.2249)					0.8380 (0.4300)	-2.8883 (1.5180)
Log monthly income	Number of employers in first 6 months			-0.0061* (0.0004)	-0.0010 (0.0007)			0.0499 (0.1396)	-0.0624 (0.3301)
	Number of employers in months 6–12			-0.0028 (0.0004)	-0.0021* (0.0008)			0.1842 (0.1478)	0.3021 (0.3727)

Table 5.2 continued

Dependent variable[1] / Early-career variable	United States[2]		France[3]		Germany[4]		Netherlands[5]	
	Men	Women	Men	Women	Men	Women	Men	Women
Number of employers in months 12–18			0.0074* (0.0005)	-0.0005 (0.0008)			0.2998* (0.1413)	0.3942 (0.3248)
Number of employers in months 18–24			-0.0030* (0.0004)	0.0076* (0.0006)			-0.0543 (0.0811)	0.0617 (0.3321)
Share of time spent in employment in first 6 months			-0.0333* (0.0055)	0.0408* (0.0095)	0.0067 (0.0048)	0.0009 (0.0056)	0.3259 (0.3413)	-1.2871 (1.0356)
Share of time spent in employment in months 6–12			0.0816* (0.0046)	0.0238* (0.0081)	-0.0047 (0.0058)	0.0030 (0.0068)	-0.2225 (0.3857)	0.0803 (0.8563)
Share of time spent in employment in months 12–18			-0.0128* (0.0047)	0.0732* (0.0093)	0.0049 (0.0053)	0.0018 (0.0064)	-0.7412* (0.2534)	-0.3143 (0.7814)
Share of time spent in employment in months 18–24			0.0455* (0.0039)	-0.0004 (0.0089)	0.0064 (0.0048)	0.0135* (0.0051)	-0.0665 (0.2874)	0.6828 (1.0285)
Average job duration during first 6 months			0.0430* (0.0137)	-0.0868* (0.0259)			-0.2871 (0.5660)	1.7682 (1.6401)
Average job duration during months 6–12			-0.1013* (0.0127)	-0.1237* (0.0211)			-0.0518 (0.6602)	0.1431 (1.4648)
Average job duration during months 12–18			-0.0042 (0.0136)	-0.1283* (0.0255)			1.0568* (0.5109)	0.5526 (1.6650)
Average job duration during months 18–24			-0.2426* (0.0143)	0.0250 (0.0287)			0.3640 (0.5019)	-2.1290 (1.8862)
Log full-year equivalent earnings								
Number of employers in first 6 months			-0.0021* (0.0003)	-0.0010* (0.0005)				
Number of employers in months 6–12			-0.0044* (0.0003)	-0.0024* (0.0005)				
Number of employers in months 12–18			0.0034* (0.0003)	0.0014* (0.0006)				

	(1)	(2)	(3)	(4)	(5)	(6)	(7)	(8)
Number of employers in months 18–24			−0.0032* (0.0002)	0.0017* (0.0005)	0.0080 (0.0061)	0.0028 (0.0071)		
Share of time spent in employment in first 6 months			−0.0417* (0.0034)	−0.0002 (0.0061)	−0.0094 (0.0076)	0.0141 (0.0086)		
Share of time spent in employment in months 6–12			0.0619* (0.0031)	−0.0028 (0.0052)	0.0002 (0.0069)	0.0024 (0.0077)		
Share of time spent in employment in months 12–18			−0.0132* (0.0032)	0.0258* (0.0061)	0.0085 (0.0061)	0.0038 (0.0063)		
Share of time spent in employment in months 18–24			0.0267* (0.0025)	0.0247* (0.0055)				
Average job duration during first 6 months			−0.0253* (0.0096)	0.0565* (0.0167)				
Average job duration during months 6–12			−0.0488* (0.0080)	−0.0944* (0.0144)				
Average job duration during months 12–18			−0.0799* (0.0083)	−0.0119 (0.0173)				
Average job duration during months 18–24			−0.1146* (0.0085)	−0.1379* (0.0149)				
Employment probability[6]								
Number of employers in first 6 months	0.0009 (0.0051)	0.0112 (0.0111)	−0.0204* (0.0102)	0.0288* (0.0111)			0.0189 (0.1147)	−0.0355 (0.1460)
Number of employers in months 6–12	−0.0109* (0.0054)	−0.0148 (0.0116)	0.0090 (0.0112)	0.0113 (0.0120)			−0.0319 (0.1084)	−0.0710 (0.1526)
Number of employers in months 12–18	0.0077 (0.0061)	0.0084 (0.0126)	−0.0042 (0.0119)	0.0427• (0.0128)			−0.0483 (0.1054)	0.0935 (0.1362)
Number of employers in months 18–24	−0.0055 (0.0055)	0.0221 (0.0118)	0.2094* (0.0095)	0.2398* (0.0101)			−0.0790 (0.0577)	−0.2044 (0.1420)
Share in time spent in employment in first 6 months	−0.0145 (0.0396)	0.0861 (0.0883)	−0.2135* (0.0798)	−0.0959 (0.0971)	−0.0683 (0.0457)	0.1389* (0.0428)	0.2880 (0.2819)	0.4336 (0.3460)
Share of time spent in employment in months 6–12	0.0610 (0.0398)	−0.0066 (0.0854)	0.3145* (0.0670)	−0.0776 (0.0798)	−0.0202 (0.0559)	−0.0077 (0.0523)	0.1190 (0.2016)	−0.3822 (0.3210)
Share of time spent in employment in months 12–18	−0.0749 (0.0436)	0.0317 (0.0914)	−0.1368 (0.0698)	−0.4607* (0.0840)	−0.0253 (0.0488)	−0.0928 (0.0495)	0.3119 (0.2087)	0.6190 (0.4289)

105

Table 5.2 continued

Dependent variable[1]	Early-career variable[1]	United States[2]		France[3]		Germany[4]		Netherlands[5]	
		Men	Women	Men	Women	Men	Women	Men	Women
	Share of time spent in employment in months 18–24	0.0974* (0.0435)	0.0558 (0.0863)	-0.2483* (0.0551)	-0.5916* (0.0738)	-0.0301 (0.0411)	0.0515 (0.0408)	-9.1522 (12.9962)	-18.8888* (9.2110)
	Average job duration during first 6 months	0.0341 (0.0373)	0.0533 (0.0804)	1.0183* (0.2160)	1.2698* (0.2587)			-0.0124 (0.4455)	-0.4417 (0.7014)
	Average job duration during months 6–12	-0.0834* (0.0355)	-0.0286 (0.0755)	-0.9072* (0.1805)	0.0640 (0.2083)			-0.9721* (0.4769)	-0.4153 (0.6159)
	Average job duation during months 12–18	0.0900* (0.0391)	0.1161 (0.0823)	0.8860* (0.1905)	2.3489* (0.2300)			-0.3040 (0.4132)	0.8430 (0.6817)
	Average job duration during months 18–24	0.0036 (0.0375)	0.1658• (0.0725)	0.3342 (0.1710)	1.0545 (0.2260)			-0.5208 (0.3616)	-1.0750 (0.7870)

*For notes and sources see Table 5.1.

early career period (the two years following school leaving by our definition) plays a role in later career outcomes.

First of all, for men and women in the Netherlands and men in the United States,[43] having had more employers at the beginning of the career is associated with higher earnings later on.[44] On the other hand, the relation is typically negative and significant for American women and the French.[45]

The question of early career stability, as measured by the number of employers, is closely linked to that of early career employability, as measured by share of time spent in employment (controlling for the time to the first job). For American, French and German women, spending more time at the beginning of one's career in employment clearly leads to higher earnings later in life. This may be reflecting a labour force attachment effect, in which women who spend less time employed at the beginning of their careers signal to future employers a possible weak labour force attachment, and thus inciting employers to invest less in these women. The lower investments bring lower returns, and thus lower earnings to these women. For men, on the other hand, the effects of spending more time employed early in the career are much less obvious.[46]

It is interesting to note, however, that employability does not seem to be an individual-specific fixed characteristic. If workers were more or less employable, and this was constant over time, we would expect to see positive coefficients on share of time spent employed everywhere for the employment probability models. This is far from being the case, as there are more negative and significant coefficients than positive and significant ones. Furthermore, it does not seem that 'employability' is learned as the labour market insertion period progresses. In fact, the United States is the only country in which the share of time spent employed during the last six months of our two-year insertion period is positively correlated with time spent employed later in the career, and this effect is only significant for men.

Finally, we also included a measure for average job duration, which is an interaction between time spent employed and the inverse of the number of employers. Our results suggest that, in general, mobility across employers has an increasingly positive effect on earnings as the amount of time spent employed increases. Coefficients on these variables are typically negative in the United States and France, but they are positive for the Netherlands. Although the Dutch result seems consistent with specific human capital theory, the American and French results require a more subtle analysis.[47]

5.3 Number of Occupations and Number of Industries Measures

Although there has been some recent work on occupation- and industry-specific human capital,[48] there is little information on whether mobility across occupations or industries early in the career is detrimental to workers.

Contrary to human capital theory, mobility across occupations or sectors may be a good thing from a matching perspective, as it is a sign that the worker is finding the most adequately suited job, rather than settling for a suboptimal career path. With these considerations in mind, Table 5.3 presents the coefficients from our various estimations[49] on the number of occupations and number of industries measures.[50]

We find that women who change occupations often during the first six months of their labour market time in the Netherlands and France tend to earn more later in life, in terms of hourly wages and monthly earnings. The negative coefficients on FYE earnings for women in France, once again, are due to an employment effect.[51] For Dutch men, changing occupations at the beginning of the career is penalized later on, while the opposite effect appears in France (given the sizes of the coefficients). The results for the United States suggest a negative link between early career occupational mobility and later career earnings, but little is significant.

Insofar as concerns industry mobility, the effects more clearly suggest that changing industries often at the beginning of one's career indicates searching for a better job, rather than dilution of human capital. Although the role of such mobility on employment probabilities is also generally positive in the United States (albeit insignificant), early career inter-industry mobility seems detrimental to later career employability in France.

6.   CONCLUSION

In this chaptr, we have considered the effects of a large variety of measures of early career experiences on later career outcomes using data drawn from four different countries. As suggested in the introduction and in Section 2, there are many different theories that link early career variables to later career outcomes, and estimation of very simplified models is likely to lead to misleading interpretations, given the complexity of the subject.

Although one might be tempted to group the four countries into sub-categories, our results suggest that this would be unwise. Even countries that might seem superficially similar in terms of institutions and certain descriptive statistics, such as France and Germany relative to the United States and the Netherlands, bear little resemblance in terms of the behavior of their labour markets as indicated by our regression results.

Furthermore, although we can find theoretical explanations that are consistent with a set of institutions in a country and certain results, these models are rarely relevant when considering a different set of results. Such a situation may be due to our use of simple econometric models, although unfortunately our data constraints are binding in this dimension.

Table 5.3 Number of occupations and number of industries measures*

Dependent variable[1]	Early-career variable	United States[2]		France[3]		Germany[4]		Netherlands[5]	
		Men	Women	Men	Women	Men	Women	Men	Women
Log hourly wage	Number of different occupations in first 6 months	-0.0126 (0.0358)	-0.0986* (0.0403)					-0.1577 (0.1123)	0.6527* (0.2571)
	Number of different occupations in months 6–12	-0.0387 (0.0288)	-0.0241 (0.0330)					-0.2954* (0.1117)	0.0388 (0.2331)
	Number of different occupations in months 12–18	0.0183 (0.0377)	0.0162 (0.0449)					-0.2940* (0.1070)	-0.1668 (0.1521)
	Number of different occupations in months 18–24	-0.0474 (0.0287)	-0.0286 (0.0338)					-0.0709 (0.0621)	-0.1602 (0.2762)
	Number of different industries in first 6 months	0.0055 (0.0407)	0.0924 (0.0414)						
	Number of different industries in months 6–12	0.0042 (0.0310)	-0.0027 (0.0403)						
	Number of different industries in months 12–18	0.0169 (0.0422)	-0.0267 (0.0505)						
	Number of different industries in months 18–24	0.0096 (0.0315)	-0.0216 (0.0420)						
Log monthly income	Number of different occupations in first 6 months			0.0118* (0.0030)	0.0120* (0.0050)			-0.1283 (0.1310)	0.6918* (0.3195)
	Number of different occupations in months 6–12			0.0387* (0.0033)	-0.0438* (0.0055)			-0.0941 (0.1304)	-0.2099 (0.2896)
	Number of different occupations in months 12–18			-0.0540* (0.0031)	-0.0176* (0.0057)			-0.1841 (0.1248)	-0.3015 (0.1890)

Table 5.3 continued

Dependent variable[1]	Early-career variable	United States[2]		France[3]		Germany[4]		Netherlands[5]	
		Men	Women	Men	Women	Men	Women	Men	Women
	Number of different occupation in months 18–24			0.0342* (0.0025)	0.0331* (0.0042)			0.0238 (0.0725)	-0.1395 (0.3432)
	Number of different industries in first 6 months			0.0134* (0.0036)	-0.0653* (0.0065)				
	Number of different industries in months 6-12			-0.0482* (0.0037)	0.0761* (0.0052)				
	Number of different industries in months 12–18			0.0299* (0.0035)	0.0254* (0.0063)				
	Number of different industries in months 18–24			-0.0044 (0.0027)	-0.0607* (0.0054)				
Log full-year equivalent earnings	Number of different occupations in first 6 months			-0.0097* (0.0020)	-0.0075* (0.0034)				
	Number of different occupations in months 6-12			0.0159* (0.0023)	-0.0089* (0.0036)				
	Number of different occupations in months 12–18			-0.0071* (0.0021)	-0.0345* (0.0040)				
	Number of different occupations in months 18–24			0.0190* (0.0014)	0.0375* (0.0033)				
	Number of different industries in first 6 months			0.0164* (0.0023)	-0.0096* (0.0044)				

Number of different industries in months 6–12			-0.0136* (0.0022)	0.0268* (0.0041)		
Number of different industries in months 12–18			0.0088* (0.0023)	0.0363* (0.0041)		
Number of different industries in months 18–24			0.0112* (0.0018)	-0.0272* (0.0037)		
Employment probability[6]						
Number of different occupations in first 6 months	-0.0090 (0.0061)	0.0010 (0.0131)	0.0849 (0.0461)	0.0181 (0.0569)	-0.0454 (0.0995)	-0.2341 (0.1285)
Number of different occupations in months 6–12	0.0034 (0.0049)	-0.0016 (0.0106)	0.1915* (0.0508)	0.0256 (0.0624)	0.0115 (0.0945)	-0.0490 (0.1252)
Number of different occupations in months 12–18	-0.0042 (0.0064)	-0.0044 (0.0144)	-0.1088* (0.0472)	-0.0830 (0.0590)	0.0133 (0.0909)	0.0486 (0.0791)
Number of different occupations in months 18–24	0.0002 (0.0048)	-0.0066 (0.0110)	-0.1354* (0.0365)	0.1445* (0.0460)	0.0751 (0.0526)	0.19733 (0.1293)
Number of different industries in first 6 months	0.0111 (0.0068)	0.0106 (0.0133)	0.0304 (0.0534)	-0.2395* (0.0690)		
Number of different industries in months 6–12	0.0023 (0.0051)	0.0016 (0.0128)	-0.2547* (0.0518)	0.1776* (0.0653)		
Number of different industries in months 12–18	0.0112 (0.0072)	0.0019 (0.0163)	0.1838* (0.0514)	0.0316 (0.0625)		
Number of different industries in months 18–24	-0.0001 (0.0053)	0.0205 (0.0134)	-0.0677 (0.0440)	-0.2105* (0.0533)		

*For notes and sources see Table 5.1

In conclusion, our results show that the subject is, indeed, very complex. There seem to be no general principles that permeate all four of our economies in the same manner, yet most theories of labour market behavior that we consider find at least some support in at least one of our countries. This implies that the appropriate model for a labour market is likely to be context-dependent, and that more attention should be devoted in the future to explicitly examining the interplay between institutions and the functioning of the labour market.

NOTES

1. See, for example, Topel and Ward (1992) for the United States and Balsan et al. (1996) for France.
2. These models do, however, generate *ex post* implications for the link between realized early-career variables and later career outcomes. For example, although *ex ante* identical, search models predict that an individual who has had a good series of wage offers is more likely to be observed later with high earnings than a worker who has had particularly low draws from the wage offer distribution.
3. Some of the earliest examples are Jovanovic (1979) and Miller (1984). More recent work includes Farber and Gibbons (1996).
4. Although the literature has not typically posed the question in these terms, related work by Farber and Gibbons (1996), Altonji (1998) and Simonnet (1997) all show that firms use initially observable characteristics less and less in determining remuneration as time goes on, which the various authors interpret as employers relying increasingly on (unobservable by the econometrician) updated beliefs induced by years of repeated observation.
5. This is because the assignment of a worker to a sector happens early, and since nothing changes after the initial assignment, the correlation between early career experiences and later career outcomes is constant.
6. Recent work has proposed that human capital may be semi-specific to the firm (of lower, yet positive value, to at least some firms other than the current employer (Stevens (1994)), occupation-specific (of equal value to all employers provided that the worker performs the same occupation as with the current employer) or sector-specific (of equal value to all firms in the same sector as the current employer). See Neal (1995, 1999), Parent (1995) and Vilhuber (1997, 1999) for tests of the different specifications.
7. See Baker et al. (1994a, 1994b) for a survey.
8. See Harris and Holmström (1982) and Macleod and Malcomson (1993), among others.
9. See Beaudry and DiNardo (1991) and Vilhuber (1999) for empirical tests of this model.
10. Collected by the U.S. Bureau of Labor Statistics.
11. An alternative solution would be to include jobs held before the permanent exit from school. This, however, runs the risk of confusing some individuals' post-school jobs, which happen to overlap with post-school ongoing education, with other individuals' high-school jobs (Ruhm (1995)).
12. This date is then refined if the individual reports the exact month of school exit. If not, the interview date is taken as the exit date.
13. Collected by the French National Institute of Statistics and Economic Studies (INSEE).
14. Since Simonnet and Ulrich (2000) have shown that there is a significant difference between simply attending a given number of years of school and finishing the year in question, we explicitly model the month of school leaving. To do so, we exploit a third data set called the Enquête Emploi, or Labour Force Survey, which contains a monthly calendar to estimate the month of school exit via a multinomial logit model conditional on sex, department of birth and month of birth (the only variables that are observable before

school leaving, exogenous and common to all data sets). We suppose that the individual left school on the last day of the month prior to the month of school exit predicted by the multinomial logit and control the quality of this imputation by comparison with the start date of the first job observed in the data.

15. Collected by the German Institute for Economic Research (DIW).

16. Although we lose observations due to missing data, most observations are lost because of the high rate of attrition in the GSOEP. Moreover, because new observations are added to the database each year, the total number of individuals available is a gross overestimate of the number of usable observations in the German data. We assume the attrition is exogenous to the processes being analyzed here, and thus do not explicitly model it in our analyses.

17. We are only able to observe earnings and hours information for people who were employed at the interview date, and thus this represents a large loss in the number of observations that will be available for the earnings regressions relative to the employment models.

18. Collected by the Dutch Institute for Labour Studies (OSA).

19. Differences in the number of individuals leaving school arise because the different waves have different time windows. The 1985 and 1986 waves cover 1980 to 1985 and 1980 to 1986, respectively. The 1988 and 1990 waves only capture two years periods, 1986 to 1988 and 1988 to 1990.

20. We do not present tables with descriptive statistics for reasons of brevity.

21. Job search theory suggests that as reservation wages increase, offer arrival rates decrease or the wage offer distribution declines, the time to first job should get longer. If the difference in time to first job and time to first job of at least 6 months is large, this suggests a high separation rate that could be either exogenous to the search process (layoffs) or endogenous (high offer arrival rates for on-the-job search).

22. Descriptive statistics on the excluded workers suggest that there are differences between the retained and excluded samples in the regressors and dependent variables. Our sample selection criteria thus introduce selection bias (relative to the full population), although our selected sample is itself of interest.

23. For those people who do not do military service (see below), the values are top-coded at 5. For all others, they are top coded at 5 minus the duration of the military service. This was done in order to maintain reasonable sample sizes, although it can also bias our estimates.

24. This should imply a low reservation wage and a subsequently faster first-job finding rate.

25. In the Dutch data, military service is observed and is not counted as time spent in the labour market. For France, military service (of 10–12 months) is not observed at all. Since it is only mandatory for men (and many men avoid it through various means) this could explain why French women find their first jobs earlier than French men. In Germany, men have the option of choosing civil service instead of military service. In our analyses, civil service is counted as employment, whereas military service is not.

26. Aside from those men exempted or disqualified from military service, the most recent statistics (1997) from the French Ministry of Defense (http://www.defense.gouv.fr/sn/dformes/dformes.html) suggest that 16 percent of those who undertake their 'national service' do not serve in the military.

27. The French calculation is 1.203 years – (84 percent * 1 year) = 0.363 years. The German calculation is 1.063 years – (50 percent * 1.25 years) = 0.438 years.

28. In fact, women should find their first jobs even sooner in countries with military service than in those without, ceteris paribus, as labour supply of their entering cohort is reduced while men are in the military.

29. Although fixed-term contracts and special youth employment programs were introduced in France in the middle of our sample period, these made up an important part of initial hiring in France (Gelot and Osbert (1995)). On the other hand, recent models estimated by van de Berg and Ridder in the Netherlands suggest that the offer arrival rate for on-the-job search is higher than that for unemployed search (van de Berg and Ridder (1993)).

30. We chose to normalize by period $t+1$ as, for all countries, the share of workers employed

increased more or less monotonically across the six-month periods during the first two years after school leaving. As such, we reduce the number of observations lost due to missing data on the earnings growth variable. One disadvantage is that, whereas this measure is bounded above by 1, it is not bounded below.

31.   The median values of the earnings growth measure (across individuals, not observations) in France were 57 percent for men and 51 percent for women, and only 21 percent of men and 20 percent of women had first year earnings that were higher than second year earnings (thus inducing a negative value for our earnings growth measure).

32.   The GSOEP does not allow us to construct this measure for our German data.

33.   Once again, the structure of the GSOEP data does not allow us to construct these measures for Germany.

34.   Since not all of the x_i, y_{it} and z_{it} variables are available for all of the data sets, the absence of a country from a results table implies that either the dependent variable or the explanatory variables were not available for that country.

35.   See, for example, Margolis (1996).

36.   Many efficiency wage models also predict the existence of such an 'ocean of small firms', where employment is readily available at a fixed wage as compared to other firms which offer seniority returns profiles.

37.   Margolis (1996) shows that including simple seniority terms in a regression is not sufficient to capture the non-linearities in earnings induced by the combination of the explicit compensation policy and the evolution of the quality of the job entry cohort.

38.   Note that these coefficients are identified off the individuals for whom the first job did not last more than 6 months, and as such refer to individuals who either accepted first jobs at low wages (and hence moved as their on-the-job search brought out better offers) or accepted unstable first jobs (signifying a preference for short-term earnings over long-term employment and earnings growth).

39.   Examples are insider–outsider models, dual labour market models and queuing/screening models. In general, these models suggest (more or less explicitly) that workers would try to keep the desirable jobs, once obtained, and thus are also consistent with the positive coefficient on the employment probability.

40.   If such an autocorrelation were present, it would have to be a very long memory process, as our right-hand side variables are measured at a minimum 3 years prior to the left-hand side variable, and in some cases as long as 18 years earlier. In addition, there would have to be an absence of an offsetting reduction in initial earnings for those with faster wage growth, whereas the literature has tended to find that faster wage growth is correlated with lower initial earnings (Abowd et al. (1999), Margolis (1996)). Still, if autocorrelation is a serious problem, then our right hand side earnings growth variables are endogenous, and we should instrument them. Unfortunately, there are few variables that suggest themselves as instruments for early career earnings growth that do not appear in the models directly.

41.   In this model, faster early career earnings growth is consistent with a high quality match, and high quality matches are less likely to end.

42.   Faster early career wage growth indicates quicker movement up the career ladder, but as the person approaches the higher rungs, the layoff risk increases. This leads to a positive correlation between early career earnings growth and later career earnings, coupled with the negative correlation between earnings growth and employment probabilities.

43.   Gardecki and Neumark (1998) found similar results for the United States.

44.   These coefficients are consistent with on the job search early in the career being a route to higher earnings later on, but since we control for early career earnings growth, early career mobility may reflect sorting workers into better suited careers, as Neal's (1999) model would suggest. Unfortunately, the results on employment probabilities, in which the early career instability is negatively related to future employment, are contrary to Neal's model.

45.   Part of this negative effect may be the result of fixed-term and youth employment promotion contracts, which some authors have suggested serve to push young people into a secondary labour market of short-term, low paying, unstable jobs. Such an explanation

would seem consistent with our data, except that the very large, positive coefficient in the employment probability model on the 18–24 month interval suggests that the jobs found later in life by these individuals may be, in fact, more stable than those found by others who had less turbulent beginnings.

46. In the Netherlands, it once again seems that the start of the first full year after school leaving (months 12–18) is the most important period, bringing with it a strongly negative relation between time spent employed and future earnings. In the United States the first six months seem the most crucial, with a significant negative coefficient, although the sum of the subsequent 18 months erases this negative effect. In France, the coefficients alternate in sign, while in Germany similar instability in the estimation coefficients is observed. Such results are difficult to interpret coherently.

47. The average duration variable in these countries may be proxying for the size of the local labour market. If the local labour market is large, an individual may test several employers for a given amount of time spent employed. Demand-side competition in the labour market may then bid up wages. If our later career data correspond to the same labour market as the early career data, or if individuals move between similar labour markets, we would expect to see a negative relation between average job duration and earnings. In addition, since workers are required to (and can) exercise the threat of leaving on occasion to remain credible, the generally positive coefficients on employment probability suggest that the more competitive labour markets experience more turnover. Superficially, it does not seem implausible that Dutch employers have more monopsony power over wages than American or French employers.

48. Neal (1999), Parent (1995), Stevens (1994), Vilhuber (1997,1999).

49. Unfortunately, these measures were not computable from the GSOEP data for Germany.

50. It should be noted that including these measures, along with the number of different employers in 6 month intervals measures, is likely to introduce significant multicollinearity in our results. The model performance statistics in table 6 indicate that this is likely to be a problem, especially for France.

51. French women who change occupations less early in their careers spend less time employed later on. Since these women also have lower monthly earnings, and since FYE earnings inflates these women's earnings more than those of women who tried more occupations, the sign on FYE earnings can switch.

REFERENCES

Abowd, J.M., F. Kramarz and D.N. Margolis (1999), 'High wage workers and high wage firms', *Econometrica*, **67** (2), 251–337.

Altonji, J. (1998), 'Employer learning and statistical discrimination', inaugural address given at the *15émes Journées de Microéconomie Appliquée*, Pointe-à-Pitre, Guadeloupe, 4 June.

Baker, G., M. Gibbs and B. Holmström (1994a), 'The internal economics of the firm: evidence from personnel data', *Quarterly Journal of Economics*, **109** (4), 881–919.

Baker, G., M. Gibbs and B. Holmström (1994b), 'The wage policy of a firm', *Quarterly Journal of Economics*, **109** (4), 921–55.

Balsan, D., S. Hanchane and P. Werquin (1996), 'Mobilité professionnelle initiale: éducation et expérience sur le marché du travail', *Economie et statistique*, **299**, 91–106.

Beaudry, P. and J. DiNardo (1991), 'The effect of implicit contracts on the movement of wages over the business cycle: evidence from micro data', *Journal of Political Economy*, **99** (4), 665–88.

Becker, G.S. (1993), *Human Capital*, Third Edition, Chicago: University of Chicago Press.

Ben-Porath, Y. (1967), 'The production of human capital and the life cycle of earnings', *Journal of Political Economy*, **75** (4), 352–65.

Farber, H.S. and R. Gibbons (1996), 'Learning and wage dynamics', *Quarterly Journal of Economics*, **111** (4), 1007–47.

Gardecki, R. and D. Neumark (1998), 'Order from chaos? The effects of early labor market experiences on adult labor market outcomes', *Industrial and Labor Relations Review*, **51** (2), 299–322.

Gelot, D. and G. Osbert (1995), 'Policies for youth employment in France over the past 20 years', presented at the *NBER Summer Institute, Franco-American Seminar*, 28 July.

Harris, M. and B. Holmström (1982), 'A theory of wage dynamics', *Review of Economic Studies*, **49** (3), 315–33.

Jovanovic, B. (1979), 'Job matching and the theory of turnover', *Journal of Political Economy*, **87** (5), 972–90.

Lazear, E.P. (1979), 'Why is there mandatory retirement?', *Journal of Political Economy*, **87** (6), 1261–84.

Lazear, E.P. and S. Rosen (1981), 'Rank-order tournaments as optimum labor contracts', *Journal of Political Economy*, **89** (5), 841–64.

MacLeod, W.B. and J.M. Malcomson (1993), 'Investments, holdup and the form of market contracts', *American Economic Review*, **83** (4), 811–37.

Margolis, D.N. (1996), 'Firm heterogeneity and worker self-selection bias estimated returns to seniority', CIRANO working paper, January.

Miller, R.A. (1984), 'Job matching and occupational choice', *Journal of Political Economy*, **92** (6), 1086–120.

Neal, D. (1995), 'Industry-Specific Human Capital: Evidence from Displaced Workers', *Journal of Labour Economics*, **13** (4), 653–77.

Neal, D. (1999), 'The complexity of job mobility among young men', *Journal of Labour Economics*, **17** (2), 237–61.

Parent, D. (1995), 'Industry-specific capital and the wage profile: evidence from the NLSY and the PSID', CRDE working paper 0895, February.

Roy, A.D. (1951), 'Some Thoughts on the Distribution of Earnings', *Oxford Economic Papers*, **3** (2), 135–46.

Ruhm, C.J. (1995), 'The extent and consequences of high school employment', *Journal of Labor Research*, **16** (3), 293–303.

Simonnet, V. (1997), 'Déterminants et rentabilité de la mobilité sur le marché du travail: Analyse théorique et empirique (Allemagne, Etats-Unis, France)', Ph.D. Thesis, Université de Paris 1 Panthéon-Sorbonne.

Simonnet, V. and V. Ulrich (2000), 'La formation professionnelle et l'insertion sur le marché du travail: une analyse multicritères', *Economie et Statistique*, **87** (3), 355–74.

Spence, M. (1973), 'Job Market Signalling', *Quarterly Journal of Economics*, **87** (3), 355–74.

Stevens, M. (1994), 'A Theoretical Model of On-the-Job Training with Imperfect Competition', *Oxford Economic Papers*, **46** (4), 537–62.

Topel, R.H. and M.P. Ward (1992), 'Job Mobility and the Careers of Young Men', *Quarterly Journal of Economics*, **107** (2), 439–79.

van den Berg, G. and G. Ridder (1993), 'An empirical equilibrium search model of the labour market', University of Amsterdam working paper, July 19.

Vilhuber, L. (1997), 'Sector-specific on-the-job training: evidence from US data', CIRANO working paper 97s–42, December.

Vilhuber, L. (1999), 'Sector-specific training and mobility in Germany', CIRANO working paper 99s–03, February.

6. Apprenticeship versus vocational school: a comparison of performances

Sylvie Mendès and Catherine Sofer

1. INTRODUCTION

Do firms value the skills resulting from in-firm training more than those acquired at school? In a number of countries, policies, particularly aimed at reducing youth unemployment, have recently been enacted to facilitate and increase the amount of time spent working in firms in the context of schooling or training programmes. Specific examples include the 1994 'School to Work Opportunities Act' in the USA and the 1995 'Modern Apprenticeship Programme' in Great Britain.

The development of apprenticeship in France, which has increased sharply over recent years, is one such policy. The question then arises whether this specific type of learning facilitates transitions from school to work, as some of the German evidence indicates. The low rate of youth unemployment in Germany (in recent years, rather a *relatively* low rate of youth unemployment) has traditionally been in part attributed to the apprenticeship system. However, other explanations are possible, such as demographic specificities, institutional arrangements which raise the returns to specific human capital for firms, or more generally the benefits from youth employment. Our focus here is not to explain why firms would invest in human capital which is not totally specific (Acemoglu and Pischke, 1999; Harhoff and Kane, 1997; Ryan, 2001). Rather, we concentrate upon the school to work transition of new labour market entrants.[1]

This chapter is organized as follows. The first section discusses the methods and French results concerning the access to first job by youths at the CAP level. Some additional results for France are presented in the second section. All of these are based on the STT Working Paper by Bonnal, Mendès and Sofer (1999) 'Access to the first job: a comparison between apprenticeship and vocational school in France', extended in Bonnal and Mendès (2000) and Bonnal, Mendès and Sofer (2002). These findings will be compared to those in the STT Working Paper of Sollogoub and Ulrich (1999a), 'Apprenticeship versus vocational school: selectivity bias and school to work transition –

evidence from France', later published as (1999b). The third section compares the French results to those obtained for other countries. The STT Working Papers using Norwegian data; Bratberg and Nilsen (1999) 'Transitions from school to work: search time and job duration' – and Dutch data – Groot and Plug (1998) 'Apprenticeship versus vocational education: exemplified by the Dutch situation'; will be examined first, and then placed into a more general international framework.

2. APPRENTICESHIP IN FRANCE

2.1 Questions Addressed and General Framework

The papers by Bonnal et al. (1999, 2002) and Bonnal and Mendès (2000) aim to measure the within-firm training effect by comparing the school-to-work transitions, at different schooling levels, of apprentices and vocational-school leavers.

Two questions are addressed: we first ask whether apprentices benefit mainly from firm-specific human capital or from positive selection. In other words, do apprentices who perform well mostly find their first job in the firm where they were apprentices (we shall call these 'stayers')? The second question relates to a possible selection effect in the educational system: young people choosing apprenticeship over vocational school may well possess some characteristic which is positively correlated with the probability of obtaining a first job rapidly. The objectives, methods and data used differ somewhat between the four STT papers. For example, Bonnal et al. (1999) and Bonnal and Mendès (2000) analyse the type of job contract obtained by different students at the end of their schooling, as well as employment versus unemployment. Bonnal et al. (1999 and 2000) also look at a (small) sample of students who choose school or apprenticeship at the high school level. We shall discuss these results later.

We first turn to the results presented in Bonnal et al. (2002). This paper combines a duration model for youth unemployment (Lynch, 1983; Dolton et al., 1994) with probit estimations, taking into account possible selection bias in the choice of training (Fougère and Sérandon, 1992; Dolton et al., 1994).

In France, the CAP, corresponding to the first exit level from vocational schools (after about 12 years of schooling), may be obtained either by following an apprenticeship or by attending a vocational school. While the diploma is the same, the schooling system is different. In both systems, there is not only general education (French, mathematics, foreign languages and so on) but also more technical courses. However, only apprenticeship provides a mix of on-the-job experience and courses at college. In vocational school, training is principally provided by teachers in the form of courses, as is general teaching. General teaching and vocational training are equally distributed in the timetable with roughly 30 hours of courses per week and are completed by a short period of work experience. An important difference between apprenticeship and vocational school concerns the status of the students. In vocational school, they are ordinary students whereas apprentices are wage earners. Hence, while the same diplomas are awarded, the content of the course is different. It is also worth noting that, although the diploma delivered by both systems is the same,[2] when considered more closely (except for a few types of jobs, hairdresser, for example), the jobs to which the training leads are often different. Another, and maybe more important, difference is that returning from apprenticeship to vocational school to continue to a higher degree is difficult and only rarely attempted, whereas a non-negligible proportion of those who obtain the CAP from a vocational school continue in the schooling system. We retain in the sample only those who leave the educational system to enter the labour market.

The data in Bonnal et al. (2002) come from the Céreq[3] survey 'Panel mesures jeunes'. This is a panel of young people who left the schooling system (including apprenticeships) in June 1989 and who were followed until December 1990. The survey gives detailed information about employment and unemployment during this period, schooling characteristics and individual characteristics. Table 6.1 provides some descriptive statistics of the sample.

2.2   A Model of Access to the First Job

Compared to vocational school, the decision to enter apprenticeship might be associated with different individual characteristics which exert diverse effects on labour market success. A first important issue is the matching of skills to labour demand. Vocational school students are thought to have a less well-developed ability to link theory to practice than apprentices. Moreover, if, as is likely, general training is more profitable for youths when it is carried out jointly with specific training, apprenticeship should be more efficient than vocational schooling in reducing the difficulties of matching the technical capacities of young workers and firms' needs. All else being equal, access to the first job as well as the quality of this first job (for example greater access to jobs with long-term contracts) should be easier for apprentices.

A second important issue is the transferability of skills acquired during apprenticeship outside of the training firm. Apprenticeship provides more specific human capital than does vocational school. Hence, apprenticeship confers an advantage on those who remain in the training firm at the end of the

Table 6.1 Descriptive statistics

	Whole sample			Apprentice			Vocational school		
	All	Women	Men	All	Women	Men	All	Women	Men
Number of observations	1399	757	642	622	332	290	777	425	352
Number of individuals (in %) who:									
Were apprentices	44.5	43.9	45.2	–	–	–	–	–	–
Obtained the diploma	63.5	65.1	61.5	64.8	67.8	61.4	62.4	63.1	61.7
Passed a higher degree (BEP) and failed	11.2	11.0	11.5	–	–	–	20.2	19.5	21.0
Are men	45.9	–	–	46.6	–	–	45.3	–	–
Are stayers	16.1	15.1	17.4	36.3	34.3	38.6	–	–	–
Were not unemployed	38.2	33.0	44.4	46.9	42.8	51.7	31.3	25.4	38.4
Age (in years)	18.7	18.8	18.7	18.8	18.8	18.7	18.7	18.7	18.7
Speciality of the diploma									
Secondary	38.5	28.0	50.8	32.3	7.8	60.3	43.4	43.8	42.9
Tertiary	59.9	69.8	49.3	67.0	91.3	39.3	54.2	52.9	55.7
Unemployment duration (in months)	3.1	3.9	2.0	2.8	3.8	1.7	3.3	4.1	2.3

apprenticeship contract, and their probability of obtaining a high-quality long-duration job should be higher. For those apprentices who leave the training firm, part of the specific human capital acquired is lost. Whether they have more trouble finding a job than do vocational-school leavers depends on the general human capital acquired. On the one hand, apprentices accumulate general capacities that cannot be acquired in school where the work environment is only simulated (obedience, work discipline, teamwork and so on). On the other hand, training received in vocational school might be transferable to a wider range of sectors. This transferability of skills may also depend on the functioning of the labour market. If job-specific skills and firm attachment are particularly important in the labour market, apprenticeship should facilitate the school-to-work transition, even if the contract with the training firm is not renewed. However, if good performance in a number of different jobs is better suited to firms' labour demands, vocational school might be more efficient. This question can be addressed by comparing the evolution of wages of apprentices and vocational-school leavers.

A third issue concerns uncertainty about the quality of the young worker who is fresh out of school. This uncertainty is obviously higher for vocational-school leavers than for ex-apprentices. For employers, there is a great deal of ignorance about young workers' capacities and future productivity. Young workers are equally uncertain about which kind of job is best suited to their capacities and desires. Such uncertainty reduces the chances of an employer and a young worker entering into a long-term relationship. Apprenticeship, compared to vocational school, should reduce uncertainty for both employers and young workers by capitalizing on the experience acquired during training; as such, ex-apprentices should be more likely to enter into long-duration contractual relationships. This latter phenomenon amounts to positive selection. Conversely, less able students may be negatively selected, that is, fired by the firm in which their apprenticeship took place; consequently, we would observe higher unemployment and lower wages for 'movers'.

A fourth and final issue refers to differences in observed and unobserved characteristics between ex-apprentices and vocational-school leavers, which may influence their school-to-work transition. It is very likely that the choice between apprenticeship and vocational school depends on young people's preferences. Participants may also be selected by the administrators of the training programmes in question, in particular by firms providing apprenticeship contracts. This leads to a selectivity bias obscuring the true benefits or disadvantages of one kind of schooling over the other. This bias will be positive if, anticipating better careers, most students prefer apprenticeships, and, as the number of contracts is limited, only the best are selected by schools and/or firms. Conversely, the bias will be negative if apprenticeship is considered to be less valuable by students and/or school teachers. This could be the case, in particular, if vocational school provides easier access to higher levels of schooling.

The model we propose allows us to correct for the selection bias resulting from the choice between apprenticeship and vocational school. We are also able to determine if apprentices' advantage in terms of access to the first job applies across the board, or mainly to stayers. However, even in the latter case, we cannot distinguish between three alternative interpretations: lack of general human capital; negative selection; and negative signalling of movers.

The model consists of the simultaneous estimation of:

1. the probability of choosing apprenticeship;
2. the probability of finding a job immediately after the end of schooling;[4]
3. the probability (among apprentices) of being a stayer; and
4. unemployment duration.

The model thus takes into account and corrects for possible correlations between observed and unobserved variables included in the different equations (this is our model 2 below). Standard probit models for (1), (2) and (3), and a standard duration model for (4), result from the special case when all of these correlations are constrained to be zero (this is what we call model (1). Further details of the statistical model are presented in Bonnal al. (2002). We estimate separate regressions for men and for women.

2.3   Results

The estimated coefficients reveal that four variables significantly affect the probability of finding a job immediately after school: the strongest effect comes from apprenticeship. Apprentices have a better chance of finding a job quickly than do vocational-school leavers, and this effect is particularly strong for young men. This effect is reinforced for men when the correlations between the equations are taken into account. The estimation of model 2 reveals a significant negative correlation between the choice of apprenticeship and the probability of an immediate job, indicating a negative selection bias for apprentices when considering their job-finding capacities. As expected, the estimated apprenticeship parameter is noticeably higher in model 2 compared to model 1. Apprenticeship thus seems to be significantly more efficient than vocational school in terms of rapid access to a job. This result does not seem to hold for women. For both genders, the diploma also exerts a strong positive influence. Firms seem to look for young people with diplomas (professional diplomas), and they consider apprenticeship as professional experience.

Considering now the probability of being a stayer (which is relevant only for apprentices), we find that diploma again has a significant positive effect. For men, model 2 shows a significant negative correlation between the probability of choosing apprenticeship and that of being a stayer. This again indicates negative selection bias against apprentices, firms mainly choosing stayers among those apprentices who do not exhibit the negative characteristics corresponding to the selection bias. Again, this result holds only for men.

The final estimation concerns unemployment duration: for both men and women, the diploma is significantly negatively correlated with unemployment duration in model 1 (in model 2, the effect is still negative but insignificant). A positive education effect only appears when its impact on the other probabilities modelled is not taken into account. The interpretation could be that, in model 1, education captures the effect of unobserved characteristics, such as IQ or work motivation, and it is these latter which have the real positive effect on unemployment exits.

Interestingly, apprenticeship has a significant positive effect upon unemployment duration for both men and women: hence apprenticeship is a penalty rather than an advantage for those apprentices who do not find a job immediately. This effect is stronger (for men) in model 2 than in model 1. Model 2 sets out the ambivalent effect of apprenticeship more clearly than model 1: a large proportion of apprentices find a job immediately, often staying in the firm where their apprenticeship took place, but with a significant number of movers also. Those apprentices are in a better situation than the average vocational-school leaver. However, a second group of apprentices do not find jobs immediately. Considering the kind of job obtained more closely (as below), one explanation can be offered: apprentices' average unemployment duration is greater than that of vocational-school leavers, as the latter are more likely to enrol in training programmes, perhaps to obtain the professional experience that they lack. Conversely, ex-apprentices would prefer longer job search in order to find more suitable jobs. An alternative interpretation is that the (small) minority of apprentices who do not find a job immediately exhibit strongly negative unobserved characteristics which prevent employers from hiring them. We find a strong positive correlation between the probability of finding a job immediately and unemployment duration for both men and women. This is consistent with the first interpretation. The calculation of probabilities associated with the parameter estimates illustrates some of these points.

2.4 Associated Probabilities

Calculating estimated probabilities from the two models helps us to understand the main results (Tables 6.2 and 6.3). These show the impact of apprenticeship and diploma on the probability of finding a job quickly and staying in the same firm. These probabilities are calculated with all other right-hand side variables held at their mean values. Table 6.2 includes the observed values in the dataset, for purposes of comparison. As there is no correction for selection bias at this stage, models 1 and 2 yield similar probabilities. It is noteworthy that the observed values underestimate the probability that apprentices find a job immediately (especially for men).

Of particular interest is apprentices' advantage in the probability of immediately finding a job compared to vocational-school leavers. The difference between men and women is also striking, with a much higher probability for the latter of unemployment, whatever the type of schooling chosen. The worst situation for women is that of vocational-school leaver. We also see a strong positive effect of education on the probability of immediate employment, with a difference of about ten percentage points in this figure between those with and without a diploma.

Table 6.3 contains some additional estimated probabilities, again evaluated at the mean level of all other right-hand side variables (but not any more conditional on the state apprentice or vocational-school leaver). Model 2 here thus corrects for initial selection bias among apprentices, so that the difference between model 1 and model 2's results can be interpreted as a measure of the negative selection bias in apprenticeship. We also calculate the probability of finding a job immediately for an average individual without apprenticeship who is not a stayer. The idea, here, is to eliminate the firm-specific human capital effect and to compare the performance in terms of access to first job of apprentices without firm-specific human capital and vocational-school leavers.

Table 6.3 shows that apprenticeship greatly facilitates immediate access to the first job compared to more traditional vocational schools, especially for men and after model 2's correction for selection bias in apprenticeship (in this case 90 per cent of male apprentices find a job immediately, compared to 55 per cent of vocational-school leavers). The correction in model 2 raises the estimated proportion of male apprentices immediately finding a job by about 8 points and reduces by 12 points the estimated proportion for vocational-school leavers, indicating the importance of the estimated selection bias. This selection bias is much smaller and works somewhat in the opposite direction for women.

It is also of interest to compare apprentices who are movers to vocational-school leavers, as both groups do not benefit from firm-specific human capital.[5] As can be seen from Table 6.3, the results again differ by sex. Male apprentice movers still have an advantage in immediate job finding (model 1), which increases sharply after correction. Firms do not seem to consider that vocational school delivers a better quality or quantity of general human capital than apprenticeship for men. The opposite situation holds for women,

Table 6.2 Conditional probabilities* of (un)employment after training

Probability of being in designated labour force status immediately after the end of schooling	Observed values		Model 1		Model 2	
	Apprentice	Voc. School	Apprentice	Voc. School	Apprentice	Voc. School
Men						
Employed						
Mean	70.7	62.5	82.8	66.9	81.9	70.3
Without diploma	62.5	58.5	76.9	59.0	75.4	62.1
With diploma	75.8	65.0	85.9	71.5	85.4	75.0
Unemployed						
Mean	29.3	37.5	17.3	33.1	18.1	29.7
Without diploma	37.5	41.5	23.1	41.0	24.6	37.9
With diploma	24.2	35.0	14.1	28.5	14.7	25.0
Women						
Employed						
Mean	59.0	51.1	66.2	52.9	67.4	54.5
Without diploma	45.8	45.9	59.6	46.0	60.9	47.6
With diploma	65.3	54.1	69.6	56.7	70.6	58.2
Unemployed						
Mean	41.0	48.9	33.8	47.1	32.6	45.5
Without diploma	54.2	54.1	40.4	54.0	39.1	52.4
With diploma	34.7	45.9	30.5	43.4	29.4	41.8

Note: * In this table the computed probabilities are conditional probabilities, i.e. they are calculated conditional on the state apprentice or vocational-school leaver.

Table 6.3   *Probability comparisons between apprenticeship and vocational school*

Probability of finding a job	Model 1		Model 2	
Immediately after	Men	Women	Men	Women
Apprenticeship	82.8	66.2	90.4	64.9
Vocational school	66.9	52.9	54.6	56.4
Apprenticeship but not stayer	70.9	47.9	76.0	48.8

where, although on the whole apprentices do better than vocational-school leavers, apprentice movers do worse. This sex difference is difficult to understand, as there is no difference in curriculum between apprenticeship and vocational school. However, there are substantial differences according to the trade that is being prepared. It is possible that apprentice training in 'female' trades (such as beauty, hairdressing, hotel trades and secretary) is more firm-specific than in 'male' occupations. Alternatively, the negative selection bias and/or signalling among movers may be stronger for women.

2.5 First Concluding Remarks

We conclude that, globally, apprentices perform better in terms of access to first job, especially for men. The positive effect of apprenticeship is mainly felt at the beginning of the period analysed: they are often hired (within two months) by the firm at which they were apprenticed. For young men, even apprentice movers perform better than vocational-school leavers. These results are stronger when the negative selection bias in apprenticeship choice is corrected. For young women, the better performance of apprentices is less pronounced, and comes only from the better performance of stayers; no significant selection bias is found.

These first results show that acquiring specific human capital pays, but also that, for men, firms value the human capital acquired in apprenticeship more highly than that acquired in vocational school. This is true even when firm-specific returns are removed amongst apprentice movers. We show that the most important variable explaining the transition from school to the first job is the diploma, both for apprentices and vocational-school leavers. While these results concerned access to the first job, very similar conclusions are drawn by Bonnal and Mendès (2000) using data for 1992 school-leavers. Other French studies comparing apprentices and vocational-school leavers have addressed questions such as the quality of the first job, employment/unemployment later in the work career, wage profiles, and differences in relative performance according to the level of schooling. These results are presented in the next section.

3. APPRENTICESHIP VERSUS VOCATIONAL SCHOOL IN FRANCE: FURTHER RESULTS

Bonnal et al. (1999, 2002) and Bonnal and Mendès (2000) consider the quality of the first job and the relative performance of higher level school leavers. We then discuss the results from Sollogoub and Ulrich (1999a, 1999b), which concentrate on the beginning of the work career.

3.1 Higher-level School Leavers

Bonnal et al. (1999) present results from similar regressions for apprentices and vocational-school leavers at the *baccalaureat professionnel* level (BACPRO in the following). This level corresponds to the last year of high school, with a higher vocational content than that contained in the general or the technical baccalaureat, which most students who stay on at school obtain at age 18, and which provides access to university. But, although corresponding to the same level, the BACPRO generally takes longer to obtain, as most students in France enter vocational schools only after having failed in the general system. The data are the same as those described above for the analysis at the CAP level, although the sample size is much smaller (314 observations). The years covered by the data correspond to the start of the development of higher level vocational diplomas through apprenticeship.

The econometric estimation is similar to that used for the data at the CAP level (see Bonnal et al., 1999). Due to the small sample size, no separate analysis by gender was undertaken. We again find that apprenticeship is a successful form of training, at least in terms of immediate access to first job. The selection bias found in model 2 implies, after correction, a significant increase in this probability for apprentices. The difference between the effectiveness of apprenticeship and vocational school is even sharper at the BACPRO level than at the CAP level. After the correction in model 2, the difference is 40 points for men and almost 30 points for women. In addition, as for men at the CAP level, but not for women, even apprentice movers have better labour market outcomes than vocational-school leavers, once selection bias is corrected. Firms thus do not seem to value apprentices' training mainly for the firm-specific human capital, but also for the general (or transferable) human capital component. This is unsurprising: it is intuitively straightforward that the higher the level of education, the larger the theoretical and thus transferable part of it.

3.2 Quality of the First Job

Bonnal et al. (1999) estimate a discrete time duration model on the same data to differentiate between different types of exits from unemployment. Discrete time modelling allows us to observe time-varying effects of apprenticeship. Four competing exits are considered:[6]

$$R = \begin{cases} 1: \text{permanent job} \\ 2: \text{temporary job} \\ 3: \text{internship} \\ 4: \text{remain out of the labour market} \end{cases} \qquad (6.1)$$

The results at the CAP level show that, for both men and women, apprenticeship: increases the probability of obtaining a permanent or (for women) a temporary job; reduces the probability of internships or of remaining unemployed. Apprenticeship is thus positively associated with favourable exits.

The diploma variable plays a similar role, significantly diminishing (and more so than apprenticeship) the probability of remaining unemployed, and increasing the probability of permanent or temporary jobs. The estimated coefficient on apprenticeship is larger than that on diploma for permanent job exits: to obtain a permanent job, apprenticeship is more effective than the CAP diploma. Apprenticeship also has a strong positive impact on the probability of obtaining a permanent job at the BACPRO level.

Considering the time-varying effects, it is found that the significant positive effect of apprenticeship on finding a permanent job is concentrated at the beginning of the time period considered. This holds for both men and women, and for education at both the CAP and BACPRO levels. A straightforward interpretation is that apprentices staying at the firm where they trained are generally hired within a few months of the end of their apprenticeship, and are very often offered permanent jobs. The same result seems to hold for those who find a job outside the firm where their apprenticeship took place. Note that the positive effect of apprenticeship on unemployment duration, found above, is entirely due to apprentices' relative disadvantage regarding internship compared to vocational-school leavers, who are often offered this kind of 'job'. This is particularly true for women at the CAP level. Conversely, at least at the CAP level, and particularly for men (where the relevant estimated coefficients are nearly always significantly positive), apprenticeship facilitates access to a permanent job over the whole period analysed.

3.3 Later in the Work Career

The main results here come from Sollogoub and Ulrich (1999a), who use a retrospective survey carried out by the Céreq on students who left apprenticeship, vocational school or secondary school in June 1989. This survey covers a four-and-a-half-year period after leaving apprenticeship or school, and provides information on the respondent's labour market situation, as well as wages.

Sollogoub and Ulrich use two criteria to study youth careers: the first is the proportion of time active in the labour market spent employed, active meaning being employed or unemployed (excluding, for example, military service for males); the second criterion is hourly wages at the end of the survey period, that is, four-and-a-half years after the end of school or apprenticeship.

They first estimate the determinants of choosing apprenticeship rather than vocational school (thus allowing any selection bias to be corrected), and then model the impact of the type of training on employment and wages. The second-stage equations are corrected for selectivity bias. Employment is estimated using a logistic model, while hourly wages are estimated using OLS. The first stage results reveal significant sample selection. In the second stage, at the CAP level, apprentices are shown to spend more time in employment than do vocational-school leavers. This holds independently of whether the apprentice is a stayer or a mover. This correlation is strengthened by the correction for the selection bias, suggesting, as found above, that apprenticeship is chosen by (relatively) less employable individuals in France. The wage results show a small but significant difference in favour of school leavers, such that the immediate positive wage effect of apprenticeship found above dissipates over the years. This difference between short-term and long-term apprenticeship effects has also been found in work covering other countries.

4.   INTERNATIONAL COMPARISONS

While the French research discussed above has much in common, in terms of the questions addressed, the data used, and the methodology employed, this is less true for the work covering other countries presented below. In addition, institutions vary from country to country. For example, the kind of job to which apprenticeship, as opposed to vocational school, leads may differ sharply between countries; the same remark may hold for the level of education at which the outcome comparisons are performed. These differences can have behavioural consequences: for example, Schwerdt (2001) finds no significant selectivity bias between apprenticeship and vocational school in German data, suggesting that apprenticeship in Germany does not attract the same kind of negative stigma as in France. As such, care is needed in making international comparisons. We first consider results from the STT research project, and then extend the comparisons to other countries.

4.1   STT Results

Bratberg and Nilsen (1999) look at the effect of apprenticeship on the transition from school to first job for youths. Using Norwegian Kirut data, their sample comprises school leavers who left education between January 1989 and September 1991. The length of the search period, the wage rate and the duration of first job are estimated simultaneously. They find that, compared to individuals with the same level of education, apprentices obtain a job relatively quickly after completing their education; they also tend to remain longer in their first job. No significant wage effect is found.

Groot and Plug (1998) use Dutch OSA-labour market survey covering the period 1985–94. Unlike the data previously discussed, which concerned recent school leavers, the Dutch sample includes individuals active in the labour market (or unemployed) at various different ages. The sample consists of 573 observations, of which 212 concern individuals from the apprenticeship system. Groot and Plug estimate a structural model in which the choice between apprenticeship and vocational school is fully endogenized. The results indicate significant differences between the two groups, as in France: apprentices are mostly male and are technically orientated. Furthermore, they are more likely to have a history of vocational education and less-educated fathers. In the second stage, a structural net earnings equation for both school types is estimated. No empirical support is found for a selection bias, nor any significant long-run earnings difference for workers with comparable levels of education. Furthermore, their results suggest no significant difference in either earnings growth or employment opportunities between vocational-school leavers and apprenticeship. These Dutch results are similar to those found in French data with respect to the short-run beneficial effects of apprenticeship, but no significant long-run effect.

4.2 Other Results

This section presents a brief overview of results from other countries. It in no way pretends to be exhaustive concerning research on apprenticeship; the objective here is to review a number of the main conclusions. Winkelmann (1996) compares apprentices' and school leavers' labour market insertion in Germany between 1984 and 1990. He looks at the beginning of the work career, where apprentices are less likely to be unemployed before they find their first full-time job. But, once found, this first job is as stable for school leavers as for apprentices. Gitter and Scheuer (1997) also stress the success of the German apprenticeship model in reducing unemployment rates and facilitating the school-to-work transition. Hanhart and Bossio (1998) find the same results for Switzerland. These results are similar to those found in the STT papers covering France and Norway.

Booth and Satchell (1994) analyse the incidence of apprenticeship in Great Britain, and, especially, the quality of the link between firms and apprentices. They analyse individual mobility, considering three exits from employment:

voluntary quits to another job; voluntary quits to unemployment; and involuntary job terminations. They use Sweep 4 of the National Child Development Study carried out in 1981. Their results show that apprenticeship reduces the three exit rates above. This suggests that both employers and apprentices are satisfied with the match. Conversely, those who do not finish apprenticeship have higher mobility. Again, very similar results are found for France in the STT papers.

Turning now to work careers, Ashenfelter et al. (1999) study the links between education and wages. They concentrate on the endogeneity of education, and its correlation with other variables that also influence labour income. This holds for the type of education chosen, including apprenticeship. Their analysis stresses the importance of the endogeneity of education and of its different types. Veum (1995), using NLSY (National Longitudinal Survey of Youth) data between 1986 and 1990 considers the effect of type of education upon wages. His results show that, in this respect, school leavers perform better than apprentices.

Using the YCS (Youth Cohort Study) survey, Dolton et al. (2001) show, conversely, a significant positive effect of apprenticeship on employment and wages. Harhoff and Kane (1997) find no significant difference between school leavers and apprentices in Germany and in the US over the life cycle, although they show evidence of different equilibria on the German and American labour markets, with notably lower specific human capital in the latter. Winkelman (1996) draws similar conclusions.

Finally, Dockery and Norris (1996) study life-cycle income in Australia, measuring the returns to apprenticeship. They find positive returns in six jobs out of ten for men, but only in one job out of three for women. These wage results, often drawing contradictory conclusions, are similar to those obtained in the STT papers: depending on the type of study, the length of time considered, and the country under consideration, apprenticeship is shown to confer no advantage, a slight positive advantage, or a slight disadvantage in terms of wages. More comparative work using the same methods is hence likely needed before any firm conclusion can be drawn.

5. CONCLUDING REMARKS

Apprenticeship seems to be an effective tool in the fight against youth unemployment. The results found in the STT papers confirm those found in other work, generally concerning different countries. Correcting for the endogenous choice of education generally strengthens the results in favour of apprenticeship. Access to the first job is easier for apprentices in every country analysed. Also, more generally, the quality of this first job is higher, with quality measured by the permanence of the job. This result is true for both women and men, although it is stronger for the latter. These are short-term findings, however. Over the longer run, the advantages of apprenticeship seem weaker, and even disappear entirely in some of the papers. The wage advantage turns to vocational-school leavers over apprentices in the longer run in a number of cases. One interpretation is that general human capital is of less value to firms at the beginning of the work career, but becomes more valuable over time as it facilitates adaptation to new types of work over the life cycle. Nevertheless, more work carried out in a comparative perspective, and with sufficient information on life-cycle comparisons is needed before any definite conclusions regarding the most appropriate form of youth training can be drawn.

NOTES

1. This question of the relative efficiency of apprenticeship and vocational training received a great deal of attention from the TSER-STT research teams, being addressed by four STT Working Papers using data from three countries: France, the Netherlands, and Norway.
2. For example the CAP in *métiers de bouche* (food sector jobs, such as baker or butcher), *mécanique auto* (car mechanic), or *comptabilité* (accounting).
3. Centre d'Etudes et de Recherches sur les Qualifications.
4. As the end of schooling generally occurs at the end of June, and July and August are a holiday period for most students, 'immediate' here means within two months.
5. They could benefit from sector-specific human capital, but then vocational school students also benefit from some specific training.
6. Exit 4, 'remain out of the labour market', refers to people who left the labour force.

REFERENCES

Acemoglu, D. and J.S. Pischke (1999), 'The structure of wages and investment in general training', *Journal of Political Economy*, **107** (3), 539–72.
Ashenfelter, O., C. Harmon and H. Oosterbeek (1999), 'A review of estimates of the schooling/earnings relationship, with tests for publication bias', *Labour Economics*, **6** (4), 453–70.
Bonnal, L. and S. Mendès (2000), 'L'accès au premier emploi des apprentis et des lycéens: peut-on parler de différences?', *Document Séminaires*, Céreq, **156**, 237–49.
Bonnal, L., S. Mendès and C. Sofer (1999), 'Access to the first job: a comparison between apprenticeship and vocational school in France', *STT Working Paper*, 02–99.
Bonnal, L., S. Mendès and C. Sofer (2002), 'School-to-work transition: apprenticeship versus vocational school in France', *International Journal of Manpower*, **23** (5), 426–42.
Booth, A.L. and S.E. Satchell (1994), 'Apprenticeships and job tenure', *Oxford Economic Papers*, **46** (4), 676–95.
Bordigoni, M. (1995), 'Jeunes en apprentissage, un besoin de confiance', *BREF*, **106**, Céreq.

Bratberg, E. and O.A. Nilsen (1999), 'Transitions from school to work: search time and job duration', *STT Working Paper,* 05–99.

Dockery, A.M. and K. Norris (1996), 'The "rewards" for apprenticeship training in Australia', *Australian Bulletin of Labour*, **22** (2), 109–25.

Dolton, P.J., G.H. Makepeace and J.G. Treble (1994), 'The youth training scheme and the school-to-work transition', *Oxford Economic Papers,* **46** (4), 629–57.

Dolton, P.J., G.H. Makepeace and B.M. Gannon (2001), 'The earnings and employment effects of young people's vocational training in Britain', *Manchester School*, **69** (4), 387–417.

Fougère, D. and A. Serandon, (1992), 'La transition du système éducatif à l'emploi en France: le rôle des variables scolaires et sociales', *Revue de l'Economie Sociale*, nos **27** and **28**, Tome 2, 89–101.

Gitter, R.J. and M. Scheuer (1997), 'US and German youths: unemployment and the transition from school to work', *Monthly Labor Review*, **120** (3), 16–20.

Groot, W. and E. Plug (1998), 'Apprenticeship versus vocational education: exemplified by the Dutch situation', *STT Working Paper*, 11–98.

Hanhart, S. and S. Bossio (1998), 'Costs and benefits of dual apprenticeship: lessons from the Swiss system', *International Labour Review*, **137** (4), 483–500.

Harhoff, D. and T.J. Kane (1997), 'Is the German apprenticeship system a panacea for the US labor market?', *Journal of Population Economics*, **10** (2), 171–96.

Lynch, L.M. (1983), 'Job search and youth unemployment', *Oxford Economic Papers*, **35**, 271–82.

Ryan, P. (2001), 'The school-to-work transition: a cross-national perspective', *Journal of Economic Literature*, **XXXIX**, 34–92.

Schwerdt, W. (2001), 'Comparaison des systèmes d'apprentissage en France et en Allemagne: une analyse économétrique', Ph.D Dissertation, Université Paris 1–Panthéon–Sorbonne, December.

Sollogoub, M. and V. Ulrich (1999a), 'Apprenticeship versus vocational school: selectivity bias and school to work transition', *STT Working Paper*, 09–99.

Sollogoub, M. and V. Ulrich (1999b), 'Les jeunes en apprentissage ou en lycée professionnel', *Economie et Statistique*, **323** (3), 31–49.

Veum, J.R. (1995), 'Sources of training and their impact on wages', *Industrial and Labor Relations Review*, **48** (4), 812–26.

Winkelmann, R. (1996), 'Employment prospects and skill acquisition of apprenticeship-trained workers in Germany', *Industrial and Labor Relations Review*, **49** (4), 658–72.

PART III

Human capital and the work career

7. Employer provided training within the European Union: a comparative review

Peter Elias and Rhys Davies

1. INTRODUCTION

There is a degree of consensus within the European Commission that a highly skilled workforce is necessary to maintain and enhance the competitiveness of the European Community (see EC, 1991, pp. 126–7). For the Community to compete successfully and hold its place in the world economy characterized by increased global competition, its enterprises need to use the latest and most efficient technology available. This in turn means that the Community has to have a labour force that is educated and trained to handle that technology. Groot (1999) notes that the European socio-economic policy debate has been dominated by a belief that the labour market should become more flexible as a means of increasing competitiveness and welfare. Access to continuing vocational training (CVT) whilst in employment is regarded as a means of enhancing the flexibility of labour by increasing the productivity and employability of workers.

Against this background, this chapter considers the role of employers in the process of skill formation within the European Union (EU). The discussion deliberately attempts to abstract from initial work-based vocational training that may be organized or provided by the State.[1] Instead, we consider the involvement of employers in the process of skill formation after periods of initial vocational training have been completed. Section 2 provides an overview of the theoretical and empirical literature regarding both the incidence of and the returns to employer provided training. In light of this discussion, Section 3 compares the contribution of employers to the process of skill formation across the EU. The difficulties associated with making international comparisons and the importance of understanding the context in which vocational training takes place is discussed in Section 4. Section 5 considers how training market failures may be addressed within a European context.

2.   WHAT DO WE KNOW ABOUT EMPLOYER PROVIDED TRAINING?

The orthodox approach of economics to education and training finds its expression through modern human capital theory (Schultz, 1961; Becker, 1964). At its simplest level, investment in human capital can be regarded as synonymous with physical capital investment and subject to conventional investment appraisal techniques. The direct and indirect costs of training are compared with the discounted future benefits of the human capital investment. In considering investment in on-the-job training,[2] Becker (1964) makes the distinction between general and specific training that has important implications for who bears the cost of vocational training. In a perfectly competitive market, general training enhances worker productivity within all firms and hence has market value. A firm that bore the costs of general training would not be able to recoup these costs by paying a wage less than the marginal product, as the employee would leave. The employee can gain the full benefits of general training and will therefore bear the costs. In contrast, specific training only raises productivity within the firm in which it is undertaken. Since such skills have no value in the external market, the employer does not necessarily have to pay a wage equal to the marginal product. The wage will lie between the marginal product and the external market wage, so that the firm and the worker will share the costs and benefits of specific training.

However, market imperfections may hinder investment in vocational training. Stevens (1994) demonstrates that while transferable skills can have value in more than one firm, the level of competition in an imperfect market may be insufficient to force wages to equal marginal product. Any firm that has a positive probability of employing a worker at a wage less than the marginal product may therefore expect to benefit from the training despite not bearing any of the costs. Where firms that do not train their employees can 'poach' workers from the collective pool of skilled labour provided by those employers undertaking training, the formation of skills by employers becomes a collective good with the associated problems of free riding. Another source of market imperfection that may hinder investment in vocational training is that arising from the capital market (see Stevens, 1999). If capital markets operated perfectly, potential trainees would be able to borrow funds up to the point where the return on the training investment would be equal to the interest on the loan. However, human capital cannot provide collateral for a loan and the returns to the human capital investment are not easily predictable. Lenders will therefore require higher rates of interest to compensate for the increased risk of default, discouraging investment in human capital.

Blundell et al. (1996), Ashton and Green (1996), Bishop (1997) and Groot (1999) provide reviews of the empirical evidence as to the determinants of employer provided training. These determinants can be broken down into job characteristics, individual characteristics and firm characteristics. Key findings from the range of studies they review reveal that, in terms of individual characteristics:

- males have better access to training than females;
- training decreases with age;
- higher educational qualifications raise the probability of receiving training;
- minority groups have a lower probability of receiving training;
- union members receive more training than non-union members do;
- training participation is higher for workers recently recruited to a new job;
- training is more likely to be taken by individuals who have ambitions to self-improvement;
- workers who are expected to have lower rates of turnover will have a higher probability of receiving training.

These studies also show that in terms of the jobs in which training is provided:

- part-time workers receive less training than full-time workers do;
- workers in regular employment receive more training than workers in temporary employment;
- the probability of training decreases with job tenure;
- workers in jobs where the skills learned are not useful at many other firms in the community will receive more training;
- training is greater in cognitively complex jobs;
- workers in jobs characterized by high value added and responsibility receive more training;
- workers who use expensive machinery receive more training.

The study of establishment characteristics that correlate with the provision of work related training reveals that:

- large establishments provide more training than small establishments;
- public sector establishments provide more training than private sector establishments;
- industries with growing or changing technology provide more training;
- training is greater where firms have strategic plans, and a fortiori training plans;
- training is greater in firms with lower turnover;
- training is greater in firms that recognize unions;

- training provision is greater within multi-establishment firms;
- firms that have long probationary periods for new hires provide more training;
- training provision is greater within firms that have not experienced a competitive crisis within the last decade;
- the incidence of training is greater amongst firms employing flexible or high performance production strategies;
- training probability is lower in firms located within areas of high unemployment.

The variations in training witnessed between individuals, occupations and establishments are generally compatible with the predictions of the human capital approach. However, these studies do not provide evidence as to the economic returns that provide the motivation for the human capital investment. The importance of the need to understand the returns from employer provided training is underlined by Barrett et al. (1998). 'Without reliable information on the relationship between the costs and benefits of training, decisions on the financing of training must be made on the basis of hunches and impressions. In such a setting, the potential for the misallocation of resources to training is large' (Barrett et al., 1998, p. 8).

In a review of the literature on rates of return to CVT in enterprises, Barret et al. (1998) draw the following conclusions:

- few studies have attempted to estimate rates of return in the strict economic/financial sense: that is relating the initial investment in training to the flow of benefits over time to produce an estimated rate of return in a manner which is done for capital assets;
- training is shown to have a positive effect on wages;
- training is shown to have a positive effect on productivity;
- there is evidence to suggest that training received from one employer increases productivity and wages with another employer;
- selection effects matter in training: people who receive training may themselves have productivity enhancing characteristics, recognized by employers but unobserved to researchers, which are confounded with the effects of training;
- different types of training matter for productivity effects, as does the combination of training with other human resource policies;
- individuals and firms have objectives for training other than wage and productivity growth.

What emerges from these research findings is the cumulative disadvantage faced by those who are not in receipt of employer provided training. It is those employees who are relatively well educated and who are employed in more skill intensive jobs – with regular contracts in industries characterized by higher rates of technological change – who will benefit from the increased wages that are associated with employer provided training. This situation will be compounded further by skill biased technological changes that have favoured the prospects of relatively skilled workers across a range of countries (see Machin and van Reenen, 1998, Berman et al., 1998). Nickell (1996) suggests that whilst the demand shift against unskilled labour has led to a widening of the earnings distribution within the UK and the US, no widening in the earnings distribution has occurred within Germany. These divergent trends are due to the presence of a more highly skilled workforce at the lower end of the ability range, a factor which has enabled German enterprises 'to respond to the relative demand shift in favour of the skilled with less dislocation' (Nickell, 1996, p. 27).

Evidence of externalities associated with transferable skills, however, suggests that there may be under-investment in employer provided training. A number of studies also point towards a general scepticism amongst employers as to the value of training within the United Kingdom (see Coopers and Lybrand (1985), Hyman (1992), Hewitt-Dundas (1996), Hillage et al. (1998)). Such views may emerge from the inability of companies to identify the costs and benefits of training programmes clearly and hence to calculate the returns from training using conventional investment appraisal techniques (Mayhew, 1991). However, reviewing the empirical literature on the effects of training within firms, Ashton and Green (1996) conclude that in so far as profit is the basic criterion of competitiveness, no empirical evidence between training and competitiveness exists. In spite of improved labour market outcomes and productivity effects, the presence of externalities and the inability to establish direct links with bottom line measures of firm performance may hinder investments in employer provided training.

3. PATTERNS OF EMPLOYER INVOLVEMENT IN SKILL FORMATION WITHIN EUROPE

In light of the overview of the literature presented in Section 2, this section reviews evidence regarding the commitment by employers across Europe to the process of skill formation. Much of our knowledge about the nature and the extent of work-related training tends to be limited in some way by constraints imposed by data collection methodologies. Evidence from larger-scale surveys primarily relies upon the response to questions about participation in work-related training during a specific reference period. Case study methods, while rich in detail and description of the training processes, cannot convey information about the extent and coverage of such events among the employed population. Apart from issues relating to data sources and related data collection methodologies, other problems stem from a more conceptual basis. Survey respondents may interpret 'Training' as an activity associated with a specific event (for instance course participation, programmed instruction), a particular status (such as as 'trainee' or 'apprentice') or with their pay (for example through the use of training pay grades). The definition of training used in a particular study may itself exclude certain types of training activity. For example, training may be defined as 'off-the-job' activity, thereby excluding training on the job. Alternatively, the recipient may not regard less formal types of training as training activities.

The most comprehensive source of data on employer provided training within Europe is the Continuing Vocational Training Survey undertaken by Eurostat. The first survey (CVTS1) was undertaken in 1994 and collected information from a representative sample of enterprises from the then 12 member states of the EU (see EC et al., 1997 for details). The second survey (CVTS2) was conducted in 2000/2001 across all member states, Norway and nine candidate countries (see EC, 2002 for details). In both surveys, CVT is defined as covering all training activities experienced by employees except for the initial training of apprentices and trainees with a special training contract. The emphasis of the Continuing Vocational Training Surveys is upon formal activities that had been planned in advance and were wholly or partly funded by the enterprise. CVT activities cover internal and external courses; staff participation in planned learning at the workplace or in the work situation using the usual work tools; instruction at conferences, workshops, lectures and seminars where the primary purpose is training; planned learning through job rotation, exchanges, secondments and quality circles; and self learning through open and distance learning.

Information from CVTS1 and CVTS2 on the percentage of enterprises offering CVT is presented in Figure 7.1.[3] It can be seen that the percentage of enterprises offering CVT is highest within the countries of Northern Europe. More than 75 per cent of establishments within Denmark, Germany, the UK and Ireland are involved in the training of employees. The extension of CVTS2 to cover Finland, Norway and Sweden has highlighted the relatively high incidence of involvement in training that exists within the Nordic countries. For each of these three countries, between 80 and 90 per cent of establishments provide CVT. In contrast, involvement in training is particularly low across the countries of Southern Europe with enterprise participation generally between 15 and 25 per cent, although Spain and Portugal have both exhibited increased rates of participation between CVTS1 and CVTS2. Comparisons over time also indicate significant increases in enterprise involvement in CVT in the Netherlands and Belgium.

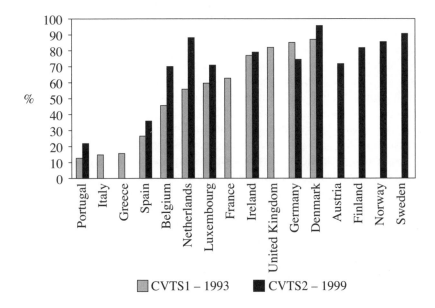

Source: EC (1997), Nestler and Kailis (2002a)

Figure 7.1   Enterprises offering continuing vocational training

Variations in training participation across Europe seem to reflect the economic heterogeneity exhibited across the Community in terms of the level of development and the distribution of sectors of economic activity between member states. These issues are considered in Table 7.1, which provides estimates of enterprise participation in continuing vocational training from CVTS2 by size and area of economic activity. Across all countries, establishment involvement in continuing vocational training is higher amongst larger establishments. It is also observed that participation in vocational training across countries is relatively uniform when considering establishments with more than 50 employees. With the exception of Spain, Portugal and Luxembourg, participation in vocational training amongst enterprises with 50 to 249 employees is approximately 90 per cent or higher. Furthermore, participation in vocational training amongst enterprises with more than 250 employees is generally above 95 per cent. The largest variations in enterprise participation rates across countries are observed amongst establishments with fewer than 50 employees. Whilst participation rates amongst these smaller enterprises are generally greater than 70 per cent across the countries of Northern Europe, participation rates within Portugal and Spain are 17 per cent and 31 per cent respectively.

Considering enterprise participation by area of activity, it can be seen that the highest incidence of involvement in CVT is observed in the area of 'finance'. In nine countries, the highest percentage of enterprises providing CVT appeared in this area of activity. The percentage of enterprises providing CVT is lowest within 'manufacturing' and amongst 'other activities' which include mining and utilities, construction, hotels and restaurants, and transport and communication. The low rates of training participation witnessed across the countries of Southern Europe are therefore generally indicative of the unresponsiveness of output per worker to training investments in low technology sectors (particularly the hospitality and tourist sectors) concentrated within these countries. However, even within 'finance', a sector that is commonly characterized by the rapid diffusion of technical progress, participation in vocational training is significantly lower within Portugal and Spain compared to the rest of the Community.

Figure 7.2 provides information from CVTS2 on the average costs per employee of CVT courses in those enterprises that provide CVT courses. Costs are presented in purchasing power standards to allow for price differences between countries. It should also be noted that this information refers only to the provision of CVT that takes place away from the place of work and not periods of instruction at the immediate place of work. CVTS2 makes the distinction between the direct costs incurred for organization of courses and the staff time costs incurred while participants in training are not engaged in productive work. These figures give an indication of the relative intensity of the formal skill acquisition process within firms. The cost of CVT is highest within the countries of Northern Europe, and in particular Norway, the Netherlands, Denmark and Sweden. Although the costs of CVT are relatively low within Spain and Portugal, it is observed that these are generally comparable with several other Northern European countries. The distinction that was observed in enterprise participation between the North and South of the Community is less evident in terms of variations in the costs of CVT.

To conclude, information from the Continuing Vocational Training Surveys indicates that there is considerable variation in the incidence of employer provided training within Europe. Training participation varies between all member states, although there is a significant divergence between the North and South of the Community. Variations in training participation appear to reflect the economic heterogeneity exhibited across the Community in terms of the level of development and the distribution of sectors of economic activity between member states. However, even within sectors of activity that are characterized by the rapid diffusion of technical progress, significant variations in enterprise involvement in CVT remain.

Table 7.1 Training enterprises as a percentage of all enterprises

Country	Industry[1]						Size			All
	Manufacturing (D)	Wholesale retail and repair (G)	Finance (J)	Property and business activities (K)	Social and personal service activites	Other (C, E, F, H, I)[2]	10–49	50–249	250+	
Portugal	19	24	67	43	29	18	17	46	78	22
Spain	38	41	74	41	33	29	31	58	86	36
Belgium	68	72	100	86	75	63	66	93	100	70
L'bourg	75	75	89	80	80	59	67	83	99	71
Austria	73	74	97	87	79	65	68	91	96	72
Germany	73	83	100	87	89	65	71	87	98	75
Ireland	90	77	90	90	58	72	75	98	100	79
Finland	77	85	100	86	93	79	78	97	99	82
Norway	85	87	98	96	92	80	84	97	100	86
N'lands	90	87	97	90	86	86	85	96	98	88
Sweden	90	94	100	90	84	84	88	99	99	91
Denmark	95	100	100	98	91	91	95	98	100	96

Notes
1. NACE categories in parenthesis.
2. Incorporating mining and quarrying; electricity, gas and water; construction; hotels and restaurants; transport and communication.

Source: Nestler and Kailis (2002a)

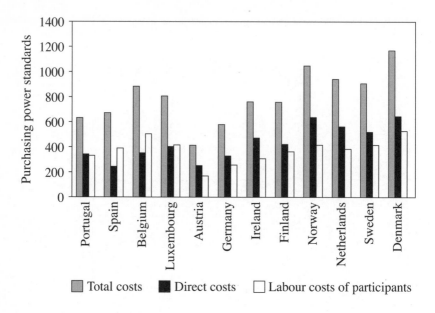

Source: Nestler and Kailis (2002b)

Figure 7.2   Costs of CVT courses per employee in enterprises with CVT courses

4.   DIFFICULTIES IN MAKING INTERNATIONAL COMPARISONS: THE CONTEXT OF CVT

The main theme to emerge from the evidence presented in Section 3 is the presence of a North/South divide in terms of employer involvement in skill formation within Europe. However, such cross-country comparisons ignore the content and purpose of vocational training undertaken by employers. CEDEFOP (1998) emphasizes the importance of the initial endowment of human capital possessed by workers in determining the role of employer provided training. In countries endowed with the apprenticeship system of initial vocational training (such as Germany, Denmark and the Netherlands), employer provided training has a largely cumulative function. Training is aimed at building upon existing skills provided by vocational qualifications to meet the needs of the enterprise. Where initial vocational education is under-taken in schools (for example in France, Italy, Ireland, Greece and Spain), employer provided training has a compensatory role. Firms adjust and adapt to the deficiencies in practical experience resulting from the theoretically orientated vocational qualifications gained within educational institutions (see CEDEFOP, 1998, pp. 150–51).

Comparisons of CVT must also be considered in terms of the context of the demand for skills across countries. Keep and Mayhew (1999) describe how underlying problems with the employer provision of vocational training can be considered in terms of market failure and systems failure. The market failure approach encompasses the conventional diagnosis as outlined earlier in Section 2, 'that work based training [is] prejudiced by a series of market failures affecting the decision taking of both employers and individual workers' (Keep and Mayhew, 1999, p. 4). In contrast, the systems failure approach is based upon the notion of the low skill equilibrium, where the demand for skills by employers was a rational reaction to incentives provided by the inherited institutional structure. The most difficult problem in gauging the importance of systems failure is the lack of firm empirical evidence to establish the extent to which countries are following different routes to competitive advantage.

Regini (1995, 1997) provides an example of such evidence in the form of case studies that consider the importance of the interaction between product market strategy, the demand for skills and the provision of employer provided training across countries. In Germany, firms were seen to compete on the basis of diversified quality production through the utilization of a highly skilled workforce. In Italy flexible mass production enabled firms to compete through the production of a variety of goods to meet changing demands. Such techniques were characterized by the polarization of skills around core occupational groups and the prevalence of external flexibility amongst the low skilled majority. In Spain production was characterized by firms who compete on the basis of price through the mass production of standardized goods by semi-skilled workers, and by traditional small firms who compete on price through the payment of low wages and the avoidance of tax and welfare contributions. Whilst highly selective, training in Germany focused upon boosting motivation and identification with the corporate culture rather than further technical development. Within Italy and Spain firms were found to provide training programmes that focus upon the skills of core occupational groups. For the majority of the labour force who receive no formal training, firms rely upon shadowing to develop the 'scant' technical skills required for the job.

In terms of systems failure, the provision and context of workplace training either builds upon or reacts to initial comparative advantages faced by employers. The predominance in a particular country or region of certain types of firm, and of the associated patterns of human resource utilization that these entail, is the outcome of long and complex processes routed in their specific history (Regini, 1995, p. 197). Whilst rich in detail and description, there are obvious difficulties in generalizing results from such studies. Even within the high skills economy of Germany, Berg (1994) describes the presence of car plants that provide technical training only to core occupational groups that resemble US plants in terms of low functional flexibility at the workplace. However, this discussion has indicated that comparisons of CVT across countries need to consider the relationship between the structure of workforce skills delivered by national systems of initial vocational training and associated patterns of production utilized by employers.

5. ADDRESSING TRAINING MARKET FAILURES WITHIN A EUROPEAN CONTEXT

In terms of addressing the problems of market failure, Groot (1999) provides an overview of the different approaches taken across Europe to the provision of skills in the workforce. At one extreme, countries such as Germany, the Netherlands and Italy leave the provision of enterprise related training to market forces. In France and to a lesser extent Spain, Belgium and Greece, central regulations govern what percentage of an establishment's wage bill must be set aside for training. However, as discussed earlier these comparisons need to be considered in the context of the provision of initial vocational training within these countries. Stevens (1999) describes how the UK has moved between both ends of this spectrum during the last 30 years. Established in 1964, the Industrial Training Boards operated a grant levy system that compelled firms to increase expenditure on training. This scheme was abolished in 1982. Since this time, greater emphasis has been placed on the individual to take responsibility for skill acquisition (for example Career Development Loans).

In comparing the effectiveness of these different approaches, recent research has focused upon the differences between France and Britain in regulating the provision of vocational training amongst the adult workforce. Greenhalgh (1999) provides a description of the interventionist training policy that has evolved in France since the early 1970s. The French Model requires that firms with more than 10 workers have to either devote a fixed proportion of their wage bill to workforce training, or to pay a tax of the same amount. These funds are either used by firms for the direct provision of training for employees or are paid into mutual funds organized by employer, union and employee representatives. The organizers of these mutual funds decide priorities and organize training to cover both sector-specific skill needs and the supply of general skills. Member firms can call upon the resources of the mutual funds to purchase training for employees, seek reimbursement for training costs and apply for training grants. The French system is in stark contrast to the UK where there is no obligation to provide training within firms. Combining rates of incidence with duration from the CVTS1,

Greenhalgh (1999) notes that the average annual hours of training per employee are longer in France at 20 hours than any other original 12 member states of the EU and well above the 15.5 hours per employees achieved in the UK. The partial deletion of poaching externalities between training and non-training firms appears to solve some aspects of the training market failure (Greenhalgh, 1999, p. 111).

Hocquet (1999) attempts to identify differences in both the incidence and impact of employer provided training in the UK and France by utilizing data from national sources. The effect of training upon wages was estimated to be 10 per cent for France and 12 per cent for the UK. However, after controlling for selectivity bias, the estimated real impact of training was estimated to be 21 per cent in France and 15 per cent in the UK. Hocquet (1999) suggests that controlling for selection effects indicates that the French system encourages the training of less efficient workers compared to the UK. Workers with lower wages are more likely to be trained in France.

In their 'matched pairs' study of food manufacturing plants, Mason et al. (1994, 1996) also found that the French legislative environment promoted the formal training of employees that was both more extensive and innovative than that observed in Britain, Germany and the Netherlands. However, the context of employer provided training is again observed to be important. Mason et al. (1994, 1996) conclude that while the relatively high volume of CVT has increased French productivity levels above those in Britain, the French system only partially offsets the productivity advantages that exist in the Netherlands and Germany through the more extensive provision of initial vocational education and training.

Studies that contrast the provision of employer provided training in France and the UK point towards the potential gains to be made from policy interventions that deal appropriately with market failure. However, to encourage the adoption of high skilled production techniques within Europe, it is also necessary to consider the factors that regulate the demand for skills by employers and contribute to systems failure. In encouraging the effective utilization of skills by employers, 'labour market institutions and state policies can influence producers to stress product innovation and operate at technological frontiers with high skills and wages' (Green et al., 1994, p. 310).

One area of potential importance has been changes to the legislative environment that have facilitated the growth in atypical forms of employment. Treu (1992) suggests that the introduction of different types of employment contracts under European law has played a leading role in labour market flexibility. The main trend has been an increase in temporary employment which has been promoted by legislation that has widened the range of acceptable reasons justifying the use of fixed term contracts (special projects, seasonal work, sickness of a permanent employee and so on). Against this background,

De Grip et al. (1997) estimate that flexible employment (defined as self-employed, part-time workers and workers with a temporary contract) increased by 15 per cent within the EU between 1985 and 1995. Marshall (1989) states that temporary jobs are not the preferred option of those in employment, but reflect the desire of employers to lay off workers during downturns in demand without any costly commitment on the part of the employer. For example, Delsen (1991) describes how temporary workers in Europe are often excluded from coverage by the systems of social security and/or protection against dismissal and other fringe benefits because of requirements for a minimum period of service or the presence of salary thresholds.

It is potentially misleading to suggest that there is a simple dichotomy between secure, regular employment and precarious atypical employment. Rodgers (1989) suggests that in any form of atypical employment, there is a distinct tendency to bi-modality in the distribution of skills. However, Grahl and Teague (1990) suggest that flexibility programmes that lead to casualized employment and low pay can discourage competition on the basis of innovation and production methods. Boyer and Caroli (1993) note that where the external mobility of labour is important, firms are not deeply involved in the skill enhancement process. This is observed both in terms of the incentives to undertake human capital investments and the encouragement of employees to participate in the workplace skill formation process as teachers. Studies have found that on-the-job training is associated with lower job-to-job mobility (for example Elias 1994). Evidence as to the importance of a stable environment in enhancing training is also provided by Claydon and Green (1992) who suggest that trade unions may have a significant indirect impact upon the provision of job-related training, via the associated reduction in labour turnover found within unionized establishments.

Leborgne and Lipietz (1990) emphasize the importance of European floors for wages, leisure and job guarantees which would 'by precluding defensive flexibility strategies, make it possible to equalise at a higher level, the conditions governing competition' (Leborgne and Lipietz, 1989, p. 197). While skill-biased technological changes have favoured the prospects of relatively skilled workers across a range of countries, institutions can also play an important role in reducing the incentive for firms to follow low skill routes to competitive advantage. This review has indicated how institutions of Europe can contribute towards addressing problems of both market failure and systems failure in the provision of skills by employers.

NOTES

1. This is an important point, given that some countries have a highly developed upper secondary educational system incorporating vocational schools (see for example the case of

Norway, Elias et al., 1994). Our intention here though is to focus particularly upon the role of the employer in the process of skill formation. We recognize, however, that employer behaviour may be affected by the role the State plays in developing vocational skills among young people in their pre-labour force entry period. Further consideration of this issue is given in Section 6.

2. There is a terminological difficulty here, between the US definition of 'on the job' training, which means any planned period of instruction related to a job and undertaken within a contract of employment. This may or may not be instruction at the workplace. The UK definition of 'on the job' training relates specifically to training undertaken at the workplace. We adopt the US definition throughout this chapter.

3. At the time of writing, published information from the second Continuing Vocational Training Survey was not available for Greece, France, Italy and the United Kingdom.

BIBLIOGRAPHY

Ashton D. and F. Green (1996), *Education, Training and the Global Economy*. Edward Elgar, Cheltenham.

Barrett A., B. Hovels, P. den Boer and G. Kraayvanger (1998), *Exploring the Returns to Continuing Vocational Training in Enterprises: a review of research within and outside of the European Union*. CEDEFOP, Thessaloniki.

Becker G. (1964), Investment in on the job training, in M. Blaug (1968), *The Economics of Education*, 1 Penguin, Harmondsworth.

Berg P. (1994), Strategic adjustments in training: a comparative analysis of the US and German automobile industries, in L. Lynch (ed.), *Training and the Private Sector: International Comparisons*. NBER Comparative Labour Market Series, Chicago.

Berman E., J. Bound and S. Machin (1998), Implications of skill-biased technological change: international evidence, *The Quarterly Journal of Economics*, **113** (4), 1245–79.

Bishop J. (1997), What do we know about employer provided training? *Research in Labour Economics*, **16**, 1–87.

Blundell R., L. Dearden and C. Meghir (1996), *The Determinants and Effects of Work Related Training in Britain*. Institute for Fiscal Studies, London.

Boyer R. and E. Caroli (1993), *Production Regimes, Education and Training Systems: from complementary to mismatch?* Paper presented at the RAND conference on Human Capital Investments and Economic Performance, Santa Barbara.

CEDEFOP (1998), *Training for a Changing Society: a report on current vocational education and training research in Europe 1998*. Office for Official Publications of the European Communities, Luxembourg.

Claydon T. and G. Green (1992), The effects of unions on training provision, *Discussion Papers in Economics*, **92** (3), University of Leicester, Leicester.

Coopers and Lybrand Associates (1985), *A Challenge to Complacency: changing attitudes to training*. Manpower Services Commission/National Economic Development Office, Sheffield.

De Grip A., J. Hoevenberg and E. Willems (1997), Atypical Employment in the European Union, *International Labour Review*, **136** (1), 49–71.

Delsen L. (1991), Atypical employment relations and government policy in Europe. *Labour*, **5** (3), pp. 123–49.

Elias P. (1994), Job related training, trade union membership, and labour mobility, *Oxford Economic Papers*, **46**, 563–78.

Elias P., E. Hernaes and M. Baker (1994), Vocational education and training in Britain and Norway, in L. Lynch (ed.), *Training and the Private Sector: international comparisons*. NBER Comparative Labour Market Series, Chicago.

European Commission (1991), *Employment in Europe – 1991*. Office for Official Publication of the European Commission, Luxembourg.

European Commission, Eurostat and CEDEFOP (1997), *Key Data on Vocational Training in the European Union*. Office for Official Publications of the European Community, Luxembourg.

European Commission (2002), *European Social Statistics: Continuing Vocational Training Survey – 1999 data*. Office for Official Publications of the European Commission, Luxembourg.

Grahl J. and P. Teague (1990), *1992 – The Big Market: the future of the European Community*. Lawrence & Wishart, London.

Green F., A. Henley and E. Tsakalotos (1994), Income inequality in corporatist and liberal economies: a comparison of trends within OECD countries, *International Review of Applied Economics*, **8**, 303–29.

Greenhalgh C. (1999), Adult vocational training and government policy in France and Britain, *Oxford Review of Economic Policy*, **15** (1), 97–113.

Groot W. (1999), Enterprise related training: a survey, in F. van Wieringen and G. Attwell (eds), *Vocational and Adult Education in Europe*, Kluwer Academic Publishers, Dordrecht.

Hewitt-Dundas (1996), *Managerial Qualifications, Training and Flexibility Within the Context of Small Firm Growth: a matched plant analysis*. Northern Ireland Economic Research Centre. Working Paper, 18.

Hillage J., J. Atkinson, B. Kersley and P. Bates (1998), *Employers' Training of Young People*. Department for Education and Employment. Research Report RR76.

Hocquet L. (1999), Vocational training as a force for equality: training opportunities and outcomes in France and Britain. *Targeted Socio-Economic Research: Schooling, Training and Transition*, Working Paper 25–99, University of Orleans.

Hyman J. (1992), *Training at Work: a critical analysis of policy and practice*. Routledge, London.

Keep E. and K. Mayhew (1999), The assessment: knowledge, skills and competitiveness, *Oxford Review of Economic Policy* **15** (1), 1–15.

Leborgne P. and A. Lipietz (1989), How to avoid a two tier Europe, *Labour and Society*, **15**, 177–99.

Machin S. and J. van Reenen (1998), Technology and changes in skill structure: evidence from seven OECD countries, *The Quarterly Journal of Economics*, **113** (4), 1215–44.

Marshall A. (1989), The sequel of unemployment: the changing role of part-time and temporary work in Western Europe, in G. Rodgers and J. Rodgers (eds), *Precarious Jobs in Labour Market Regulation: the growth of atypical employment in Western Europe*. International Institute for Labour Studies, Geneva.

Mason G., B. van Ark and K. Wagner (1994), Productivity, product quality and workforce skills: food processing in four European Countries, *National Institute Economic Review*, **147**, 62–82.

Mason G., B. van Ark and K. Wagner (1996), Workforce skills, product quality and economic performance, in A. Booth and D. Snower, *Acquiring Skills: market failures, their symptoms and policy responses*. Centre for Economic Policy Research, Cambridge.

Mayhew K. (1991), *Training – The Problem for Employers*. Employment Institute Economic Report, **5** (10).

Nestler K. and E. Kailis (2002a), *Continuing Vocational Training in Enterprises in the European Union and Norway (CVTS2)*. Statistics in Focus: Theme 3, 3/2002. Eurostat.

Nestler K. and E. Kailis (2002b), *Costs and Funding of Continuing Vocational Training in Enterprises in Europe (CVTS2)*. Statistics in Focus: Theme 3, 8/2002. Eurostat.

Nickell S. (1996), *Sectorial Structural Change and the State of the Labour Market in Great Britain*. The Labour Market Consequences of Technical and Structural Change Discussion Paper Series, Centre for Economic Performance, 2.

OECD (1993), Enterprise tenure, labour turnover and skill training. *Employment Outlook*, pp. 119–55. OECD, Paris.

Regini M. (1995), Firms and institutions: the demand for skills and their social production in Europe, *European Journal of Industrial Relations*, **1** (2), 191–202.

Regini M. (1997), Different responses to common demands: firms, institutions and training in Europe, *European Sociological Review*, **13** (3), 267–82.

Rodgers G. (1989), Precarious work in Western Europe: the state of the debate, in G. Rodgers and J. Rodgers (eds), *Precarious Jobs in Labour Market Regulation: the growth of atypical employment in Western Europe*. International Institute for Labour Studies, Geneva.

Schultz T. (1961), Investment in human capital, in M. Blaug (ed.) (1968), *The Economics of Education* Vol. 1. Penguin, Harmondsworth.

Stevens M. (1994), A theoretical model of on-the-job training with imperfect competition, *Oxford Economic Papers*, **46** (4), 537–62.

Stevens M. (1999), Human capital theory and UK vocational training policy, *Oxford Review of Economic Policy*, **15** (1), 16–32.

Treu T. (1992), Labour flexibility in Europe, *International Labour Review*, **114** (3), 10–18.

8. Labour contracts and economic performance: Spain and France

Juan Cañada Vicinay and Michel Sollogoub

1. INTRODUCTION

Institutional regulations of the labour markets have been the subject of controversy concerning the role they play in the market's functioning.[1] As computed by the OECD in 1994, Spain and France stand at the higher end of the labour standard index describing the strength of legislation governing a number of aspects of the labour markets related to working time, employment protection, minimum wages, employees' representation rights and fixed-term contracts. On a scale ranging from 0 to 10, Spain has the highest score among the described countries (7) and France comes just behind (6).[2] At the same time, the performances of these two countries, as described in Table 8.1, show divergent results relatively to the UK and the Netherlands. While France presents similar figures to the EU-15 average, Spain is an extreme case of low performance, since the incidence of temporary jobs and unemployment are almost double the EU average, while part-time work is less then half the EU rate and less than a fifth of the Dutch percentage. France is more in accordance with the European average, exhibiting a slightly higher unemployment rate. Moreover, atypical employment and unemployment generally follow separate trends, since the former is monotonically increasing while the latter exhibits a maximum in the middle of the decade and then declines markedly in the most recent years. Women are more affected than men, since they are more exposed to unemployment and to temporary and part-time jobs.

In this chapter, we focus on the nature of the labour contract that regulates the relationship between employers and employees. In Spain and France, essentially two types of labour contract are used to define the relationships between the employers and the employees: fixed-term and open-ended labour contracts. We analyse the reactions to the establishment of these two types of contract in the two countries. As we shall show, in Spain, public governmental measures were taken in 1997 in order to react to the negative consequences of the fixed term contracts. In France, the co-contracting private parties – the employers and the workers – react to the incentive structure of the contracts

Table 8.1 *Labour macroeconomic variables in selected EU countries*

	Both genders					Females					Males				
	EU-15	E	F	NL	UK	EU-15	E	F	NL	UK	EU-15	E	F	NL	UK
Temporary employees as percentage of the total employees															
1992	10.7*	33.7	10.4	9.7	5.4	11.9*	39.1	12.1	13.8	6.6	9.8*	30.7	9.0	6.9	4.3
1996	11.7	33.6	12.5	12.0	6.9	12.6	36.7	12.7	15.9	8.1	11.0	31.8	11.4	9.1	5.9
2000	13.4	32.1	15.0	14.0	6.7	14.5	34.5	15.7	17.2	7.7	12.6	30.5	14.3	11.5	5.9
Part-time employment as percentage of total employment															
1992	14.7*	5.0	12.9	34.2	23.8	29.6*	12.3	24.6	63.0	43.9	3.7*	1.4	3.5	14.9	5.7
1996	17.0	7.6	16.2	38.4	25.0	32.2	16.5	30.0	68.4	44.2	5.2	2.6	5.4	16.7	7.5
2000	18.0	8.2	16.9	41.2	24.9	33.7	17.2	31.0	70.6	44.5	6.3	2.9	5.4	19.3	9.0
Unemployment rate															
1992	9.2*	17.7	10.2	5.6	9.7	11.1*	25.4	12.9	7.8	7.3	7.9*	13.5	8.1	4.0	11.6
1996	10.9	22.2	12.4	6.4	8.2	12.4	29.5	14.5	8.1	6.3	9.8	17.7	10.6	5.2	9.7
2000	8.4	14.1	10.3	2.7	5.5	9.9	20.5	12.3	3.5	4.9	7.3	9.2	8.6	2.2	6.2
Proportion of long-term unemployment (≥12 months) to all unemployment															
1992	40.9*	43.9	34.2	42.4	35.4	41.8*	52.6	36.3	40.0	26.6	39.9*	34.7	31.7	45.6	39.6
1996	47.7	52.8	38.0	45.0	39.8	49.7	59.5	39.6	41.8	28.0	45.8	45.8	36.1	49.1	45.8
2000	45.2	42.4	39.6	32.7	28.0	46.3	48.6	40.8	33.4	19.0	44.2	36.6	38.3	31.7	33.7

Note: *EU-12; Country codes: E Spain; F France; NL Netherlands; UK United Kingdom.

Source: EUROSTAT, Labour Force Survey (1993, 1997, 2001). Tables 14, 54, 64, 92 and 98 for 1992 and 1996; tables 28, 34, 53 and 57 for 2000.

by adjusting their behaviour. By focussing on labour contracts we provide a complementary topic to human capital in explanation of both labour market performance as a whole and individual labour trajectories. Given the labour market precariousness of French and Spanish youths, we will pay special attention to the influence of education on the probability of reaching permanent employment. This is a major life event for young people because it determines their economic independence, encourages their decisions relating to family formation and thus marks their access to adulthood. In other words, the labour stability of young people influences the size and quality of the forthcoming generation, which becomes a central issue since one can observe a general trend to delay these life cycle events.[3] In what follows, we present an analysis of the effects of the legal framework on the type of contracts defining the employment relation in Spain and on the quality of the employment relation in France. We first present the Spanish case, reporting the results obtained by Cañada Vicinay (2002a).[4] We then turn to the analysis of the French case using Pénard et al.'s (1999) results. We conclude by drawing some policy indications.

2.   THE SPANISH STORY

2.1   An Overview

Ever since its initiation two decades ago, Spanish labour market reform has been focussed on the regulation of labour contracts. The central objective was to gain flexibility as a necessary condition to stimulate the flow of job creation. The basic instrument was to reduce the price of work via non-wage costs. Following the French experience in 1979, the 1984 reform introduced the non-causal fixed-term contract as a regulation at the margin (Bentolila and Dolado, 1994). The reform had no effect on either the job protection and bargaining power of insiders or unemployment benefits. The evolution of economic indicators during the late 1980s created an image of great success for this reform since the average yearly GDP growth rate increased from 1.15 per cent in 1980–85 to 4.4 per cent in 1985–90. At the same time, the temporary worker rate grew from around 10 per cent in the early 1980s, to 17 per cent in 1987 and reached 29 per cent in 1990. However, this image quickly vanished with economic recession in the early 1990s when the situation was particularly alarming, since the proportion of temporary workers was over 33 per cent (37 per cent for women; 60 per cent for those under the age of 30) and the unemployment rate was over 23 per cent (women 30 per cent, men 19 per cent; 44 per cent and 27 per cent below the age of 30 respectively). The general strikes of December 1988, May 1992 and January 1994 resulted in some partial institutional reforms in 1994[5] and paved the way for reforms of open ended contracts (OEC henceforth) and voluntary part-time jobs (P-TJ henceforth) which occurred in the second quarter of 1997 (2Q1997) and the fourth quarter of 1998 (4Q1998) respectively. The former promoted company demand for open-ended contracts by reducing both hiring costs (that is, social contributions) and firing costs in its monetary (severance pay) and non-monetary (dismissal procedure) components. The latter encouraged the workers' supply side through the participation of women and young people by increasing their interest for more protected part-time jobs.

Job stability is a serious problem in Spain which concerns employees and employers as much as policy makers and analysts. Diverse criticisms of the 1984 reform have addressed issues such as the negative influence of non-causal fixed term contracts on segmentation, wage formation and productivity (Bentolila and Dolado, 1993 and 1994, Bentolila and Saint Paul, 1992, Jimeno and Toharia, 1993, Segura et al., 1992). Recent papers by Alba-Ramirez (1998a, b) and Petrongolo and Güell-Rotlan (1999) focus on transitions to permanent employment during the period 2Q1987–2Q1996 which cover a full cycle of the Spanish economy. However, there is a lack of research into the effects of the legal changes that occurred in the late 1990s. Dolado et al. (2002) do present a panel study of the evolution of the proportion of FTC between 1987 and 2000 for 17 sectors and 17 regions with a CES function for OEC and FTC. These authors do not find a significant effect of the OEC reform in 1997 and verify that the fraction of temporary jobs is positively correlated with the weight of young workers and public employment between 1998 and 2000.[6]

It would therefore seem desirable to carry out a microanalysis in order to assess to what extent the reforms of 1997 and 1998 have influenced the relevant changes in the structure of the labour market. To this end we will focus on the evolution of transitions to permanent employment during the period from 2Q1994 to 1Q2001. This period covers the recent expansive phase of the Spanish business cycle (from the recovery in 1994 to the slowdown in 2000) and presents an homogeneous legal framework which enables us to isolate the effects of these reforms. As a subsidiary issue we will also look at the evolution of the part-time jobs inflow during the same period.

2.2 Data and Methods

As in Alba-Ramirez (1998a, b) and Petrongolo and Güel-Rotlan (1999) we use the panel files of the Spanish Labour Force Survey (EPA enlazada) in which a sixth of the sample (some 60 000 households) updates every quarter. This enables us to follow the trajectory of an individual for up to six quarters. The questionnaire focusses on the situation at the moment in time that the survey is carried out with respect to the educational, training and labour characteristics of the individual. We restrict the sample to individuals who were surveyed for all six quarters. Therefore, we exclude individuals who have changed address or abandoned the initial household during the 18 months of the observation period. The analysed calendar period from 2Q1994 to 1Q2001 allows a full monitoring of 23 consecutive EPA cohorts (from 2Q1994–3Q1995 to 4Q1999–1Q2001) and covers 26 consecutive calendar quarters of transition time (from 3Q1994 to 1Q2001). Furthermore we will control some variables related to the economic situation such as the quarterly evolution of the annual growth of real GDP and real wages, and employment firms' expectations.

Given that our purpose is to evaluate the evolution of inflows into open ended contracts (OEC) and part-time jobs (P-TJ) in relation to legal changes, we will use a parametric duration model in which the transitions to both OEC and P-TJ receive a competing risk treatment under the hypothesis of independence of alternative destinations.[7] We estimate an accelerated event time model, $\log t = \beta_z Z + \omega$, where ω is a random error variable of zero mean with a distribution not depending on Z (see Cox and Oakes, 1984). Here we fit a Weibull distribution[8] whose cumulated probability function of achieved transitions $F(t)$ at any moment t of the process is (for instance, $F(12)$ at 12 months, see Figure 8.1 below):

$$F(t)=1 - \exp(- (\exp(- \beta_0 - \beta_z Z)\, t)^{1/\alpha}) \qquad (8.1)$$

being $F(0)=0$ and $F(T)=1$ at the start and end of the process. The parameter α determines the time dependency of the hazard function through the process (positive if $\alpha<1$ and vice versa); positive (negative) β coefficients correspond with variables which reduce (increase) the hazard function and cumulated transitions at any moment t of the process, or alternatively increase (reduce) the duration of the current spell.

2.3 Assessing the Efficiency of the Reforms of 1997 and 1998

The four panels in Figure 8.1 explore the quarterly evolution of transitions to OEC and P-TJ destinations from different origins. The statistic plotted is $F(12)$ which evaluates the cumulated transitions after the first 12 months of the process. The upward, horizontal and downward profiles refer respectively to increasing trends, stability or decreasing trends. A sensitive effect of a reform will be expressed by a change of profiles after the reform: from bottom to top if the reform increases the cumulated transitions, and vice versa. Each profile has been estimated separately, controlling by 26 calendar quarters (from 3Q1994 to 1Q2001) dummy variables of eventual time of transition.

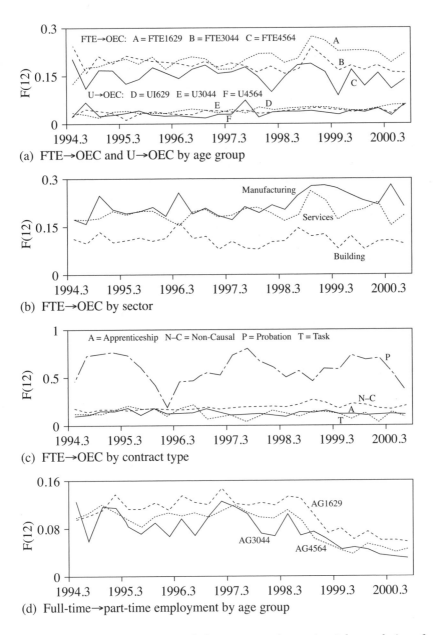

Figure 8.1   Inflow into open-ended contracts and part-time jobs: evolution of transitions during the first 12 months, F(12)

Panel A of Figure 8.1 focuses on transitions from fixed term contracts (FTC) and unemployment (U) to OEC by age groups. As expected from the expansive phase, we observe a (weak) upward trend in all the cases, except for the transitions from FTC for senior workers. FTC→OEC flows show a negative effect of age that is increasing after 1997: young (old) fixed term workers are more (less) likely to achieve permanent employment. The comparative analysis shows that the probability of reaching an OEC during the first year of the current spell is four times higher from FTC than from U (18 per cent vs. 4.4 per cent at sample means).[9]

The differentiation by sectors in Panel B demonstrates that the transitions are high and increase in sectors with no specific task contracts (passing from 20.3 per cent b–2Q1997 to 23.5 per cent a–2Q1997 in manufacturing and from 18.9 per cent to 20.2 per cent in the service sector) while there is a decrease in the building industry where specific task contracts dominate. The analysis by type of contract in Panel C shows a weak upward and continuous profile for non-causal fixed-term contracts and a weak downward trend for apprenticeship and specific task contracts. Notice the high performance of probation period contracts since almost two-thirds of them end up in OEC during the first year. The continuity of profiles in Panels A, B and C does not reveal any important effects of the 2Q1997 reform, which lower the price of new permanent employment among the two extreme age groups. This result suggests a corridor effect of a dual labour market: a reduction in the cost of hiring and firing is not enough to encourage new hiring.[10] Nevertheless the evolution of different profiles suggests the desirability of examining the influence of the business cycle.

Panel D looks at the transitions from full-time to part-time work by age groups. Here things are quite different, since all the profiles exhibit a discontinuity at the point of the reform 4Q1998, in such a way that the transitions to P-TJ decrease by more than a half after the date of the reform. Separate estimates for women and men exhibit a similar pattern for each age group, with the influence of the reform being greater for women who were the most important objective. This is an apparent surprise, since this reform was addressed at improving the attractiveness of P-TJs from the workers' perspective by increasing rights and protection in terms of the common eventualities (for example industrial accident, occupational disease, unemployment and retirement).[11] Consequently, the reason for the failure of the P-TJ reform must be connected to the fact that the increasing protection was coupled with increasing social contributions, and hence part-time jobs became less attractive for employers.

Summarizing, we have observed an asymmetrical effect of labour reforms on company hiring policies. The contracting activity that becomes more expensive is adversely affected, while there is no effect of the opposite measures to reduce the labour costs of OEC. As mentioned above, these results suggest that the corridor effect (1) works in the OEC equilibrium and (2) does not work in the P-TJ equilibrium. In the first case, the 2Q1997 reform tends to reduce wages but does not move the OEC level. In the second case, the equilibrium is outside the corridor area and the 4Q1998 reform tends to increase wages and reduce part-time employment.

These results would indicate that a more in-depth study of the influence of the 2Q1997 and 4Q1998 reforms be carried out. In order to connect the Spanish and French cases, we will concentrate here on the transitions to OEC from FTC and from short-term and long-term unemployment of young people aged 16–29. The econometric estimations and the definition of variables are presented in Table 8A.1 of the Appendix. We verify an important effect of the business cycle in such a way that the growth rate of real GDP increases the transitions to permanent employment in all the cases.[12] Furthermore, the growth rate of real wages accelerates the transitions from unemployment and impedes those from temporary employment. This is an important finding that verifies the unemployment pressure on deflating wages. The variation between the present and the next quarter of the employment expectations of employers captures the fluctuations of vacancies and shows that employers are on average right about the future and undertake the changes they forecast.

Concerning the human capital point of view, we observe a positive effect of education on the conversion of temporary contracts on a permanent basis (Petrongolo and Güell-Rotlan, 1999) and on reaching a permanent job from long-term unemployment. (Alba-Ramirez, 1998a). As expected, the odds of reaching a regular job increase with age and with the elapsed time on the current spell (positive time dependency of hazard rate) for temporary workers and the short-term unemployed, while there is no effect for long-term unemployed who are mainly seeking their first job. Notice that participating in training programmes reflects a negative probability on access to an OEC in all the cases. Contrary to the human capital framework, this result reveals the unsuitable system of training in Spain which is in urgent need of a major reform.

Furthermore, the active seeking for an OEC causes the desired effects, which suggests that, in spite of the alarming nature of the situation, FTC workers can profit from a co-operative behaviour as in the Pénard et al. (1999) model. The unskilled and skilled workers' estimates reflect that OEC is less likely for blue collar than for white collar workers, which corresponds to the 'tertiarization' process of the Spanish economy. The negative incidence of the public sector is in agreement with Dolado, et al. (2002) in such a way that when splitting this variable by periods (before and after 2Q1997) one verifies the change of hiring policy in the public sector, where the use of FTC intensifies after the reform. Concerning the transitions from unemployment, the negative relationship between OEC inflow and willingness to accept a job seems to be counterintuitive, since willingness is directly related to the reduction of the reservation wage.[13] This requires further analysis to establish the causal relationship. The coefficient of seeking first job (SFJ) captures the entry barrier by comparing the difficulties faced by new entrants with their coequals with previous labour experience.

2.4   Concluding Remarks

In this approach to establishing the effectiveness of partial reforms on improving the performance of the labour market, we have found an asymmetrical response depending on whether the measure reduces or increases labour costs. In fact, the 2Q1997 reform promoting a low cost permanent contract has had a positive although very limited influence. In contrast with this the 4Q1998 reform – that attempted to foster the labour market insertion of new entrants and women by means of part-time jobs with full rights – has not encouraged the commitment of employers since it involves a substantial increase in their costs in terms of social contributions. As expected, we find a positive influence of human capital variables with the exception of specific skills learned through adult education courses, since the individuals trained in such programmes are less likely to reach permanent employment. The analysis of the influence of the business cycle shows a positive effect of growth rate GDP in all the cases, and thus permanent employment inflows are cumulative from alternative origins. In contrast, the effect of growth rate of wages is negative from temporary work and positive from short-term and long-term unemployment, which verifies the unemployment pressure on deflating wages growth.

3.   THE QUALITY OF THE EMPLOYMENT RELATIONSHIP: THE CASE OF FRANCE

This section evaluates the implications of fixed-term contracts (FTCs), in comparison to open-ended contracts (OECs), on the quality of the employer–employee relationship. In France, where FTCs have become increasingly common in the last ten years, employers can mitigate the effects of legally imposed firing regulations by using fixed short-term contracts instead of contracts of open and indefinite duration. We shall look at the issue of the quality of the employment relationship from a theoretical and an empirical perspective.

3.1   The Employment Relationship as a Repeated Game

In any employment relationship the employer and the worker need to make decisions concerning their level of effort, their commitment to the relationship, and their investment in training. These repeated decisions, which impact on the conditions and the quality of the work, cannot be fully delineated *ex ante* in the labour contract. Only commitments which can be verified by a third party and which are enforceable in a court of law can be formalized in a contract and establish each party's commitment to issues like minimal levels of effort, working conditions, and training. Either party can have recourse to the courts of law to enforce these minimal expectations. However, the intensity of effort or the quality of the training cannot be fixed in a contract. For this reason there is some interest in modelling the employment relationship as a repeated, non-cooperative game in which, for each period, the worker chooses his or her level of effort and the employer sets the working conditions and the level of training, under constraint of respecting the minima set out in the legal contract. The question which immediately arises is: can the employer and the employee use the repeated nature of their relationship to obtain commitments to a greater level and quality of effort and investment?

Clearly, when there is no repetition, co-operation is impossible. If each party expects that the other will supply no effort, then mistrust will prevail and any hope for co-operation disappears. If the relationship is repeated, however, opportunistic behaviour can be deterred by the threat of retaliation in subsequent periods.[14] The two parties might agree on co-operative strategies which dictate the level of effort and investment expected from each and which provide for penalties in case these commitments are not respected. This is tantamount to an implicit contract between the employer and the worker. This contract is inherently self-enforceable, as the parties to the contract ensure that it is honoured. Each will co-operate as long as the benefits corresponding to opportunistic behaviour are less than the costs associated with the penalties for cheating. We find these notions of self-enforcing implicit contracts and repeated games in recent efficiency-wage models.[15]

The existence of co-operation and of an efficiency wage depends upon many factors related to the characteristics of the wage, the job and conditions in the labour market. One factor that is rarely accounted for in efficiency–wage models is the cost of terminating a contract. This has a significant impact on the severity and the credibility of the sanctions that can be used against a party engaging in opportunistic behaviour. For example, the worst penalty that an employer can impose on a worker is to not renew the contract. However, this threat is only credible if the costs of terminating the contract and of recruiting and training a new employee are not too high. Pénard et al. (1999) developed a model of employer– employee co-operation allowing a precise evaluation of the costs of breaking the employment contract. This model demonstrates that the possibilities for co-operation between employer and employee with a given seniority increase with the level of severance benefits that would be payable if the contract were terminated at the end of the period. This result is of interest in the framework of the French labour market due to its institutional peculiarities.

3.2 The Impact of FTCs and OECs on Co-operation

After a trial period of variable length,[16] the employer needs 'just cause' (labour law) in order to terminate an OEC, especially when the firing is attributed to the character of the worker.[17] Furthermore, the employer must pay severance benefits to the employee if the layoff occurs after at least two years of uninterrupted service with the employer (regardless of the type of contract), except in the case of serious misconduct by the employee. Because of these institutional arrangements, it is reasonable to state that terminating an OEC represents a supplementary cost to the employer compared to not rolling over an FTC into an OEC. Employers' threats to terminate OECs are thus less credible than those to not renew FTCs.

An employee, on the other hand, can leave a job governed by an OEC by simply giving notice. The credibility of such a threat, presented in response to opportunistic behaviour by the employer, relies on the same conditions as the threat to not accept an OEC at the end of an FTC. Though the direct costs of leaving an OEC are low for the worker, the opportunity costs (indirect costs) remain substantial in periods of high unemployment.

It is then possible to derive a second testable proposition. This says that in a low-skill employment relationship, the possibilities for co-operation are greater and the wages higher during the initial periods if the hiring occurs under an OEC rather than under a FTC. According to this proposition, the expected wage profile for hiring directly under an OEC is, on average, higher for two reasons: (1) co-operation is more likely under an OEC than under an FTC; and (2) the employer is committed to paying a co-operative wage, or an efficiency wage, which is higher under an OEC than an FTC. If we are studying young workers with few skills employed under an OEC, we may expect wage rates to vary with the initial contract, all other things being equal. Youths initially hired under an FTC will reduce their wage expectations in order to see their contract transformed into an OEC and to counter the risk of being the victim of opportunistic behaviour by their employers. These qualitative predictions concerning the profile of wages[18] among young employees are tested in the following section.

3.3 Empirical Estimation

Our data are taken from the CEREQ[19] survey *Devenir Professionel des Jeunes Sortis de l'Enseignement Secondaire Général ou Technique ou de l'Apprentissage en 1989.* This survey covers 13 100 individuals who finished school in 1989, with a level of education strictly lower than the French baccalauréat.[20] These data are augmented with information from the *Atlas des Zones d'Emploi de l'INSEE*, which provides a series of 81 economic indicators for 348 geographic employment zones in France. These indicators include demographics, production facilities, employment, the initial training system and the labour market characteristics of each zone. This information enables us to characterize the hiring firm's local environment. In this study we focus on a sample of 4602 individuals under OECs at the time of the survey. Some 1000 of them were initially hired under FTCs, while 3602 went directly into OECs. In the jobs occupied at the time of the survey, mean wages are quite similar across individuals regardless of the nature of the hiring contract. Econometric estimation will allow us to test whether, in keeping with our theoretical predictions, the wages of youths who followed the FTC–OEC trajectory are lower than those of individuals hired directly into OECs, after controlling for characteristics specific to the individuals, the jobs, and the local environment.

Different econometric specifications have been used, and the possibility that the hiring contract type introduces a selectivity bias has been carefully discussed.[21] Column 1 in Table 8.2 (below) presents the results of the standard specification of the wage equation[22] from which the variable for the type of hiring contract is excluded. The logarithm of the wage at the time of the survey is regressed on a set of individual characteristics: age, sex, marital status, the presence of children, the level of qualification[23] and the educational history (age at which primary school is completed, grade-repeating in secondary school). Variables characterizing the job are also introduced: the amount of training received,[24] seniority, seniority squared, an index for part-time work and the size and sector of activity of the firm. We also account for the potential impact of the length of unemployment spells preceding the job, earlier episodes of job training and the number of jobs held since leaving school. Finally, we account for factors relevant to the local environment: the unemployment rate among the active population, the rate of firm creation, school attendance among 16–19-year-olds, the mean wage in the employment zone, the proportion of the population of adult graduates having a vocational diploma of CAP or BEP type, and the evolution of this ratio between 1982 and 1990. This first specification is estimated to generate a benchmark for comparisons.

Table 8.2 shows the estimated coefficient and, in parenthesis, the Student's *t*. For each specification the following control variables have been added: individual characteristics (18 variables); local environmental variables (6); and characteristics of the job occupied at the time of the survey (22).

The specification in column 2 includes the nature of the hiring contract

Table 8.2   Log of the wage at the time of the survey

	(1)	(2)	Specification (3)	(4)
Constant	3.112 (19.837)	3.121 (19.887)	3.043 (19.082)	3.050 (19.177)
FTC	–	*0.012 (1.661)*	– 0.074 (2.249)	–0.118 (3.144)
Nbchg	–	–	–	0.051 (5.219
Nbchg × FTC	–	–	–	*–0.026 (1.719)*
Lambda	–	–	0.052 (2.666)	0.064 (3.261)
R²	0.20	0.21	0.21	0.21

Note: Significant at the 5% level, *significant at the 10% level.*

(denoted FTC). We see in specification (2) that being hired under an FTC has an effect on the wage which is positive and statistically significant at the 10 per cent level. This initial result contradicts our theoretical predictions. Estimates from specification (3) indicate that this coefficient is biased. Once the correction for selectivity bias has been made, the estimated coefficient of the variable FTC does, in fact, become negative and significant at the 5 per cent level. For given seniority, and all other things being equal, individuals initially hired under FTCs earn 7.4 per cent less than those hired directly into OECs. The significance (at 5 per cent) of the correction factor lambda confirms the existence of a selectivity bias in interpreting the effect of hiring contract on earnings. The positive lambda term has the following interpretation: the unobserved characteristics that positively affect the probability of being hired also contribute to a higher wage. When taking these factors into account, being hired under an FTC contract contributes to lower earnings.

Finally, it appears in specification (4) that the greater the number of changes of contract, of position, of duties, or of firm, described by the variable *nbchg*, the higher the wage. However, this effect is weaker for the FTC–OEC trajectory than for the simple *OEC* path (the composite variable *nbchg × FTC* is significantly negative at the 10 per cent level). This result reveals that the rollover of an FTC into an OEC eventually leads to a change of position within the firm and frequently, though not always, to a substantial pay raise. This increase is, nonetheless, less than in the case of a youth hired directly into an OEC initially. In this latter case, the change in position is more likely to coincide with a raise. Introducing these two variables causes the coefficient for the type of contract to be lower than in specification (3). The wage is now 10.9 per cent lower for the FTC–OEC trajectory than for the simple OEC course.

3.4   Concluding Remarks

Thus, the allocation of the benefits from co-operation appears somewhat more favourable to workers under an OEC. Under FTCs, workers reduce their wage claims in order to have their contract transformed into OECs. After this transfer, the balance of credible threats shifts in favour of the worker, resulting in an increase in wages. Nonetheless, for given seniority, wages remain lower among those having begun with an FTC. The wage profiles thus appear quite different, depending on whether the hiring occurred under an FTC or an OEC. These results support the notion that FTCs tend to create employment relationships under which employees and employers have less incentive to realize investments and efforts than under OECs.

4. CONCLUSION

The conclusions we can draw from these studies are twofold. On one hand, it appears that the employers consider the legal framework to exploit the opportunity it offers in their own interest. This is not new, but it has to be taken in consideration when rules are established that regulate labour markets. The mere difference in rules creates a possibility which is exploited when possible. On the other hand, the Spanish example in the 1990s shows that the inflow into permanent contracts is driven more by the individual human capital endowment and business cycle variables than by legal changes. For France, even if the FTC facilitates integration into the labour market, and sometimes provides a matching process leading to an OEC, it is also liable to create inefficient working conditions in which employers and employees are insufficiently committed. These results lead us to question the usefulness of government programmes aimed at integrating youths into the workforce (youth-employment contracts) that are generally based on FTCs. The limited duration of these contracts creates the risk of opportunistic behaviour by employers. To avoid this, government employment programmes should account for concerns relating to employers' levels of commitment to the employment relationship. Disincentives – such as the limited duration of the contract, and the ease with which the employment relationship can be terminated at the end of the contract – may be compensated for by an obligation to provide training, as in training-oriented contracts for example.

APPENDIX

Weibull Estimates of the Probability of Reaching an Open-Ended Contract in Spain 2Q1994–1Q2001

Table 8A.1 contains the competing risk estimations of transitions to OEC from FTE, short-term and long-term unemployment for young people aged 16–29. The exogenous variables in this table

Table 8A.1   Transitions to open-ended contract from:

	A) Fixed-term contract: Weibull est.		sample charac.		B) Short-term unemployment: Weibull est.		Sample charac.		C) Long-term unemployment: Weibull est.		sample charac.	
	β	Chi2	Means	std err.	β	Chi2	Means	std err.	β	Chi2	means	std err
2Q94–1Q95	-0.24	7.30	0.08		1.67	49.12	0.09		3.95	85.06	0.14	
2Q95–1Q96	-0.40	24.77	0.14		1.34	40.54	0.15		2.95	67.24	0.19	
2Q96–1Q97	-0.21	10.40	0.15		1.10	36.90	0.15		1.83	35.27	0.17	
2Q97–1Q98			0.15				0.15				0.15	
2Q98–1Q99	-0.12	4.72	0.15		-0.56	23.20	0.15		-0.78	16.73	0.13	
2Q99–1Q00	-0.01	0.06	0.16		-0.35	10.58	0.15		-0.39	3.92	0.12	
2Q00–1Q01	-0.14	4.85	0.16		-0.77	27.37	0.16		-0.79	8.99	0.10	
Female	-0.01	0.20	0.42		-0.07	1.20	0.47		-0.15	1.78	0.58	
Married	0.03	0.33	0.08		0.17	3.20	0.10		0.26	2.31	0.11	
Univ.	-0.11	3.23	0.16		0.01	0.00	0.20		-0.69	10.51	0.20	
Up. second	-0.04	0.69	0.54		0.04	0.22	0.53		-0.36	3.98	0.51	
Vocational	-0.18	11.01	0.19		0.06	0.24	0.16		-0.40	3.38	0.17	
AG1619	0.32	24.25	0.12		0.40	13.79	0.18		-0.47	3.89	0.11	
AG2024	0.00	0.02	0.47		0.07	1.14	0.48		-0.47	18.66	0.45	
Training	0.15	9.23	0.14		0.50	37.71	0.24		0.60	17.72	0.27	
BC-Sk	0.08	3.83	0.29		0.11	1.64	0.17		0.08	0.20	0.11	
BC-Usk	0.23	28.72	0.24		0.15	3.24	0.21		0.20	1.29	0.15	
Seek for PE	-0.21	20.36	0.88									
Fsize>50	-0.11	10.32	0.22									
Public	0.66	113.16	0.08									
SFJ					0.42	28.68	0.31		0.36	8.19	0.49	
RUB					0.16	1.82	0.05		-0.76	10.68	0.06	
N-RUB					0.03	0.26	0.29		0.02	0.02	0.63	
Accept					0.15	56.17	2.22	1.25	0.24	46.76	2.32	1.25
AG-GDP	-0.11	11.78	3.59	0.68	-0.32	20.03	3.59	0.68	-0.12	0.96	3.53	0.71
AG-Wage	0.09	23.59	3.20	0.89	-0.95	76.09	3.04	0.85	-1.58	75.25	3.20	0.89
VE-Exp	-0.04	7.32	0.00	0.79	-0.14	12.04	0.01	0.61	-0.14	3.47	-0.02	0.59
INTERCPT	4.46	653.8			7.23	178.70			11.04	141.96		
Scale α	0.90				0.72				1.03			
α Std err.	0.01				0.02				0.04			
Llk int only	-15303.4				-3117.4				-2185.1			
Llk int+cov	-15127.4				-2960.1				-2040.8			
Nc	5496				790				502			
Rc	55626				24426				18597			

are grouped according to: (1) Calendar time dummies – seven year variables relating the age in which the eventual transition took place; (2) Personal characteristics – such as gender, marital status, achieved education level (upper secondary, vocational and university) and five-year age groups; (3) Individual characteristics related to the labour market – such as participating in training programmes, blue collar position by differentiating skilled (BC-Sk) and unskilled workers (BC-Usk). Furthermore, the transition FTE→OEC adds three dummies: the active seeking for an OEC from the current FTE (Seek for OEC); public vs. private sector (public); and the size of the firm that differentiates firms with 50 or more wage earners (FSize ≥ (50). The additional variables for flows from unemployment concern searching for first job (SFJ), the registration at the National Agency of Employment, receiving and not receiving unemployment benefits (RUB and N-RUB), and an aggregate variable for willingness to accept a job that involves change of residence, change of job, reduction of wage and reduction of professional category (accept); (4) Business cycle indicators – such as the annual growth rates of real GDP (AG-GDP) and real wages (AG-Wage) and the variation of quarterly employment expectations of employers (VE-Exp). These covariates receive a time-varying variable treatment.

NOTES

1. See for instance Nickell (1997) and Siebert (1997). Cross-country studies carried out by the OECD in 1997, 1998 and 1999 respectively did not support the hypothesis of the damaging effects on labour performance of rigidities in collective bargaining, minimum wages (see also Dolado et al., 1996), and employment protection.
2. As computed by OECD, quoted by Nickell (1997).
3. For instance, Spain is an extreme case in such a way that in the year 2000 the age of access to marriage was 28.7 years for women and 30.95 years for men, while these figures were respectively 23.7 and 26.4 in the year 1978 (see Cañada-Vicinay 2002b).
4. We will also refer to Petrongolo and Güell-Rotlan (1999) which was also realized in the framework of this study.
5. For instance, the decentralization of the INEM (Government Employment Agency), the relaxation of Government supervision of bargaining process, the introduction of economic causes for firing, and the regulation of temporary work agencies. For details see Sebastian (1994), Jimeno (1996) and Bentolila and Jimeno (2002)
6. In fact, authors observe a change on hiring in the public sector after the reform of 1997 where temporary jobs are significantly increasing while declining in the private sector.
7. In fact, this is a separate study of the reforms of 1997 and 1998. In the former case we estimate the flux from unemployment and FTC to OEC (with no differentiation between full-time and part-time jobs) as an independent destination of alternative transitions (that is, from FTC to OEC, Unemployment and out of the market). In the latter case we focus on inflows to PT-J independently of the OEC or FTC nature of the contract. A more detailed analysis requires the merging of both the nature and time intensity dimensions of the contract as well as adding the desired or involuntary PT-J. We will focus on these aspects in future issues.
8. A non-parametric approach should be suitable to identify the time dependence of a particular cohort and its evolution across consecutive cohorts. See Petrongolo and Güell-Rotlan for such a specification.
9. As an alternative measure, direct calculus by Segura et al. (1992, p. 106) has shown that 22 per cent of the total number of temporary workers in 2Q1987 had achieved a PE one year later. With the same method Alba-Ramirez (1998b) shows that the transitions from FTC to OEC declined to an average of 12 per cent in the period 1993–96.
10. The corridor effect works when the firm equilibrium is on the discontinuity (step) of marginal cost of labour. See Lindbeck and Snower (1989) for an insider–outsider version, and Saint Paul (1996) for an efficiency wages interpretation.
11. In fact, the number of workers looking for a P-TJ increased by 20 per cent after this reform.

12. Alba-Ramirez (1998b) found a positive effect of GDP growth on the transitions U→OEC using a multinomial logit model.
13. Worth mentioning here is the fact that the EPA computes four factors of willingness to accept a job involving a change of residence, a change of job, lower status and small wage for the category, which separate treatment with dummy variable always produces a negative effect and its treatment as a class variable (values 0–4 of affirmative responses) produce a monotonic negative effect.
14. For an introduction to repeated games, see Friedman (1986).
15. See for instance MacLeod and Malcomson (1998) and also Shapiro and Stiglitz (1984), which is the seminal article in this literature.
16. This may vary from several weeks to nearly six months, depending on the job. The greater the qualifications for the job, the longer the trial period may be. During this period, the employer may terminate the contract freely and without penalty.
17. However, loss of confidence can be invoked as a reason for terminating the employment contract. Thus, the existence of a poor relationship or of diverging opinions is sufficient to confer 'just cause' on the termination of employment. This possibility undermines the guarantees provided by the OEC contract.
18. We do not report the satisfaction results.
19. Centre d'Etudes et de REcherche sur les Qualifications.
20. The baccalauréat is a degree obtained after 12 years of schooling.
21. The selectivity problem occurs when observed and unobservable characteristics affecting the wage also impact on the nature of the hiring contract. The correction used is explained in the paper written for the contract (Pénard et al., 1999). The variables used to estimate the probability of initially being hired into an FTC include several sets of variables which are not included in the wage equation, namely duty in the firm (10 dummies), position in the firm (5 dummies), year of hiring (5 dummies). The complete list is available from the authors.
22. Experience and experience squared, usually included in wage equations, were found not to be significant in our model. This is explained by the strong correlation between the variables for experience, seniority and previous unemployment.
23. We distinguish 7 levels of qualification: (1) No diploma (leaving secondary school); (2) apprentice did not obtain the vocational diploma prepared; (3) vocational school leaver did not obtain the vocational diploma prepared; (4) apprentice obtained the vocational diploma prepared and was kept in the training firm for first job; (5) apprentice obtained the vocational diploma prepared and not kept in the training firm for first job,; (6) vocational school leaver obtained the vocational diploma prepared; (7) high school leaver did not obtain the baccalauréat.
24. This pertains to formal training given in the firm. Some 15 per cent of individuals hired under OECs and 8 per cent of those under FTCs receive some.

REFERENCES

Alba-Ramírez (1998a), 'Re-employment probabilities of young workers in Spain', *Investigacones Económicas*, **XXVI** (2), 201–24.
Alba-Ramírez, A. (1998b), 'How temporary is temporary employment in Spain?', *Journal of Labour Research*, **19** (4), 695–709.
Bentolila, S. and J. Dolado (1993), 'Fixed-Term Contracts and Wage Setting in Spanish Manufacturing Firms', *Banco de Espana Economic Bulletin*, January 0(0), 59–64.
Bentolila, S. and J. Dolado (1994), 'Labour flexibility and wages: lessons from Spain', *Economic Policy*, **18**, 53–99.
Bentolila, S. and F. Jimeno Juan (2002), 'La reforma de la negociación colectiva en España', Documento de Trabajo, 2002–03, FEDEA.

Bentolila, S. and G. Saint-Paul (1992), 'The macroeconomic impact of flexible labor contracts, with an application to Spain', *European Economic Review*, **36**, 1013–53.

Cañada Vicinay, J. (2002a), 'Is permanent employment an accessible aim for young people? Assessing the labour market reform in Spain 1997', XI AEDE meeting, Lisbon.

Cañada Vicinay, J. (2002b), 'Higher education, labour insertion and first marriage in Spain', SRHE Annual conference, Glasgow.

Cox, D.R. and D. Oakes (1984), The Analysis of Survival Data, Chapman & Hall, London.

Dolado, J., F. Kramarz, S. Machin, A. Manning, D. Margolis and C. Teulings (1996), 'The economic impact of minimum wages in Europe', *Economic Policy*, **23**, 53–99.

Dolado, Juan J., Garcia Serrano C. and Juan F. Jimeno (2002), 'Drawing Lessons from the Boom of Temporary Jobs in Spain', *The Economic Journal*, **112** (480), 270–95.

EUROSTAT (1993), *Labour Force Survey*, Luxembourg.

EUROSTAT (1997), *Labour Force Survey*, Luxembourg.

EUROSTAT (2001), *Labour Force Survey*, Luxembourg.

Friedman, J.W. (1986), *Game Theory with Applications to Economics*, Oxford University Press, Oxford.

Heckman, J.J. (1979), 'Sample selection bias as specification error', *Econometrica*, January, **47**, 153–61.

Jimeno, J. and L. Toharia (1993), 'The effects of fixed-term employment on wages. Theory and evidence from Spain', *Investigaciones Económicas*, **17** (3), 475–94.

Jimeno, J. (1996), 'Los efectos visibles de la reforma laboral de 1994', *Cuadernos de Información Económica*, **108**, 1–10.

Lindbeck, A. and D. Snower (1989), *The Insider–Outsider Theory of Employment and Unemployment*, The MIT Press, Cambridge, Massachusetts.

MacLeod, W.B. and J.M. Malcomson (1989), 'Implicit Contracts, Incentive Compatibility, and Involuntary Unemployment', *Econometrica*, **57**, 447–80.

Narendranathan, W. and M. Stewart (1993), 'Modelling probability of leaving unemployment: competing risk model with flexible base-line hazards', *Applied Statistics*, **42**, 63–83.

Nickell, S. (1997), 'Unemployment and labor market rigidities: Europe versus North America', *Journal of Economic Perspectives*, **11** (3), 55–74.

OECD (1994), The *OECD Jobs Study, Evidence and Explanations, Part II – The Adjustment Potential of the Labour Market*, Chapter 6, OECD, Paris.

OECD (1995), *The OECD Jobs Study*, Paris.

OECD (1997), 'Economic performance and the structure of collective bargaining', *Employment Outlook*, ch. 3, Paris.

OECD (1998), 'Making the most of the minimum: statutory minimum wages, employment and poverty', *Employment Outlook*, ch. 2, Paris.

OECD (1999), 'Employment protection and labour performance', *Employment Outlook*, ch. 2, Paris.

Pénard, T., M. Sollogoub and V. Ulrich (1999), 'Hiring contracts, wage and job satisfaction: theory and evidence on French low qualified youth', STT Working Paper, 30–99.

Petrongolo B. and M. Güell-Rotlan (1999), 'The transition of workers from temporary to permanent employment: the Spanish case', STT Working Paper, 07–99.

Saint Paul, G. (1999), 'Assessing the political viability of labor market reforms: the case of employment protection', *Review Federal Reserve Bank of St Louis*, **81** (3), 73–87.

Saint-Paul, G. (1996), 'Exploring the political economy of labour market institutions', *European Policy*, **23**, 265–315.

Sebastian, C. (1994), 'Un análisis de la reforma laboral', *Cuadernos de Información Económica*, **90**, 112–116.

Segura, J., F. Duran, L. Toharia and S. Bentolila (1992), *Análisis de la Contratación Temporal en España*, Ministerio de Trabajo y Seguridad Social, Madrid.

Shapiro, C. and J. Stiglitz (1984), 'Equilibrium unemployment as a worker discipline device', *American Economic Review*, **77**, 443–4.

Siebert, N. (1997), 'Labor market rigidities: at the root of unemployment in Europe', *Journal of Economic Perspectives*, **11** (3), 37–54.

9. Education, gender and labour mobility

Kjell G. Salvanes[1]

1. INTRODUCTION

Labour markets are in constant flux. Plants expand, contract and replace workers who quit or get fired. Many of the recent insights on the massive gross flows in the labour market stem from the recent literature on gross job flows (hiring due to expansion of plants and plant entry and firing due to a decline in incumbents and plant exit) and worker flows above job changes (churning or replacement of workers for a given number of jobs).[2] However, very little is known about what is behind the extensive aggregate flows, and the heterogeneity in employment practices is a particularly ill-treated issue. For instance, when both a high degree of hires and separations are observed at the same time, it could be due to hires of highly educated workers and fires of low-educated workers, hires of young workers and fires of old workers and so on, and not at all to churning of homogeneous workers. When assuming homogeneous workers, which is done in most of this literature, it is impossible to distinguish between these two types of employment policies.[3] Another observation emerging from this literature is that there is a large degree of plant-specific heterogeneity in turnover patterns in that expanding plants also fire workers and plants reducing employment also hire new workers to a large degree. Thus, whether the job flows and churning are two distinct processes or used interchangeably by firms, is also an open question.

In this chapter we first present the aggregate worker and job flows for Norway and compare the results to results for other European countries and the US. Then we study in detail the question of human resource management policies for heterogeneous workers. We use a panel data set for Norway for 1986–94 which matches workers and plants, a necessary data characteristic for the analysis of job and worker flows for heterogeneous workers.

The main focus of this chapter is to analyse worker and job flows by education level by separating workers in three levels of education. Distinguishing between education categories of workers allows analysis of whether high job creation/destruction rates and churning rates are due to job creation for highly educated workers and job destruction for low-educated workers, or whether hires and separations are high for all skill levels. Labour flows are then decomposed by age and gender, as well as the combination of these variables.

Next, we test whether job and churning processes are different for the three education groups of workers, that is, whether net employment changes at the plant level (job reallocation) are determined by the same factors as worker flows. In particular, we compare the role of the business cycle on job destruction and re-employment separations and examine whether the processes determining job and worker flows are different for the three types of workers.

2.   DEFINITIONS AND DATA SET

2.1   Definitions

When considering the turnover of heterogeneous workers at the plant level, using the gross flows approach has some advantages over the earlier literature on quits and fires. From this perspective, worker turnover, or flow, at the plant level consists of job flows due to changes in the size of plants, workers being dismissed, workers quitting, and workers being replaced by other workers for a given number of jobs. Worker flows ($WF_{e,j,t}$) of skill type j for plant e equal the sum of total hires of skill type j ($H_{e,j,t}$) and total separations of skill type j ($S_{e,j,t}$). Job flows ($JF_{e,j,t}$) at the plant level consist of net changes in the size, $L_{e,j,t}$, of the plant: $dL_{e,j,t} = L_{e,j,t} - L_{e,j,t-1}$. Since the net change in the size of the plant must equal the difference between hirings and separations, $dL_{e,j,t} = H_{e,j,t} - S_{e,j,t}$, worker flows can be written as consisting of worker flows due to changes in the size of the plant and to the replacement of existing jobs: $WF_{e,j,t} = JF_{e,j,t} + CF_{e,j,t}$.[4] The second term on the right-hand side is called churning or replacement flows in the literature, and consists of the sum of hires and separations (equal in equilibrium) due to replacement, $R_{e,j,t} + S^R{e,j,t}$. The change net change in the employment of worker type j for plant e from $t-1$ to t can then be decomposed as:[5]

$$dL_{e,j,t} = H_{e,j,t} - S_{e,j,t} = C_{e,j,t} + R_{e,j,t} - D_{e,j,t} - S^R_{e,j,t} \qquad (9.1)$$
$$= C_{e,j,t} - D_{e,j,t} + R_{e,j,t} - Q_{e,j,t} - F_{e,j,t}$$

From the first line of equation 9.1, we see that total hires, $H_{e,j,t}$, of worker type j for the firm can be decomposed into job creation, $C_{e,j,t}$, and re-employment hires, $R_{e,j,t}$. Total separations, $S_{e,j,t}$, can be decomposed into separations due to job destruction, $D_{e,j,t}$, and replacement separations, $S^R_{e,j,t}$.[6] From the second line of the equation we notice that replacement separations can further be split into quits, $Q_{e,j,t}$, and fires, $F_{e,j,t}$. However, the data set does not allow for a distinction between quits and fires, and thus in the econometric analysis we will use a business cycle indicator as a rough way to distinguish to test whether quits or fires dominate this part of separations.[7] The aggregate job and worker flow rates (sector, industry and so on) are given in the Appendix.

2.2 Data

The empirical analysis is based on different administrative register files from Statistics Norway. For manufacturing, the data was supplemented with economic information at the plant level from the 'Time Series Files' for manufacturing based on the annual censuses. (For a description of these data, see Halvorsen et al., 1991.) The data period covers 1986 to 1994. In these administrative registers, individuals are characterized by their personal identity code and plants with an identification code. This enables us to match persons to plants and to combine information on education, age, tenure and so on with employer characteristics at the individual level. Our database contains yearly information for all employed individuals over the age of 16 and all plants in Norway. The employers are defined at the plant level by an identification code dependent on geographical location and independent of ownership conditions. When merging in the data from the Time Series Files for the econometric analysis, the match by plant numbers is about 90 per cent.

In the administrative registers, individuals are characterized by their personal identity code and plants with an identification code. In the second quarter each year every worker is matched to the individual's main employer. The start date of this match is provided by the main employer, as is the stop date if it finishes within the year. For each worker, the following information is available for the period 1986 to 1995: hours worked per week, union membership, whether the worker holds multiple jobs, annual income, education and basic demographic background variables. Hours worked per week are only reported in three discrete categories; 4–19 hours, 20–29 hours and 30 hours or more. Education level is based on the normal duration of the education and includes only the highest attained, completed programmes of education. All courses of formal education exceeding 300 hours are registered. The following selection criteria were used when defining the estimation sample. Only workers with full-time jobs (30 hours or more per week) were included in the estimation, and workers who held more than one job per year were excluded. For the descriptive statistics all workers were used. See the Appendix for precise definitions of how the variables are defined and descriptive statistics of the data.

3.   WORKER AND JOB FLOWS IN NORWAY: DESCRIPTIVE STATISTICS

We first present descriptive statistics on the aggregate worker and job flows for both the financial and manufacturing sectors, in order to compare the mobility in the labour market in Norway to that in other countries. The financial sector was used in addition to the manufacturing sector in order to compare the standard results for manufacturing to a high skill service sector. We then, using the matched employer–employee properties of our data set, decompose the flows by worker categories. The worker and job flows are primarily decomposed into educational categories but also by gender and age groups. We also analyse the degree to which plants that are expanding also fire workers, and plants that are decreasing in size also hire new workers. This approach allows us to see whether the personnel policies of churning workers and changing the size of the plant by expanding or decreasing the size are used at the same time

3.1   General Worker and Job Flows in Norway

In order to make comparisons with studies from other countries, we first present the general results of worker flows for all education groups taken together. Table 9.1 provides the mean values of worker and job flows per year in the period from 1987 to 1994, by level of general education.

In manufacturing, the annual worker turnover rate (WFR) rate is 44 per cent on average over the data period, as can be seen from the upper panel of Table 9.1. The hiring rate (HR) and separation rate (SR) constitute on average 21 and 23 per cent of the worker turnover, respectively. Note that both hiring and separations are high in all years. The total churning rate (CFR) – the rate of workers changing positions in excess of job destruction or job creation – accounts for 21 per cent of worker turnover, and job reallocation rate (JRR), measuring employment changes due to plants expanding by job creation or declining by job destruction, is 24 per cent. The ratio between worker turnover due to worker churning and total worker reallocation (CHR/WFR) provides a measure of the importance of quits and dismissals in total worker flows. This ratio is 48 per cent on average, which means that the fraction of worker turnover due to churning is 48 per cent.

There are some differences between manufacturing and the service sector (banking and insurance) studied here. The level of worker turnover is about the same, 43 per cent for banking and insurance. However, worker reallocation due to churning is far less important than in manufacturing; 38 per cent is due to churning (CHR/WFR) as compared to 48 per cent in manufacturing. Although both job turnover and churning flows are at the same order of magnitude in

Table 9.1   Worker turnover by year and by general education level, 1987–94

Year	Manufacturing							Finance sector						
	HR	SR	WFR	JRR	CFR	JFR	ES	HR	SR	WFR	JRR	CFR	JFR	ES
1987	0.24	0.25	0.49	0.21	0.28	-0.01		0.25	0.21	0.46	0.23	0.23	0.04	
1988	0.23	0.27	0.50	0.25	0.24	-0.04		0.27	0.23	0.50	0.29	0.20	0.04	
1989	0.18	0.25	0.43	0.25	0.19	-0.07		0.18	0.24	0.41	0.26	0.16	-0.06	
1990	0.19	0.20	0.39	0.21	0.18	-0.01		0.25	0.28	0.54	0.38	0.16	-0.04	
1991	0.19	0.21	0.41	0.21	0.20	-0.04		0.20	0.22	0.42	0.28	0.15	-0.02	
1992	0.20	0.24	0.43	0.25	0.18	-0.04		0.19	0.20	0.39	0.32	0.15	-0.01	
1993	0.18	0.22	0.40	0.22	0.18	-0.03		0.13	0.21	0.35	0.21	0.14	-0.09	
1994	0.22	0.19	0.41	0.23	0.19	0.03		0.15	0.18	0.33	0.22	0.11	-0.03	
Mean	0.21	0.23	0.44	0.24	0.21	-0.02		0.21	0.22	0.43	0.27	0.16	-0.02	
Ed.	H	S	WF	JRR	CF	JFR		H	S	WF	JRR	CF	JFR	
Low	0.19	0.23	0.43	0.25	0.18	-0.04	0.58	0.19	0.23	0.42	0.31	0.11	-0.04	0.29
Med.	0.24	0.23	0.47	0.27	0.20	0.01	0.38	0.22	0.22	0.44	0.28	0.16	-0.01	0.61
High	0.31	0.25	0.56	0.40	0.16	0.05	0.04	0.27	0.25	0.51	0.36	0.15	0.02	0.10

Note: *These calculations are based on the total (not selected) samples. ES = employment share

both sectors, there are differences between banking and insurance both in the general characteristics and in the development of employment in this time period. One obvious difference is the level of human capital, which is one reason why we chose banking and insurance for comparison in the first place. From Table 9A.1 in the Appendix I note that the share of workers with medium and high education levels is on average 72 per cent in banking and insurance, while it is only 42 per cent in manufacturing. Hence, the difference in worker turnover rates between a service sector and manufacturing may indicate that both education and industry differences matter in explaining turnover.[8]

The results for Norway are comparable to studies undertaken for the US and Denmark. Burgess et al. (1995) present worker turnover rates for all sectors, including services and the public sector, for Maryland, based on quarterly data for the period 1985:3–1993:3. They state that their job reallocation rate or gross job flow rate is comparable to the results given in Davis and Haltiwanger (1992), which is 20.5 per cent. The result for Norway is 24 per cent (for manufacturing) based on this data set.[9] Given this, we can compare the importance of worker flow given the number of jobs, (CFR/WFR), between the two countries. Churning as a proportion of total worker flow is 46 per cent for the US and 48 per cent for Norway, implying processes of the same magnitude. Albæk and Sørensen's (1998) study of Danish manufacturing, based on annual data for the 1980–91 period, provides a worker reallocation rate of 56.5 per cent with a job flow rate of 23.5 per cent and a churning rate of 33 per cent. Hence, for Denmark the worker flow due to churning is higher than for Norway and the US, and the CFR/WFR ratio of 58 per cent for Denmark is also somewhat higher.

3.2　Worker Flow by General Education Level

The lower panel of Table 9.1 presents the average annual turnover figures for the two sectors by educational level. These figures allow us to analyse whether the high job creation/destruction and churning rates are due to high job creation for workers in one education class and job destruction for workers in another, such as replacing less educated workers with more highly educated ones, or whether hires and separations are high for all skill levels.

When comparing the mean values, it is clear that worker turnover in manufacturing is highest for the upper education group (56 per cent), while it is 43 per cent for the lower education group. The corresponding results for banking and insurance are 51 and 42 per cent. Most interesting is the finding that hires and separations – both due to job creation and destruction and due to replacement – take place simultaneously for all education levels.

Gross job turnover, that is, job creation and job destruction, drives the monotone increasing relationship between worker flows and education levels.

Calculating the ratio of job reallocation to the worker turnover rate (JRR/WF) shows that 66 per cent of worker flows are due to job turnover within the high education group and the corresponding number is 56 per cent for the low education group. Furthermore, the component of gross job turnover that drives higher worker turnover in the high education group, relative to the low education group, is not job destruction for less educated workers but rather new hires of highly educated workers, that is, gross job creation. This leads to a net job creation rate of 5 (2) per cent for the highly educated group and −4 (−4) per cent for the low educated group in the manufacturing (financial) sector. This pattern suggests that structural changes in labour demand across education levels due to, for instance, skill-biased technical change, may be important for explaining differences in worker turnover by education and employment policies at the plant level.[10]

When the pure churning flows are isolated by education, an interesting pattern evolves, as shown in Figure 9.1. The figure presents the key results from Table 9.1. Both means and standard deviations from annual variation are presented. The churning rate for medium educated workers is highest for both sectors, which is reflected in an inverse U-shape for churning with respect to education. For manufacturing, churning is also lower for highly educated than for less educated, causing an asymmetric curve. Churning in the high-skill financial sector is higher for less educated workers than for highly educated ones, with a slightly higher churning rate being observable for the medium educated. Both the inverse U-shape and the asymmetry of the curve may be rationalized by theory, which we come back to in Section 5.

3.3 Cohort and Gender Differences

If we consider the pattern of worker flows across cohorts of workers from Table 9.2, there is a strong impression of high turnover among young workers. Different explanations for this phenomenon are possible. Job shopping is obviously one explanation. Another possibility is that employers learn about workers by churning (see Margolis et al., 2002). Still another explanation for age differences in employee turnover could be age differences in employee protection legislation. In the Norwegian case this is plausible since seniority protects workers against layoffs (see Nilsen et al., 2003). An inverse relationship exists between the age of a worker and the churning rate, both in manufacturing and in the financial sector. For instance, in manufacturing the rate varies from 29 per cent for 25–34 year-old workers in 1986 to 6 per cent for workers aged 55–64. The high turnover among young workers and quite low turnover for older workers, who were also eligible for early retirement pensions in this period, shows that the labour market is in persistently high flux and that this situation is not merely an artefact of workers entering the labour market from

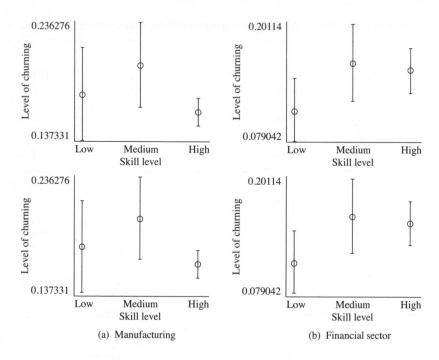

Figure 9.1   Churning rates for low, medium and high educated in Norway,
*   1987–94*

school and leaving the labour market through retirement. The implication of
the latter would be high separation rates for old workers, which is obviously
not confirmed by Table 9.2.

From the middle panel of Table 9.2, we note that women represent 26 per
cent of those employed in manufacturing, while women are a majority in the
financial sector, in that they constitute 56 per cent of all those employed.
Surprisingly, there is no difference in churning rates over gender in either
manufacturing or in banking and insurance. A slightly higher total worker flow
for women is found, 48 per cent for women compared to 42 per cent for men
in manufacturing, and 44 per cent for women versus 42 per cent for men in the
service sector. Both higher simultaneous gross job creation and job destruction
for women account for the fact that the difference does not lead to a gender
difference in net job creation.

A ready explanation of gender differences in turnover is that young women
take extended maternity leaves, which are counted here as churning separations. Were this true, it would lead to higher churning rates for young women
relative to men of comparable age. In the lower part of Table 9.2, the results

Table 9.2 Worker flows by cohort, gender, gender/cohort and gender/education for the manufacturing and financial sectors

	Manufacturing							Financial sector						
	HR	SR	WFR	JRR	CFR	JFR	ES	HR	SE	WFR	JRR	CFR	JFR	ES
Cohort														
1961–90	0.33	0.32	0.65	0.36	0.29	0.02		0.31	0.31	0.62	0.39	0.24	0.01	
1951–60	0.19	0.21	0.41	0.26	0.14	−0.02		0.21	0.22	0.43	0.29	0.14	−0.01	
1941–50	0.16	0.18	0.33	0.24	0.10	−0.02		0.17	0.18	0.36	0.28	0.08	−0.01	
1931–40	0.12	0.17	0.29	0.23	0.06	−0.04		0.15	0.17	0.33	0.28	0.04	−0.02	
Gender														
Female	0.23	0.25	0.48	0.28	0.20	−0.02	**0.26**	0.21	0.23	0.44	0.28	0.16	−0.02	**0.56**
Male	0.20	0.22	0.42	0.23	0.19	−0.02	**0.74**	0.20	0.22	0.42	0.28	0.14	−0.02	**0.44**
Gender/cohort														
Female														
1961–70	0.37	0.35	0.72	0.45	0.27	0.02	**0.07**	0.31	0.32	0.63	0.40	0.23	−0.01	**0.15**
1951–60	0.24	0.25	0.49	0.35	0.14	−0.01	**0.06**	0.21	0.23	0.44	0.31	0.12	−0.02	**0.17**
1941–50	0.18	0.20	0.38	0.30	0.08	−0.02	**0.06**	0.17	0.18	0.36	0.29	0.07	−0.01	**0.14**
1931–40	0.13	0.19	0.32	0.27	0.05	−0.06	**0.04**	0.15	0.17	0.32	0.29	0.03	−0.02	**0.07**

Table 9.2 continued

| | Manufacturing | | | | | | | | | Financial sector | | | | | |
	HR	SR	WFR	JRR	CFR	JFR	ES	HR	SE	WFR	JRR	CFR	JFR	ES
Male														
1961–70	0.34	0.31	0.65	0.38	0.27	0.03	**0.17**	0.35	0.31	0.66	0.46	0.20	0.04	**0.08**
1951–60	0.19	0.20	0.39	0.27	0.12	−0.01	**0.18**	0.22	0.22	0.44	0.32	0.12	0.00	**0.14**
1941–50	0.15	0.17	0.32	0.24	0.08	−0.02	**0.17**	0.18	0.19	0.37	0.29	0.08	−0.01	**0.13**
1931–40	0.12	0.16	0.28	0.23	0.05	−0.04	**0.12**	0.16	0.18	0.34	0.30	0.04	−0.02	**0.06**
Gender/Education														
Female														
Low	0.21	0.25	0.46	0.30	0.16	−0.04	0.18	0.19	0.23	0.42	0.32	0.10	−0.04	0.21
Medium	0.31	0.29	0.60	0.39	0.21	0.02	0.07	0.23	0.24	0.47	0.31	0.16	−0.01	0.34
High	0.45	0.31	0.76	0.60	0.16	0.14	0.01	0.32	0.26	0.58	0.45	0.13	0.06	0.02
Male														
Low	0.19	0.23	0.42	0.26	0.16	−0.04	0.40	0.20	0.23	0.43	0.34	0.09	−0.03	0.08
Medium	0.23	0.22	0.45	0.28	0.17	0.01	0.31	0.21	0.22	0.43	0.30	0.13	−0.01	0.27
High	0.29	0.24	0.53	0.39	0.14	0.05	0.03	0.26	0.25	0.51	0.36	0.15	0.01	0.08

Note: *These calculations are based on the total (not selected) samples

182

by cohort show that in both manufacturing and banking and insurance there are strong differences in churning over cohorts, but no differences over gender. Young women do have higher churning rates than other women, possibly due to extended maternity leaves. However, young men also have high churning rates. Among the many possible explanations for this phenomenon is that extended maternity leaves by young women induce more job shopping among young men, or that they incite men, especially well educated young men, to accept a different career profile. Such behaviour would even out the gender difference.

A decomposition of worker flows by gender and general education is presented in Table 9.2. Concentrating first on churning rates, the characteristic inverse U-shape over skills is present both for males and females, thus confirming the results in Section 3.2. For the financial sector, this particular churning pattern is found for women, while churning is an increasing function of education level for men. The latter result is an indication that young men with high education may be frequent quitters and job shoppers, an explanation which would be consistent with the idea that job shopping among well educated young men compensates for the high turnover rates among young women. Looking at gender differences in job turnover, we notice that gross job flows, and especially gross job creation, are particularly elevated for highly educated women in both sectors, leading to a much higher net job creation rate for highly educated women than for men. The net job creation rate is 14 per cent for highly educated women in manufacturing compared to 5 per cent for men, and 6 per cent compared to 1 per cent in banking and insurance. Hence, an important part of the high job creation rate for highly educated workers is the hiring of highly educated women.

In sum, the level of total worker flows in Norway is comparable to that in other countries, although it is slightly lower in terms of churning flows. We also find differences in job destruction, job creation and re-employment rates over education levels and over cohorts of workers. This may, of course, partly explain the observed simultaneity of hires and separations at the plant level found in many studies. Further, we also find (but do not report here) that the hiring and separation processes are interrelated, since plants increasing in size also retain highly educated workers to a greater extent. For contracting plants the opposite is true: they are left with less educated workers. Somewhat surprisingly, we find no gender difference in worker flows for the Norwegian economy despite the gender–wage differential that has been shown elsewhere. In particular, the patterns in job turnover found for educationally-heterogeneous labour also hold when conditioning on gender. The absence of a difference across genders in job flows in Norway may be due to institutional factors. Specifically, maternity leave is relatively liberal in Norway where (until recently) one year of leave compensated at 80 per cent of reference earnings was available; such a system makes it less likely that a woman will quit a job and start in a new job around childbirth.

4. RE-EMPLOYMENT SEPARATIONS AND JOB DESTRUCTION ARE DISTINCT PROCESSES

4.1 Econometric Specification

The aim of this section is to analyse whether the churning process differs from the job reallocation process, and to see how these processes differ by education level. We base our analyses on a simple econometric model.

We define the replacement rate – previously defined as separations for a given number of jobs – and the job destruction rate at the plant level for three classes of general education for workers. Plants are indexed by e and education levels by $j =$ low (until 10 years), medium (between 10 and 14 years) and high (15 years and above).[11] The following definitions are used for the replacement and job destruction rates, respectively: $SR^R_{e,j,t} = (S^R_{e,j,t})/[(L_{e,j,t} + L_{e,j,t})/]2$ for the former and $JDR_{e,j,t} = (D_{e,j,t})/[(L_{e,j,t} + L_{e,j,t})]/2$.

The same econometric models will be estimated both for replacement separations and for job destruction, in order to compare the results. The most general model to be estimated – presented in terms of $SR^R_{e,j,t}$ for convenience – is the following:[12]

$$SR^R_{e,j,t} = \gamma_{ejt} + \beta_c I^c_t + \mu_{jc} (\gamma_{ejt} \times I^c_t) + \beta_h X^s_{et} + \mu_{jh} (\gamma_{ejt} \times X^s_{et}) + \varepsilon_{ejt} \quad (9.2)$$

In this specification, γ_{ejt} is an indicator variable for general education level corresponding to the one of the three re-employment rates per plant in each time period and I^c_t is a business cycle variable which allows us to test the cyclical properties of re-employment separations and thereby consider whether quits or layoffs dominate. As is standard in the job flows literature, the manufacturing wide net job creation rate was used as the indicator of the state of the business cycle.[13] Together with the interaction term between education level and the business cycle interaction term, we use this simplified model to analyse the different patterns of job destruction and replacement over the business cycle and across education types.

In order to test the effects of plant level characteristics on job destruction and replacement rates we introduce some plant level variables. X^s_{et} is a two-dimensional vector of plant and firm size (defined by the number of workers). Precise definitions are given in the Appendix.

4.2 Econometric Issues

A couple of econometric issues require attention. First, the ranges of the dependent variables $SR^R_{e,j,t}$ and $JDR_{e,j,t}$ are [0,1] and [0,2], respectively. This means that a standard linear regression, which allows variation in the dependent variable between $-\infty$ and $+\infty$, may be inappropriate. One way to take into account the limited range of variation for $SR^R_{e,j,t}$ and $JDR_{e,j,t}$ is to use limited dependent variable models.[14] Define the following variable, which we only present for replacement separations for convenience:

$$\hat{SR}^R_{e,j,t} = \ln \left(\frac{c + S_{e,j,t}}{c - S_{e,j,t}} \right), \tag{9.3}$$

where c is a number larger than 2. Arbitrarily c was chosen to be 2, although different values were experimented with, without giving much difference in results.[15]

An alternative specification of the truncated dependent variable problem was also considered. A Tobit model restricted between 0 and 1 for replacements and 0 and 2 for job destruction was specified as an alternative to the specification in equation (9.2). In addition, and in relation to the aforementioned specification problem, the distributions for SR^R and JDR are skewed with a lot of zeros. The zero replacement and zero job destruction observations are real phenomena; they represent plants not churning workers and not eliminating jobs for a particular type of worker. The question is whether the no-replacement observations and observations with positive replacement should be considered as two separate processes.

One could argue that due to adjustment costs one decision of the plant is whether to churn workers or not, and given this first step, the next decision is how much to churn. This implies that we have two different but related underlying processes and that they should be modelled as such. On the other hand, although there are clearly adjustment costs, such as search costs, for these types of changes, an important part of these adjustment costs (such as a personnel department) are independent of the churning decision and a lesser share is dependent on how many workers are churned. This view is supported by the adjustment cost literature, which stresses the distinction between gross worker adjustment costs and adjustment costs from changing the size of a plant (Hamermesh and Pfann, 1996). For this reason, we only consider a single process of job replacement.

On the other hand, there might be differences in adjustment costs relative to job destruction between reducing the work force by only a few workers and reducing on a larger scale, since large changes in employment may also be associated with changes in investment in capital. However, in order to keep identical specifications of replacements and job destruction, we maintain the same specification for job destruction as for churning. Furthermore, since we expect the replacement rate to vary systematically with the number of workers present in a plant at each education level, a robust Huber–White estimator for the variance–covariance matrix was used allowing for plant specific clustering in the variance–covariance matrix.

4.3 Different Patterns for Job Destruction and Re-employment Separations

The econometric results are reported in Table 9.3 for re-employment separations and for job destruction. Three differences are worth noticing. First, it is clear from the pattern over the business cycle for all model specifications that replacements and job destruction are two distinct turnover processes. Job destruction has the expected counter-cyclical pattern, since it basically represents fires or employer-initiated separations. The pattern of job replacement is pro-cyclical, which is a strong indication that quits dominate layoffs. Institutional characteristics, as well as previous studies, suggest that such a result for churning is to be expected in Norway. For one thing, there exists a relatively high degree of labour protection in Norway, which reduces the potential for layoffs.[16] Mass reduction of employment in a plant, or downsizing, is possible for economic reasons, but this will be measured as job destruction. Dismissals for cause are possible, but likely comprise only a small share of the total. Hence, it is expected that most of the churning flow is due to workers quitting a job.[17]

Second, it is also apparent that job destruction becomes increasingly stable over the cycle as education increases, an effect which can be seen in the interaction terms between the business cycle and education indicators. For replacement rates no difference exists. Third, when conditioning on tenure and experience, the replacement pattern is decreasing in the education level rather than hump shaped as we saw in Figure 9.1. A plausible explanation for the disappearance of the hump shape is complementarity between general and specific human capital. Based on the relative strength of two opposing forces, that is, a lock-in effect of specific training (which is assumed to be complementary with general education) and an outside option effect (which is assumed to be stronger for more highly educated workers), a reasonable prediction for medium educated workers is that they will have a higher turnover rate than both higher and lower educated workers. Medium educated workers have higher general education than low educated workers and thus a higher relative quit rate. They may also have a lower degree of specific-training/general education complementarity than the most educated workers, which

Table 9.3   *Estimates of re-employment and job destruction equations for three education categories for Norwegian manufacturing, 1987–94*

	Re-employment separations				Job destruction			
Ed. Low	10.4	34.9	14.1	25.4	7.51	22.4	7.16	8.93
Ed. Med	10.9	34.7	11.5	21.3	7.01	20.6	7.89	12.8
Ed. High	8.01	20.9	6.91	9.24	5.53	12.5	–0.48	0.51
Bus. Cycle	0.15	4.92	0.20	6.93	0.41	8.71	–0.40	8.74
Ed. Med × Bus. Cycle	0.03	0.78	0.04	1.10	0.16	2.95	0.16	2.97
Ed. High × Bus. Cycle	0.07	0.92	0.02	0.31	0.33	3.68	0.35	3.28
Tenure			0.10	3.09			–0.05	1.38
Experience			0.24	25.5			0.12	1.61
Root MSE	0.236		0.150		0.20		0.20	
R^2-adj	0.15		0.26		0.16		0.16	

Note: The dependent variable is the re-empolyment separation rate (i.e. separations above job destructions) for each plant for three education levels of workers: low (<10 years). medium (10–14 years), and high (15+ years). All parameter estimates are multiplied by 100. The variance–covariance matrix is estimated by a robust estimator. Three-digit ISIC indicators are regional dummies are included. T-values are provided next to parameter estimates for each column.

leads to a higher turnover rate relative to these workers as well. Alternatively, it may be the case that medium educated workers have skills covering parts of low skill jobs and parts of high skill jobs. In other words, medium skilled workers can search over a wider set of jobs, and the additional offers this generates may lead to a higher expected quit rate for this group.[18] On the other hand, no sign of a hump shape with respect to education levels exists in job destruction prior to introducing tenure and experience. When tenure and experience are introduced in these models, however, the pattern changes and a hump shape in job destruction appears. The main conclusion that can be drawn from these general results is that the job destruction and churning separation processes should be analysed separately, implying that different effects of firm level personnel policies are expected for the two processes.

5.   CONCLUDING REMARKS

The focus of this chapter has been to examine differences in re-employment and job destruction rates across worker types using a panel of matched employer–employee data for the Norwegian manufacturing and financial services sectors.

We chose the manufacturing and banking and insurance sectors in part because the gender composition is very different. However, when analysing worker turnover by gender, no difference was detected for replacement flows. Furthermore, young women and young men seem to have the same replacement rates. One possible explanation here is that extended maternity leaves by young women are compensated for by more job shopping or a steeper career ladder for young men, leading to many job shifts, particularly among the well educated. Some support is found for this interpretation in that the replacement flow for highly skilled men is higher than for women, especially in the service sector. Another striking finding is that the net job creation for highly educated women is much higher than for highly educated men.

Our descriptive statistics show that re-employment separation rates follow a hump shape across education levels, while job destruction is declining in education. These results are found for the financial sector, and not just the manufacturing sector that has been the focus of many previous studies. In the econometric analyses this inverse U-shape is less pronounced and even disappears when conditioning on years of job tenure. Complementarity between general and specific education may be driving this pattern for re-employment separations or quits. We also find differences in job creation and destruction rates, as well as for re-employment rates, over education levels, cohorts and gender. This may, of course, partly explain the observed simultaneity of hires and separations of workers at the plant level found in many studies.

Finally, using an econometric framework, we find that re-employment separations are pro-cyclical, which suggests that this process consists mainly of quits. We also find that job destruction is counter-cyclical, which implies that this is driven mainly by employer-initiated separations or layoffs, as one would expect. Furthermore, these two processes also demonstrate different patterns depending on the educational level of the workers involved. Job destruction rates for high educated workers are more stable over the business cycle than for less educated workers, while no difference is visible for re-employment separations.

APPENDIX

Variable Definitions

In order to aggregate worker flows to a sector level, the following formulas are used. The rates for job creation (entry, increase), and job destruction (exit, decrease for established plants) for skill type j, can be defined as:

$$ENTRY_{j,t} = \frac{2}{L_{j,t-1} + L_{j,t}} \sum_{\substack{e \in E_{e,t-1} \\ e \notin E_{e,t}}} L_{e,j,t} \qquad INCR_{j,t} = \frac{2}{L_{j,t-1} + L_{j,t}} \sum_{\substack{e \notin E_{e,j,t-1}, E_{e,j,t} \\ dL_{e,j,t} \geq 0}} \left| L_{e,j,t} - L_{e,j,t-1} \right|$$

$$DECR_{j,t} = \frac{2}{L_{j,t-1} + L_{j,t}} \sum_{\substack{e \notin E_{e,t-1}, E_{e,j,t} \\ dL_{e,j,t} \leq 0}} \left| L_{e,j,t} - L_{e,j,t-1} \right| \qquad EXIT_{j,t} = \frac{2}{L_{j,t-1} + L_{j,t}} \sum_{\substack{e \in E_{e,j,t-1} \\ e \notin E_{e,t}}} L_{e,j,t-1}$$

respectively, where $E_{e,j,t}$ is the set of establishments with employment of skill type j in year t, and $L_{j,t}$ is the total employment of type j, defined by: $L_{j,t} = \sum_{e \notin E_{e,j,t}} L_{e,j,t}$

The gross job creation and gross job destruction rates of industry i in year t are given by:

$$JCR_{j,t} = INCR_{j,t} + ENTRY_{j,t}, \quad JDR_{j,t} = DECR_{j,t} + EXIT_{j,t}$$

The net employment change (or job flow rate) and gross job reallocation rate (or job reallocation rate) are given by:

$$JRR_{j,t} = JCR_{j,t} + JDR_{j,t} \qquad JFR_{j,t} = JCR_{j,t} - JDR_{j,t},$$

Similar definitions are used for churning flow and worker flow rates:

$$CFR_{j,t} = \frac{2}{L_{j,t-1} + L_{j,t}} \sum_{\substack{e \notin E_{e,j,t-1}, E_{e,j,t} \\ dL_{e,j,t} \geq 0}} \left| R_{e,j,t} + S^R_{e,j,t-1} \right|$$

$$WFR_{j,t} = JRR_{j,t} + CFR_{j,t}$$

where $R_{e,j,t}$ are hires in excess of job creation at the plant level for each type of workers and S^R are separations in excess of job destruction.

Worker Categories by General Education Level

Education level is based on the normal duration of the education and includes completed (and highest attained) education and all formal education courses exceeding 300 hours. We also use a three category discrete measure of skill, based on the level of education. These levels of education are calculated according to the Nordic Key for Classification of Education comparable to the International Standard of Classification of Education (ISCED). The grouping of individual educational courses by educational level is based on observation of the normal duration of the educational activities. The standard is organized with nine educational levels. Following this standard we have defined 'low educated' as up to the third level, which is equivalent to 10 years of education. 'Medium educated' is defined as education from the third up to the fifth level, which is equivalent to normal education duration of 14 years, not leading to a degree. 'High educated' is three years of college/university leading to a degree. Low educated includes primary education plus one year of secondary education in the post-1970 educational system, or seven years plus three years (*realskole*) in the pre-1970 educational system, medium education includes high school, both vocational and general high school preparing for college/university, plus two years of college/university.

Table 9A.1   Summary statistics for variables used

Variables	Mean	St. dev.
Low educ. (share)	0.60	0.21
Medium educ.	0.35	0.20
Highly educ.	0.05	0.08
Tenure (low ed.)	9.81	2.04
Tenure (med ed.)	9.61	2.11
Tenure (high ed.)	9.62	2.76
Experience (low ed.)	25.28	7.29
Experience (med. ed.)	17.78	7.39
Experience (high ed.)	16.33	8.25
Firm size	19.10	66.42

Note: All means of plant specific variables are calculated at plant level. All values in 1990 NOK

NOTES

1. Acknowledgement: I would like to thank Chris Ferrall, Dan Gordon, Øyvind A. Nilsen, Fabio Sciantarelli, a referee and participants at the EEA and EALE conferences, workshops at London School of Economics and University of Amsterdam, and seminars at the University of Bergen and Norwegian School of Economics and Business Administration for their helpful comments on previous versions of this paper. Svein Erik Førre is thanked for excellent research assistance.
2. For work on job flows see Davis and Haltiwanger (1992), Dunne et al. (1989), Leonard (1987) and Wedervang (1965) for an early contribution. Work focussing on gross worker flows includes Abowd et al. (1999), Albæk and Sørensen (1998), Hamermesh et al. (1996) and Burgess et al. (1995).
3. A couple of exceptions are Hamermesh et al. (1996), who distinguish between blue and white collar workers, and Lane et al. (1998), who distinguish between worker flows over firm size and plant age. Nilsen et al. (2003) analyse the pattern of adjustment costs for different categories of workers.
4. See Burgess et al. (1995) and Hamermesh et al. (1996) for a discussion of the difference between job and labour turnover for homogeneous workers and the distinction between different labour turnover measures.
5. We follow the literature here and assume no vacancies, which implies that replacement hires, $R_{e,j,t}$, and replacement separations, $S_{e,j,t}^{R}$, are equal in equilibrium.
6. Given that we observe our plants on an annual basis, we will not observe creation (destruction) of a job of the same skill if a different job is destroyed (created) at the same plant within a year.
7. The voluntary–involuntary distinction in separations requires some type of wage rigidity, for instance because it is too costly to renegotiate an employment contract. Otherwise a separation is only the result of optimizing behaviour of workers and plants, as predicted by matching theory or efficient turnover (see, for example, McLauglin (1991) for a discussion of this issue).
8. For both manufacturing and banking and insurance there has been a steady downward trend in churning flows from 1987 to 1994. This reduction coincides with a steady reduction in net employment from at least 1986 until recently, with an annual reduction of 2 per cent in our data period for both sectors.
9. Job reallocation has been analysed in two previous studies for manufacturing in Norway using a different data set (Klette and Mathiassen (1996), and Salvanes (1997)). For the period from 1987 to 1994, the job reallocation rate is 19.1. The job reallocation rate has

increased over time in our data period, mostly as a result of the countercyclical pattern of job turnover. The period 1989–93, which comprised most of our data period, is a downturn.

10. See Salvanes and Førre (2003) for an analysis of skill-biased technological change and competition from abroad and the pattern in job creation/destruction for different skills.

11. Note that the job reallocation rates for each skill group may be higher than the job reallocation rates at the plant level for all skills taken together. The reason, of course, is that changes in the skill mix within plants can take place without changing the size of the plant. An evaluation of the importance of between- and within-plant job reallocation may be obtained by deriving the between-plant and the total job reallocation measures (Salvanes and Førre, 2003).

12. An alternative specification for estimating these gross flows of workers is used in Salvanes and Førre (2003), where the gross flows are estimated separately for each worker type to avoid imposing a common error structure across all worker types. Salvanes and Førre (2003) also estimate a Tobit specification of a similar model.

13. Obviously, the net job creation rate used as a business cycle indicator is not without problems. GDP growth is arguably a better measure as it avoids the obvious endogeneity problem inherent in the net job creation measure for a small economy. Different measures of the business cycle are tested in Salvanes and Tveterås (2003), and they all generate very similar implications. The advantage of the net job creation rate is that it better captures the timing of the impact of macroeconomic fluctuations on the labour market.

14. See, for example, Wallis (1987).

15. This was only feasible because our data contained no observations with $S_{e,j,t}=2$.

16. See Nilsen et al. (2003), for an analysis of labour adjustment costs in Norway.

17. This is also confirmed in Hamermesh et al. (1996), where the authors found that quits comprised 68 per cent of annual separations while fires represented only 13 per cent in the Netherlands.

18. It is not clear how strong this effect may be. Further, it may be argued that the most highly educated should be the most flexible and thus have the largest set of job options. However, it is likely that there exists a limit to how low a highly educated employee can go down the job ladder without signalling that he or she is a bad quality or low effort worker.

REFERENCES

Askildsen, J.E. and Øyvind Anti Nilsen (1998), 'Union membership and wage formation', Discussion paper, Department of Economics, University of Bergen.

Abowd, J.M., P. Corbel and F. Kramarz (1999), 'The entry and exit of workers and the growth of employment', *Review of Economics and Statistics*, **81** (2), 170–87.

Albæk, S. and B.E. Sørensen (1998), 'Worker flows and job flows in Danish manufacturing, 1980–91', *Economic Journal*, **108** (November), 1750–71.

Burgess, S., J. Lane and D. Stevens (1995), 'Job flows, worker flows and churning', CEPR working paper, 1125.

Davis, S. and J. Haltiwanger (1992), 'Gross job creation, gross job destruction, and employment reallocation', *Quarterly Journal of Economics*, **107**, 819–63.

Dunne, T., M.J. Roberts and L. Samuelson (1989), 'Plant turnover and gross employment flows in the US manufacturing sector', *Journal of Labor Economics*, **7**, 48–71.

Hamermesh D.S., W.H.J. Hassink and J.C. van Ours (1996), 'New facts about factor demand dynamics: employment, jobs and workers', *Annales d'Economie et de Statistique*, 41/42, 21–40.

Hamermesh, D.S. and Pfann (1996), 'Adjustment costs in factor demand', *Journal of Economic Literature*, **34**, 1264–92.

Halvorsen, R., R. Jenssen and F. Foyn (1991), 'Dokumentasjon av industristatistikkens tidsseriebase', Oslo: Statistics Norway.

Klette, T.J. and Mathiassen, A. (1996), 'Job creation, job destruction and plant turnover in Norwegian manufacturing', *Annales d'Economie et de Statistique*, 41/42, 97–125.

Lane J., A.G. Isaac and D.W. Stevens (1998), 'Firm heterogeneity and worker turnover', *Review of Industrial Organisation*, **13**, 113–25.

Leonard, J. (1987), 'In the wrong place at the wrong time: the extent of frictional and structural unemployment', in K. Lang and J. Leonard (eds), *Unemployment and the Structure of Labor Markets*, London: Blackwell.

Margolis, D.N., V. Simmonet and L. Vilhuber (2002), 'Technical/professional versus general education, labor market networks and labor market outcomes', *International Journal of Manpower*, **5** (23).

McLaughlin, K.J. (1991), 'A theory of quits and layoff with efficient turnover', *Journal of Political Economy*, **99** (1), 1–29.

Nilsen, Ø.A., K.G. Salvanes and F. Schiantarelli (2003), 'Employment adjustment, the structure of adjustment costs, and firm's size', working paper 16/03, Norwegian School of Economics and Business Administration.

Salvanes, K.G. (1997), 'Market rigidities and labour market flexibility: an international comparison', *Scandinavian Journal of Economics*, **2**, 315–33.

Salvanes, K.G. and S.E. Førre (2003), 'Employment effects of trade and technical change. Evidence from Norway', *Economica*, **70** (2), 293–330.

Salvanes, K.G. and R. Tveterås (2003), 'Plant exit, vintage effect and the business cycle in Norway', *Journal of Industrial Economics*, (forthcoming).

Wallis, K.F. (1987), 'Time series of bounded economic variables', *Journal of Time Series Analysis*, **8** (1), 115–23.

Wedervang, F. (1965), *Development of a Population of Industrial Firms*, Bergen: Universitetsforlaget.

Index